CORNELL STUDIES IN SECURITY AFFAIRS

edited by Robert J. Art *and* Robert Jervis

A Substitute for Victory

THE POLITICS OF PEACEMAKING AT THE KOREAN ARMISTICE TALKS

ROSEMARY FOOT

Cornell University Press

ITHACA AND LONDON

To T.C.S.K.

Contents

Preface

The Korean armistice negotiations, conducted between U.S. military officers representing the U.N. Command and Chinese and North Korean military personnel, lasted more than two years and required some 575 meetings before agreement could be reached. During this period, ground action—though more limited than in the first year of the conflict—continued, and U.S. bombing entered its most destructive phase. Some 45 percent of American casualties were inflicted over these two years, and Chinese, North Korean, and South Korean losses were massive as well. The horrendous experiences of Korean civilians during this heavily destructive phase of the war should also never be forgotten.

In my previous book on the Korean conflict, *The Wrong War*, the detail of the armistice negotiations was given scant attention. I noted that the protracted discussions were the source of much frustration and tension within the Truman and Eisenhower administrations; that the prolonged nature of these talks caused the restrictions placed on the fighting gradually to be lifted and contributed to the militarization of U.S. foreign policy elsewhere in the world; and that the difficulty in settling this conflict through political means fueled a debate in Washington about expanding the war into China. I also suggested that there might have been some attempt in the United States to calibrate bombing policy with the various phases of the truce talks and that the growing disillusionment with the negotiations—along with America's steadily increasing air force and atomic capabilities—created additional barriers to the idea of a negotiated settlement.

These changes in capabilities and the growing sense of frustration over the course of the conflict provided the context for President Dwight D. Eisenhower's decision to terminate the negotiations if agreement was not reached shortly after his election. This context also led his administration to contemplate utilizing nuclear weapons in any expansion of hostilities brought about by a Chinese and North Korean refusal to concede the one remaining issue at the talks: that prisoners of war should not be forcibly repatriated. It is striking to consider that this prisoner-repatriation policy, which held up the conclusion of the armistice agreement for fifteen months—with all that meant for U.S./U.N. troops in the line and for those in the prisoner-of-war (POW) camps—could be so strictly adhered to in Washington and in allied capitals. It is even more astonishing to consider that the U.S. administration would contemplate unleashing nuclear war against a supposedly secondary enemy, ostensibly in response to the failure to agree on this one outstanding point. Determining why this policy was deemed to be so important forms a central part of any explanation of the prolonged nature of the truce negotiations.

In this book, therefore, the armistice talks and the formulation of U.S. policy for these negotiations are at the center of the analysis. A wide range of factors designed to explain the tortuous path to the framing of the agreement will be considered. Earlier accounts of these talks, dominated by those who were directly involved at the time, have depicted these discussions as a most telling example of the perfidious nature of Communist bargaining tactics and have advised that such an experience should never, or only rarely, be repeated. This study shows, however, that this portrayal of Communist intransigence, against an implied flexibility on the part of U.S. officials, has never been an adequate explanation for the protracted length of these negotiations; above all, it neglects detailed consideration of the complex domestic and international environments in which these talks took place. For example, it does not consider the difficulties of negotiating for the United States—a major power that, in the past, had always been extraordinarily successful in its employment of force. Neither does this assumption consider the additional problems that might have been introduced through the decision to use U.S. military personnel in talks that were essentially political. Such a depiction of a U.S. willingness to compromise also ignores the presence of domestic political critics in America who were only too ready to equate compromise with that negative term "appeasement" and to revive support for General Douglas MacArthur's argument that there was "no substitute for victory." This portrayal of U.S. flexibility pitted against Communist intransigence also does not take into account the complicated decision-making structure present during the Korean negotiations. As head of the U.N. Command, the United States did play the dominant role in the talks but was still subject to constraints imposed not only by Western allies who favored compromise but also Asian allies, notably South Korea, who encouraged inflexibility. Finally, such a depiction of the U.S. role in the discussions does not consider the delay that policy divisions within the administration caused—divisions between officials in Korea and those in Washington, in addition to those among officials from the various executive departments in the nation's capital. As will be shown, these opposing positions were frequently to be forged into a policy consensus during the course of the negotiations rather than prior to them, with negative psychological consequences for those charged with the task of negotiating.

A major aim of this book is to demonstrate the complexity of this negotiating environment, but a further objective is to suggest that the significance of these negotiations has tended to be neglected. Their significance should be contemplated in the context of the casualties and destruction incurred in relation to the issues at stake in the talks; in the manner by which these discussions fashioned future negotiations between the Chinese and American governments; and the means by which they helped to generate a level of acrimony between the two states that made serious dialogue difficult to contemplate or initiate. Of more general relevance to the discipline of international relations, an examination of these talks sheds additional light on the process by which conflicts are settled and illustrates the various bargaining methods adopted by states that are divided racially, culturally, and ideologically.

The completion of this book owes much to the kind assistance of friends and colleagues. Robert Jervis, Tim Kennedy, and Christopher Thorne read through the entire manuscript raising questions, asking for clarification, and generally giving support and encouragement. The care and attention they each devoted to this study is a testimony to their generosity and professionalism. A second reader for Cornell University Press judiciously combined encouragement with criticism and sent me back to a number of my sources, thus helping to deepen my understanding of the period. William Stueck very kindly shared some of the documents in his possession; I have enjoyed the debates we have had on this topic over the past few years. Further trips to the archives and presidential libraries have enabled me to renew acquaintance with those who were so helpful to me in the past. Once again, they were unstinting in their efforts to track down sources and to put me in touch with valuable documentary material. I particularly acknowledge the help of Wilbert Mahoney, Sally Marks, and Kathryn Nicastro of the National Archives, David Haight of the Dwight D. Eisenhower Library, and Warren Ohrvall of the Harry S. Truman Library. Visits to Washington, D.C., were made infinitely more enjoyable through the warm hospitality of Marcus Cunliffe and Phyllis Palmer. I value greatly the time I have spent with them in their home.

Parts of chapter 7 appeared earlier in *International Security* 13, no. 3 (1988/89). The journal has kindly given permission to reprint some sections of that article in this work. My thanks are also due to the Bancroft Library, University of California, Berkeley, for permission to make use of the William F. Knowland papers. Cambridge University Press has kindly granted permission to reproduce the map of Korea from Kalicki's *The Pattern of Sino-American Crises*.

It would not have been possible to undertake this research without the generous assistance of the British Academy in London and the University of Sussex. As British universities and other academic institutions grapple with the enervating problems associated with ever-diminishing budgets, I am especially grateful for their continuing support of my efforts to gain a better understanding of Britain's most significant ally.

ROSEMARY FOOT

Sussex, England

A NOTE ON TRANSLITERATION

The system of transliteration that has been adopted for Chinese place and personal names is in keeping with the documents of the period.

Chronology

Jan. 17	China rejects the ceasefire proposal.
Feb. 1	The United Nations declares China to be an aggressor in Korea.
Mar. 24	General MacArthur issues his unauthorized statement to Communist commanders suggesting the time is right to "confer in the field."
Apr. 11	President Harry S. Truman relieves MacArthur from his command and appoints Gen. Matthew B. Ridgway to succeed him.
May 3	Hearings on the military situation in the Far East begin before the joint Senate Committees on Armed Services and Foreign Relations.
May 31	America's Soviet expert, George Kennan, meets the Soviet ambassador to the United Nations, Jacob Malik, to discuss ways of ending the conflict.
June 23	Malik's radio address calls for "a ceasefire and an armistice providing for the mutual withdrawal of forces from the 38th Parallel."
July 10	The Korean armistice negotiations begin at Kaesong.
July 26	Agreement on the agenda for the armistice talks is reached.
Aug. 23	Talks are suspended after Communist delegates allege U.N. Command violation of the neutral zone at Kaesong.
Oct. 25	Ceasefire discussions resume at new site of Panmunjom.
Nov. 26	The demarcation line is established and will hold, provided other issues outstanding at the talks are settled within 30 days.

1952

Jan. 2	The U.N. Command proposes nonforcible repatriation for prisoners of war.
Jan. 8	The Communists reject this proposal.
Feb. 16	Communist negotiators suggest that Moscow should be a member of the commission established to supervise the armistice arrangements.
Feb. 19	Delegates agree to the holding of a political conference 90 days after the signing of the armistice agreement.
Apr. 19	U.N. Command delegation informs the Communists that only 70,000 of 132,000 prisoners in U.N. Command camps are willing to return home.
Apr. 28	The U.N. Command delegation puts forward a "package" proposal to be rejected or accepted in full: (1) no prohibition on the rebuilding of airfields; (2) Poland and Czechoslovakia but not the Soviet Union to serve on a neutral nations supervisory commission; (3) prisoners of war not to be repatriated forcibly.
May 2	The Communist delegation accepts all but the last point.
May 7	Both sides announce a stalemate over the POW issue. Gen. Francis T. Dodd, in charge of the U.N. Command POW camps, is seized by prisoners at Koje.
May 12	Gen. Mark W. Clark formally succeeds General Ridgway as U.N. commander.

Sept. 28	The U.N. Command delegation puts forward three versions of the nonforcible repatriation policy.
Oct. 8	These terms are rejected, and the talks go into recess.
Oct. 24	The United States introduces the 21-power resolution at the United Nations.
Nov. 4	General Eisenhower wins 55 percent of the popular vote in the presidential election.
Dec. 4	The U.N. General Assembly endorses the amended Indian resolution on nonforcible repatriation for prisoners of war.

1953

Feb. 22	General Clark proposes an exchange of sick and wounded prisoners.
Mar. 5	Joseph Stalin dies.
Mar. 28	The exchange of sick prisoners is accepted, and Premier Chou En-lai also proposes, two days later, that those prisoners who are unwilling to be repatriated should be transferred to a neutral state.
Apr. 20	The exchange of sick and wounded begins.
Apr. 26	Armistice talks resume at Panmunjom.
May 7	Communist delegates put forward an eight-point plan designed to solve the POW issue.
May 20	The U.S. National Security Council decides that "if conditions arise requiring more positive action in Korea," air and naval operations will be extended to China and ground operations in Korea will be intensified.
May 22	The U.S. secretary of state meets with the Indian premier and hints at future expansion of the war.
May 25	The U.N. Command negotiating team puts forward its final terms and is given permission to break off the talks if these are rejected.
May 28	The U.S. ambassador to Moscow explains to the Soviet foreign minister the final U.N. Command negotiating proposal.
June 8	The POW question is resolved.
June 17	A revised demarcation line is settled. President Syngman Rhee orders the release of those North Korean prisoners resisting repatriation.
July 27	The armistice agreement is signed.

A Substitute for Victory

The Korean peninsula. Reprinted, by permission, from Jan Kalicki, *The Pattern of Sino-American Crises* (London: Cambridge University Press, 1975).

[1]

Introduction: The Negotiations in Their Global and Domestic Settings

The Korean armistice negotiations were one of the most difficult bargaining processes of the Cold War period. With the improvement in U.S./U.N. battlefield fortunes after the defeats in the winter of 1950–51 and the failure of the Chinese offensives of April and May, the time had seemed ripe in mid-1951 for settling the conflict. The Truman administration's aim of maintaining the support of its Western allies, coupled with the realization that any significant push into North Korean territory would encounter stiffer enemy resistance, encouraged a tempering of American objectives. The Chinese inability to overcome the problems associated with extended supply lines, and perhaps a suspicion that the outcome of their most recent offensives owed something to America's successful adaptation of one of their own strategies—that of luring the enemy deep into hostile territory—also convinced Pyongyang and Peking of the need to contract their goals. Nevertheless, though the initiation of talks implied a common perception that a ceasefire would now be advisable and desirable, many more features of the era—those both intrinsic and contextual to the negotiations— served to make this conflict difficult to resolve. Even after interests had converged enough to allow an armistice agreement to be signed, the United States, in particular, would experience a strong sense of dissatisfaction with the exercise it had been engaged in for so long. Many Americans would believe more firmly than ever that there was, as General Douglas MacArthur had said, "no substitute for victory."

THE GLOBAL SETTING

As the head of the U.N. Command, the U.S. government played the dominant role in the negotiations with their Chinese and North Korean protagonists, formulating and transmitting policy positions to the negotiating team through national administrative channels, rather than through broader U.N. machinery. This is not to imply that world opinion and more particularly those nations contributing to the war effort did not constrain or influence U.S. policy choices, but the institutional arrangements indicate the extent to which the United States was able to keep Korean developments under its own control.

The degree of acquiescence among Western and pro-Western nations in this dominant U.S. role owed much to the range of measures that the United States had at its disposal after 1945 to persuade other states to conform to its preferences. Two related events left Washington in a position to provide such incentives: the enormous growth in American capabilities over the course of World War II, coupled with the economic decline or even collapse of former "great powers." America's GNP, for example, increased from $88.6 billion in 1939 to $198.7 billion in 1945. It controlled some 70 percent of the world's gold and foreign exchange reserves. The economy experienced a threefold increase in the output of manufactured goods and a 60 percent increase in the extraction of raw materials. Agricultural output also rose by one-quarter, despite a 17 percent reduction in those working on the land. Whereas in 1940 the United States had ranked nineteenth in world military terms, by 1945 the description "great power" was no longer seen as sufficient to depict such overwhelming strength, which included the world's most powerful navy, a sophisticated air force, a well-equipped ground army, and a monopoly in nuclear weaponry.[1]

In contrast to such burgeoning power, America's major ally, Britain, on retreat from empire in Asia and the Middle East, had been required to expend approximately one-quarter of its national wealth in order to support its efforts between 1939 and 1945. John Maynard

[2]

Keynes was convinced that, in the immediate postwar period, Britain would need between $1 billion and $2 billion in financial aid from the United States, a country that it already owed some $30 billion under Lend Lease. Over the course of World War II, London was totally eclipsed on the international scene as Washington took over its investment, trading, and security roles in, for example, Australia and New Zealand. It was hardly easy for Britain "after centuries of leading others, to resign [itself] to the position of allowing another and greater power to lead [it]," and make do with the role of "counsellor and moderator," as one foreign office official in London put it.[2]

Obviously, such strength as America enjoyed carried with it enormous enforcement potential for a state that had distinct preferences about the world political order it wished to see established, together with a deep-rooted sense that American ideals would guarantee future international peace and prosperity. The possession of the potential for enforcement did not mean, however, that coercion had to be employed to make others conform to its vision. The American approach to constructing an international order did not require dictatorial methods; rather, its hegemonic position depended on what has been described as a subtle blend of concessions to the weak, together with the projection of its leadership in terms of universal or general interests, and not in support of goals that were simply self-serving.[3]

Indeed, there was a strong ideological consensus among the United States and its Western allies concerning their economic and security needs after 1945 which carried them through into the 1950s. This was expressed tangibly in generalized terms through organizations such as the United Nations, the North Atlantic Treaty Organization (NATO), the International Monetary Fund (IMF), and the World Bank. In certain respects the outbreak of the Korean War cemented this cooperation still further, since all of Washington's major allies agreed that the North Korean attack on South Korea was Soviet-inspired and represented a test of the American will to resist Communist expansion. More particularly, the armed intervention was also perceived as a test of America's willingness to protect its weakened partners.

Certainly, the rapid demobilization of U.S. armed forces immediately after World War II did raise difficulties for the Truman administration as it strove to implement such a broad range of policy objectives; and although the Korean conflict occasioned a speedy revival in America's military capabilities, the United States still experienced shortages in men and materiel until late in 1952. Thus, on the heels of the Truman administration's decision to place its military resources at the disposal of South Korea, vastly increased defense budgets had to be voted through Congress. By 1953 the defense budget had more than trebled over the pre-1950 level, representing a massive 14 percent of U.S. GNP, which now stood at more than $350 billion. These extra resources allowed American administrations to make their military containment policies global in their application, for not only did America's own naval, air, ground, and atomic forces increase as a result, but security relations with allies were also transformed. NATO became a far more effective organization with the appointment of a supreme commander and the establishment of a unified command structure; a solution was found to the problem of West German rearmament; financial and military assistance to Indochina and the Philippines was accelerated and increased; defense treaties were signed in 1951 with Australia and New Zealand; the United States bolstered its commitment to Chiang Kai-shek's regime on Taiwan; and it moved forward to end its occupation of Japan in order to integrate that country more firmly into the U.S. security system in the Pacific. Before the Korean conflict the United States, which for so long had tried to avoid "entangling alliances," had only one commitment outside the Western hemisphere, and that was the North Atlantic Treaty. By the mid-1950s it had "about 450 bases in 36 countries and was linked by political and military pacts with some 20 countries outside Latin America,"[4] including Australia, New Zealand, South Korea, Taiwan, and Japan. For these reasons, the period of the Korean War has been described as the most active phase of the Cold War, a critical event that sharpened U.S. policy perceptions and clarified its objectives.[5]

As indicated above, many states recognized these new policies as representing a significant break with America's past stance of international involvement without commitment. These developments were indications that the United States did not intend to retreat once more into political isolation but instead demonstrated that its claims that it would be ready to defend countries against Commu-

[4]

nist aggression were meaningful. The dominant reaction to U.S. intervention in the Korean conflict in Western Europe and in Japan was therefore one of relief, combined with the belief that action taken under U.N. auspices boosted both the organization's and the West's prestige.[6]

This broad consensus on the Korean War's origins and meaning, however, was not to be sufficient to rule out all conflicts of interest between Washington and its allies during the course of the fighting. Tensions arose throughout between the allies' need for America's military and economic largesse, and their concern that Washington's new commitments and active participation in Asian affairs would detract from more pressing security concerns in Europe and the Middle East. Moreover, these same governments feared that this involvement in Asia could lead to a dangerously violent outcome that would spare no state.

Britain, for example, spent the Korean War years concerned about Soviet retaliation in Europe while America was preoccupied in Asia, and found its own attention increasingly diverted away from that area of conflict and toward the rising tide of nationalism in Iraq, Iran, and Egypt that threatened to disrupt vital oil supplies from the region. The Attlee and Churchill governments both hoped for a relatively speedy end to the Korean hostilities, and indications are that if they had been given a more direct voice in the truce negotiations, they would have been more flexible than U.S. administrations proved to be (perhaps displaying what one scholar has described as the "shopkeeper" approach to diplomacy, characteristic of the British diplomat).[7] In December 1950 and again in November 1952, to name but two of a number of occasions when it tried to use what influence it could muster, London first tried to persuade Washington to open negotiations with the Chinese and then later on to soften its bargaining terms.[8] The Canadian government worked in a similar fashion to the British: Lester Pearson, the foreign minister, frequently attempted to enhance his bargaining power with the United States by using his position in 1950 as a member of the U.N. ceasefire group, his role (also in 1950) as president of the Seventh Regular Session of the General Assembly, and his time in 1952 and 1953 as chair of the Canadian U.N. delegation, all as a means of persuading Washington to adopt certain less rigid policy positions. Australia, too, though cognizant of its junior position in the Western alliance, and keen to find favor in the United States in order to obtain a bilateral security commitment, also made it known that it viewed Korea as a relatively minor conflict when compared with the greater threats to Australian security that emanated from the Middle East and Malaya.[9] And although nonaligned India, unlike these other states, had no close linkage with the United States, it worked hard to make its position understood in Washington. Its policy of nonalignment in some senses increased its value to the United States during the war, as shown, for example, when New Delhi alone proved acceptable to both East and West as the pivotal member of the repatriation commission set up to deal with the exchange of prisoners of war, otherwise made up of two pro-Western neutrals (Sweden and Switzerland) and two pro-Eastern ones (Czechoslovakia and Poland). This concrete recognition of the value of nonalignment made Indian acceptance of Korean policy positions desirable (though not crucial) for both sides in the Cold War.

Nevertheless, though these states at various times tried to modify U.S. behavior during the armistice negotiations, Washington, as a result of its dominant global role, could still gain acceptance of policy positions it held firmly. When allies proved too vigorous in their requests for modifications in U.S. policies, the Truman and Eisenhower administrations would remind its Western friends of their continuing dependence and warn them of the strong hold that isolationist ideas still had within the United States. The U.S. secretary of state, Dean Acheson, told Britain's foreign minister, Ernest Bevin, for example, in the winter of 1950–51, during their disagreement over the U.N. resolution labeling China an aggressor in Korea, that failure to recognize this aggression in the U.N. body would create such a wave of isolationist sentiment in the United States that all the plans made for the Atlantic pact countries would be put in jeopardy. He repeated that same threat in November 1952 when London announced its support for an Indian U.N. resolution that sought a way out of the impasse over the POW repatriation issue. President Dwight D. Eisenhower, too, was to show a similar willingness to bring pressure on Britain and other allies should they step too far out of line on China policy. In July 1953 he urged his cabinet officers to use every lever against these governments should they attempt to break ranks in the post-Korean War era.[10]

Policy toward the People's Republic of China (P.R.C.) was at the center of America's disagreement with its Western allies during the course of the truce negotiations. Dislike of Washington's increasing entanglement with Chiang Kai-shek, and fears that the United States might too readily expand the war into the P.R.C., leaving Europe vulnerable to Soviet retaliation, lay at the heart of most other states' desire for a quick diplomatic solution in Korea. In these governments' views, an intransigent policy toward the P.R.C. only served to cement Peking's alliance with Moscow. In calmer moments U.S. administrations noted the logic of aspects of this argument and acknowledged the drawbacks of continuing to fight a secondary enemy in an area of lesser strategic significance; but the price that Washington was willing to pay for a settlement in Korea was much smaller than the one that most other states seemed willing to give.

There were a number of compelling reasons why the United States found it difficult to satisfy the demands for greater flexibility at the talks that were being made by their Western allies. Not least among these were the unpredictable and at times uncontrollable actions of the South Korean government, which would frequently attempt to subvert the negotiating process. Syngman Rhee, the South Korean president, in response to the continuing negotiations regularly threatened to withdraw his troops from the U.N. Command, a threat of some significance since these forces held two-thirds of the front line. He also made it clear that any attempt to reestablish the 38th Parallel as the dividing line between North and South Korea would meet with a violent reaction throughout the South. At various points in the negotiations Rhee would intervene to slow the pace of agreement or to try to scuttle the discussions entirely. When it was agreed, for example, that Indian troops would supervise prisoner repatriation, he refused to let them land in his country; and when the end of the negotiations were in sight, he nearly wrecked the whole agreement by organizing the release from U.N. custody of those North Korean prisoners who had recorded that they were unwilling to be repatriated. Maintaining allied unity among a group that included at one end of the continuum Syngman Rhee and at the other (say) Lester Pearson and Clement Attlee would prove to be a consuming task for officials in Washington throughout the Korean hostilities.

Fears of Rhee's ability to jeopardize the lives of U.S. soldiers, and constant accusations from domestic political critics that the administration had never done enough to support such staunch anti-Communist allies in Asia, tempered the executive branch's willingness to pressure Rhee. Indeed, throughout the period of the Korean armistice negotiations, U.S. administrations formulated policy in a divisive political atmosphere that had been sharpened by the many unfounded accusations Senator Joseph McCarthy had been making against executive officers.[11] This atmosphere served to harden the U.S. response to the P.R.C., to tighten U.S. bonds with Taiwan, and to maintain the public representation that South Korea was a worthy and valuable ally. Although the threats emanating from the neo-isolationist bloc in Congress could prove useful to U.S. administrations when Atlantic allies became recalcitrant over China policy, its sentiments could also make it difficult for the executive branch to compromise at the truce negotiations, for fear of being labeled "soft on communism." Frequently, these administration critics would take advantage of the adversarial nature of American politics and claim presidential weakness in the face of alleged threats to national security.[12]

As will be shown in later chapters, the Republican party, having decided after their election defeat in 1948 to make foreign policy a central part of their criticism of the Truman administration, attacked the armistice talks the moment they began, describing a prospective truce at or near the 38th Parallel (much as Rhee did) as an "appeasement peace." And these critics could also draw on the continuing popularity of General MacArthur, who at the hearings held to investigate his dismissal from Far East and U.N. commands alleged that the Democrats were waging war with "no hope for victory." In 1952, a presidential election year, Republicans, including the presidential candidate Dwight D. Eisenhower, would claim that Harry S. Truman had fallen into a trap when he had agreed to negotiations, and that he was showing rank timidity in the face of clear evidence that the Communists were using the time to build up their forces in Korea. Republicans would also turn the apparent economic health of the nation against the Truman administration by claiming that the "prosperity had at its foundation the coffins of the Korean war dead," slaughter that as yet seemed to have no end. The search for an armistice agreement in a political climate where negotiation was equated with the pejorative term "appeasement" would contribute to a harshness of approach and to the sense of frustration that such a lengthy procedure invoked.[13]

Despite President Eisenhower's popularity and solid win in the 1952 election, he, too, was not immune to such domestic influences. The outspoken group within the Republican party, headed by Senators Robert A. Taft and William F. Knowland, that had been calling for an end to negotiations to be followed by expanded war against China and the attempted unification of Korea now came into positions of prominence within Congress. They expected from Eisenhower, and urged upon him, decisive courses of action, indirectly contributing to his administration's decision in May 1953 to present its final terms at Panmunjom and, in the event of their rejection, to make ready for a spread of hostilities into China and intensified activities on the peninsula.[14]

Though this retaliatory sentiment was not generally supported in liberal sections of the American press, other voices—such as that of *Time* magazine's—could often be heard in support of such a policy. Mass public sentiment was much closer to the views espoused by General MacArthur and was generally impatient with the conduct of Truman administration policy. Opinion polls had shown initially that there had been a high level of support for Truman's decision to intervene in Korea, but once Chinese forces had entered the fighting in November 1950, this approval rating dropped markedly. For similar reasons (also having to do with the length of time U.S. citizens believed their country would be involved on the peninsula), when truce negotiations began, 74 percent of respondents thought that it had been a good idea for the U.N. Command to agree to participate in these talks; but as the discussions bogged down, enthusiasm waned among the public. Moreover, it began to revert to its previous level of support for MacArthur and his policy of an expanded war. At the end of December 1951, for example, as many as 60 percent thought Truman to have been wrong in dismissing the general, and only 29 percent agreed with the decision. From late 1951 through 1952, there was a steady increase in the numbers of those wanting to break off the truce negotiations, though never a majority.[15]

[9]

At the root of this pro-MacArthur sentiment was a basic desire to teach the Chinese a lesson after the shock of their intervention in Korea and their early military successes; but it was also an expression of a more general "intolerance of ambiguous policy" and "an impatience with complicated long-term solutions to difficult policy problems."[16] Such a reaction was not confined, however, to an overemotional public. This resentment at the evidence of Chinese military prowess, and the disillusionment with the tortuous negotiations, also would be reflected within the Truman and Eisenhower administrations themselves. Most frequently, the military branch would express such views, especially those commanders in Tokyo at U.N. Command headquarters or in Korea itself who came to regard the decision to negotiate as nothing less than a "colossal blunder" on Washington's part.[17] These officials would be far less tolerant of any allied call for compromise at the talks, since they believed that increased military pressure and greater firmness would more readily secure the U.N. Command's desired objectives.

Though it was politically useful for the United States to be able to confine the armistice discussions to military matters between field commanders—as Acheson said, it avoided the issue of U.S. non-recognition of the P.R.C. and the Democratic People's Republic of Korea (D.P.R.K.), and prevented overtly political questions such as the membership of Taiwan and the P.R.C. in the United Nations from being raised[18]—it did mean that those directly engaged in the discussions had little or no stomach for the task.[19] The military voiced its suspicions of any proposal for talks as soon as the Soviet U.N. ambassador, Jacob Malik, made his statement suggesting a ceasefire. The Defense Department's Joint Intelligence Committee (JIC) believed a ceasefire would allow the Communists to regain the military initiative in Asia, and the Far Eastern Air Force commander expressed serious objections to the idea of entering into negotiations without adequate guarantees as to future Communist behavior.[20] Not everyone in the Pentagon reacted in this manner, of course, and many realized that a ceasefire at a strong defensive position represented the only sensible solution, unless the United States was willing to take extensive casualties. But there was little joy expressed about the prospects of negotiating; distaste for the Communists was too strong for that. Over the course of the negotiations and immediately on their conclusion, many who had seen service out in Korea described their opponents in virulently hostile and racist terms, unfortunately recalling those epithets that had so recently been widely applied to the Japanese in World War II, if not over a longer period to the nonwhite in general.[21] General Ridgway, for example, the U.N. commander from April 1951 to May 1952, called the Communist negotiators "treacherous savages"; General William K. Harrison, chief U.N. negotiator from May 1952 to July 1953, described them as "common criminals;" and Admiral Ruthven E. Libby told the president that he had spent seven months dealing with people who "had the quality of talking animals." The prevailing opinion was that the Chinese and North Koreans were "sons of bitches and outside the pale of normal gentlemanly humanity."[22]

This stark depiction of America's battlefield enemies was hardly conducive to the supposed search for common ground. But there was little inherent in military training that was appropriate to a bargaining process, and there is some evidence that those charged with the task believed themselves incapable of it.[23] It has been said that military elites are perceived as "the repository of the honor of the country and of the armed forces,"[24] and if that honor is besmirched in any manner, then the primary objective is to remove that stain. The passivity involved in the long and complex negotiating process that would occur in Korea was completely foreign to military training, with its emphasis on action and concrete achievement. The U.N. Command team's preference for issuing ultimatums to the Communist negotiators was partly a response to this intolerance of inactivity. U. Alexis Johnson, the deputy assistant secretary of state for Far Eastern affairs during the Korean conflict, subsequently claimed that for these kinds of reasons he had been against the military's being used in the truce talks: "They were not practiced in foiling propaganda ploys or keeping cool during deliberately offensive harangues about themselves and their country," he recorded in his memoirs. Furthermore, he regretted their lack of negotiating experience and the need for their instructions to come through "military channels as orders, which tended to produce a certain rigidity in how they were implemented."[25] However, the State Department should bear primary responsibility for contributing to this outcome, since it was that organization which rejected Ridgway's request that his armistice delegation be provided with political advisers. Not until May 1952 did State officials change their minds on that and decide to improve the political advice being made available. (Interestingly, the Chinese were not to make a similar mistake. Chiao Kuan-hua, who headed a department at the foreign ministry and had had experience of dealing with Americans at the time of the Marshall mission to China, was kept in the background at Kaesong—later Panmunjom—throughout. He was joined by Vice–Foreign Minister Li Kenong, who was replaced for a while when ill by Ke Bonian, director of the American and Oceanian department in China's foreign ministry, and by General Wu Hsiu-chuan, who had headed the Chinese special delegation to the United Nations in December 1950.)[26]

The U.S. military's lack of sympathy for negotiations as well as its tendency to adhere to regular bureaucratic channels and proce-dures were influential in leading it to develop contingency plans in the event that the discussions broke down. Three days after the formal start of talks, for example, the Joint Chiefs of Staff forwarded proposals to the secretary of defense which recommended an ex-panded war into North Korea and into China should negotiations be seen to have failed. Their thinking had no doubt been influenced by recorded developments in tactical atomic weapons and the re-cent production of a report that recommended use of these missiles in the event of a deadlock at the talks. Later in the year the Pentagon put forward various suggestions to cover the contingency of a long, drawn-out negotiating process. These recommendations, consid-ered at the level of the National Security Council (NSC), led to the observation that if "after a reasonable period" the talks were still at an inconclusive stage, then additional measures, including those against Chinese territory, would probably have to be taken.[27]

Against this background of a possibly expanded war, a number of military personnel began to discuss the necessity of setting a date for the termination of the negotiations, and, as will be seen in subsequent chapters, all those at U.N. Command Headquarters would at one time or another recommend the breaking off of discus-sions. Alongside the expression of these views, bombing restric-tions against a number of previously embargoed targets gradually came to be lifted. Though it was argued that such decisions were taken in order to force concessions at the truce talks, such action also meant that the notion of a negotiated compromise now faced serious competition from an active military policy.

The military branch expressed its frustrations with Korean War policy in a relatively straightforward manner—military leaders had been asked to do a job in Korea and were not being permitted to complete that task in the manner they thought most appropriate. When civilian members of the Truman and Eisenhower administrations described their attitudes, they demonstrated a more complex set of priorities, which often were somewhat in conflict with each other. Both administrations recognized that, on the one hand, the long, drawn-out negotiations were tying U.S. resources down in East Asia, a theater of supposedly secondary importance. On the other hand, there was the fear that peace in Korea could slow down allied and domestic rearmament efforts. Moreover, a ceasefire would foreclose the much-needed opportunity, in Washington's view, to attempt to deflate the military prestige of the Chinese Communists. Yet, on the other hand, an expanded conventional war could lead to unacceptable levels of U.S./U.N. casualties, would occasion extreme hostility from North Atlantic allies, and would demonstrate the deep fissure between them and America's anti-Communist allies in Asia who would welcome an expansion of the conflict.[28] The administration thus sought an incompatible set of objectives involving the preservation of domestic unity, the maintenance of the broad U.N. coalition of nations, and at the same time the diminution of Communist power in Asia.

The contradictory nature of these goals was of greater consequence, not only because comparisons could be made with the "simpler" formula expressed by some members of the Defense Department, but also because of the fragmented nature of the decision-making structure applicable to the Korean armistice negotiations. The U.N. Command negotiators in Korea were mainly subjected to those influences that encouraged a harsher approach toward the negotiations. As a result, therefore, they often criticized the passive process of negotiation and advocated an approach toward the talks that involved making the U.N. Command positions clear to the Communists and utilizing military pressure as the main means of gaining acceptance of that stance. Such officials found they had support for this approach from certain of the most vocal

[13]

members of Congress, from increasing numbers of the public, from the South Korean government, and from some officials in Washington who either thought it necessary to support the man in the field, or who likewise believed that it was useless to attempt to negotiate a "just" settlement with Communists.

However, the U.S. decision to adopt a U.N. framework for its actions on the peninsula meant that there was another level to the decision-making structure, one that encouraged a more concessionary approach in the talks. The U.N. involvement required a responsiveness to international opinion (and especially to the views of America's most important allies), which could sometimes cut across the demands issuing from the Asia-firsters in Congress, from Rhee in Seoul, or from those in the bureaucracy who preferred force and inflexibility to diplomatic compromise. As will become clear, forming a consensus among these different constituencies was a significant feature of the Korean War period and often required complex sets of negotiations with a disparate group of allies, and between the executive branch in Washington and the U.N. commander in the field.[29]

As the negotiations went into their second year, for a variety of psychological, cultural, and bureaucratic reasons the consensus that emerged tended to concentrate at the end of the negotiating continuum that advocated inflexibility and increased military pressure. In part, the president's personal predilection for appearing tough and decisive accounted for this tendency. Truman's increasing frustration with the negotiating process was made plain on a number of occasions in 1952—in its most extreme form causing him to fantasize in his private diary that he had issued an ultimatum to the Communists and had threatened action, on a range from destruction of military bases in northern China through to all-out war.[30] To a man who was an "impulsive" decision maker, born out of a lack of self-esteem, and who had once complained that it had taken 17 days to negotiate the great issues at Potsdam ("why in 17 days you can decide anything"),[31] the 18 months that he spent dealing with negotiating positions concerning Korea must have been intolerable.

Acheson's particular dislike of negotiating with adversaries except from a position of recognizable strength has often been noted. The joint State-Defense study, NSC 68, described by one of Acheson's biographers as a "thoroughly Achesonian exposition," eschewed diplomacy as a means of dealing with Moscow and saw it as a "dangerous detraction from building positions of strength around the Soviet periphery."[32] His negative attitude toward negotiation, coupled with his responsiveness to presidential predilections, encouraged the secretary to argue for stricter armistice provisions than those that some of his departmental colleagues thought appropriate. Acheson's Republican successor, John Foster Dulles, was also considered to be generally fearful of entering into negotiations, believing that when an opponent sought to negotiate, this was "a sign of weakness and/or failure."[33] In these circumstances, Dulles believed, the best course of action was to drive home the advantage, a course of action that he briefly recommended when final agreement came near.

These men's observations of Hitlerian tactics and the policy of appeasement followed in the 1930s, and dealings with Stalin during wartime conferences reinforced these psychological attributes. But the explanation for U.S. discomfiture with the negotiating process runs even deeper than this and owes much to the values and orientations that have come to be associated with the American political culture.

Many scholars have noted the U.S. lack of attachment to and suspicion of negotiation.[34] From 1776 until 1950 the United States had been extraordinarily successful in its employment of force and thus had no particular need to develop the art of diplomacy and compromise. Each success had encouraged an attitude of invincibility, which was further boosted by isolation from truly serious security dangers and the presence on America's borders of weak, nonthreatening states.[35] The most recent experiences of administration officials involved U.S. participation in world wars in which one of the primary diplomatic questions concerned the type of peace settlement to impose. Such individuals had never faced the need to establish a compromise settlement dictated by a stalemate on the battlefield.

Furthermore, America's success on its own continent, which imparted to it a missionary zeal to make others over in its image, also included the belief that Americans would wage war only for the purest of motives.[36] In both world wars the United States had depicted itself as being involved in a crusade against evil, in support of democratic freedoms. As others have noted, there was "little room in such an image [of warfare] for limiting one's objectives or limiting the means employed to achieve them."[37] Thus, when members of Congress criticized the executive branch for subjecting U.S. armed forces to their first defeat, for abandoning objectives "before the battle was fought and decisively won," or charged that fighting a limited war with limited means shocked the nation's "sense of decency,"[38] beyond their political motives, they were also probing a deeper sense of wrong felt by people that had believed America would always prevail against opponents.

It could be argued, of course, that this attitude of moral rectitude when engaged in conflict was probably mirrored on the Communist side during the armistice talks. China's pride in its ancient civilization, and its sense of triumph and unity after the establishment of the P.R.C., gave its leaders a strength of purpose and resolve and reinforced the belief that history was on its side. Communist political ideology, with its negative conception of capitalist nations and its depiction of wars as struggles of the just against the unjust, could also be said to have made the idea of compromise a difficult one for the North Koreans and Chinese. (Indeed, in the Chinese language, the word for "compromise" has negative overtones; hence, their preference for thinking in terms of mutual interests.)[39] Yet, unlike the United States, China's ideology had its pragmatic side in its acceptance of the need to seek temporary accommodation with imperialist nations at times of relative weakness. Indeed, its recent history was full of examples where such temporary arrangements had been made in the hopes of gaining some respite from the plunderings of the strong.[40] The United States, on the other hand, was the most powerful state in 1950, claimed a hegemonic role in the international system, and espoused a belief in the moral superiority of its ideology over that of the Communist nations. In these circumstances, the requirement for it to negotiate with an ideological adversary and with a nation that had so recently been depicted in the West as being weak and in chaos would surely have exacerbated the difficulties of coming to any agreement at Panmumjom.

It could also be argued that the U.S. distrust of negotiation encouraged a more generally remarked proneness to emphasize details, the technicalities, the fine print, and the need to close all loopholes at the armistice talks. It is also likely that the U.S. attitude

[16]

toward bargaining reinforced a preference for a more combative style of negotiating, involving a firm and clear commitment to a position, which would be put forward in the form of an ultimatum, in the expectation that the opponent would be forced to recognize the "fairness" of that position. The Chinese, on the other hand, and again probably for historical and cultural reasons, were especially concerned to establish general principles at the start of the talks, to maintain equality of status in the negotiations, and to arrive at parallel advantages by offsetting mutual risks, gains, and losses. They adopted a kind of "tit-for-tat" strategy involving mutual concessions, a process that tended to be disliked by the U.N. Command negotiating team, which saw itself as being forced into one retreat after another.[41] These differing negotiating styles, themselves intimately linked with the respective political cultures, undoubtedly increased the difficulty of coming to a speedy agreement.

Viewed from the perspectives of the U.S. relationship with its allies, of the domestic political environment, and of certain psychological and bureaucratic features of the era that themselves were underpinned by a deeper dislike of all negotiation, it is hardly surprising that the Korean armistice negotiations should have been such a long and tortuous process. Moreover, it now seems somewhat absurd that some of those involved on the eve of talks should have seen the reaching of agreement as a relatively straightforward procedure. Western newsmen, for example, are said to have set up a betting pool on the likely length of negotiations, with the pessimists estimating six weeks. A Chinese diplomat who was kept in the background at Kaesong (Chiao Kuan-hua) told his friend, the correspondent Wilfred Burchett, that he thought the talks would last about three weeks. Diplomats at the United Nations, four days before the start of the negotiations, also acted as though a settlement were a foregone conclusion and quickly began to consider the steps that should follow the conclusion of a ceasefire.[42] But their optimism ignored the many factors that would prevent the move toward a swift resolution of the conflict. Mutual suspicions and conflicting national values were magnified on the U.S. side by a domestic political atmosphere generally hostile to the formulation of agreements with the Communist world, especially an accord that was based on such an inconclusive military outcome. America's allies, though wanting the United States to sustain the new postwar economic and political order, still perceived a need to restrain Washington from carrying through its more aggressive policies in Asia, and thus often gave contradictory advice to their senior partner. U.S. administrations had conflicting priorities also: they wanted to be rid of the need to negotiate with a secondary power on the basis of effective equality, did not want their resources drained in an area of less than primary strategic significance, and yet realized that continuing tension helped maintain allied unity and congressional acceptance of large defense budgets.

Though this study will concentrate on the complex domestic and international environments in which U.S. policies were formulated, it is apparent, too, that a range of motivations and problems also existed on the Communist side. Certainly, the decision-making structure that they faced was less complicated than for the United States; yet strains were likely to have arisen from the presence of the two military commands in Korea, the Chinese People's Volunteers and the North Korean army. Though it is much more difficult to establish the relationship between the Communist powers, indications are that the Chinese dominated the formulation of policy objectives but were not unresponsive to North Korean preferences. More generally, it has been suggested that the Chinese prefer a group method of diplomacy, requiring extensive discussion among a large delegation before proposals are advanced, and it seems possible that behind the scenes in Korea they adopted this approach. (Certainly, Gen. Wu Hsiu-chuan has confirmed this preference when referring to the activities of the Chinese delegation at the United Nations, where "before and after each speech, discussions were held and opinions solicited within the delegation.") This would have made it difficult for their senior negotiator at Panmunjom to be immediately adaptable or flexible, further contributing to the slow pace of the negotiations.[43]

The Soviet role in the bargaining process also merits consideration. It was clear that the Soviet Union, as head of the socialist camp and as the sole supplier of North Korean and Chinese military equipment, would believe it appropriate for it to intervene at significant moments in the negotiating process—as shown, for example, by Malik's broadcast in June 1951 and again in November 1952 when armistice issues were discussed at the United Nations. Thus, the relationship between all three Communist governments,

[18]

though difficult to discern, does warrant examination when attempting to understand the path to the armistice agreement.

Furthermore, and, again, as with the United States, there was also a mixture of often incompatible objectives on the Communist side. China's intervention in Korea had gained it considerable prestige, both within and beyond the socialist bloc; and its continuing ability to hold American ground forces to a stalemate enhanced this position. There are also some indications that its leaders initially believed that wider benefits could be derived from this increase in power, as will be seen below, which would involve Taiwan and U.N. representation. The presence of American forces on its borders, and the "Resist America—Aid Korea" campaign that resulted from it, helped unify the nation, mobilize political support, and root out political opponents. Yet, on the negative side of the equation, intervention in Korea and its inability to sign a ceasefire agreement made the P.R.C. more dependent on the Soviet Union for its economic, political, and security needs and took vast budgetary resources away from its domestic economy (48 percent of spending was on defense in 1951, for example). The longer the war lasted, the more concerned Chinese leaders would become about this delay in the implementation of its economic plans.

From the Soviet Union's perspective, it would find the long, drawn-out negotiations useful to the promotion of its international peace offensive, would welcome the diversion of American resources to East Asia, but would be alarmed at the way in which the United States could use the resultant international tension to establish its global containment policy. Perhaps only the junior partner, North Korea, had a relatively straightforward set of priorities and a desire to end the war quickly; but that required equitable terms in the form of little or no loss of territory, protection from the devastating might of American air power, and the unfettered opportunity to rebuild the country. Establishing an early peace would prove difficult for all.

[2]

Early Opportunities:
June 1950 to June 1951

The four distinct phases evident in the first year of the Korean conflict each produced opportunities to explore ways of ending the war on that peninsula. In the first phase, with the U.S. commitment to South Korea and more generally to anti-Communist containment policies made tangible, Britain and India launched separate initiatives to ensure that the conflict would quickly be resolved and not be enlarged in geographical scope. These efforts foundered on the U.S. argument that no political price should be paid to the aggressor, especially when U.S./U.N. military forces were in such a disadvantageous military position. However, with the improvement in U.S./U.N. battlefield fortunes between September and early November 1950, neutral, allied, and Communist voices were again raised in the search for a way of ending hostilities and to prevent the war's further expansion as U.S./U.N. forces prepared to advance across the 38th Parallel into North Korea. But "roll-back" and the possible achievement of the military unification of Korea proved too great an attraction, and the movement north continued, thus precipitating an entirely new phase of the fighting as the Chinese People's Volunteers entered in support of the North Korean army.

The augmentation of North Korean strength immediately paid dividends for Pyongyang on the battlefield as U.S./U.N. armies in the winter of 1950–51 were forced into a retreat. In these new circumstances Britain, again supported most ardently by India, pressed the Truman administration to negotiate a ceasefire, in exchange for which Peking would be offered a seat in the United

Nations and the return of Taiwan, an exchange that Washington would not countenance, however. Only as the U.S./U.N. military position began to revive, and with the emergence of a military stalemate between March and June of 1951, would the U.S. administration actively contemplate opening negotiations for a ceasefire and armistice. Over these four phases of the war, therefore, all blocs—Western, Eastern, and nonaligned—were at one time engaged in the search for a settlement, and in the course of this search the U.S. administration determined certain positions that were to influence the nature of the truce arrangements finally arrived at in July 1953, as well as its policies toward China over a longer period.

CHINA POLICY AS THE PATH TO A SETTLEMENT

In the first weeks of the war, with South Korean troops in retreat and American combat forces newly committed to the defense of the Republic of Korea (R.O.K.), diplomats in London, Moscow, and New Delhi were most active in exploring the means to bring about a ceasefire. London's interest stemmed from one general and one specific source: from its belief that Washington, having shown its resolve, should not be trapped into diverting too many of its resources toward Asia, to the neglect of Europe; and, more particularly, from the United Kingdom's disapproval of the U.S. attempt to contain any future Communist moves in that area by interposing the Seventh Fleet between the Chinese mainland and the island of Taiwan, thereby entangling the Taiwan issue with the progress of the Korean hostilities. In an attempt to derive some positive outcome from an action involving Taiwan that did not receive much international approbation, the British government of Prime Minister Clement Attlee seized on the status of Taiwan as the possible basis for a bargain with the Soviet Union, at the same time solving the issues of the future of the island, the Soviet return to the Security Council, and the P.R.C.'s entry into the United Nations. The cessation of hostilities in Korea would be used to underpin progress on these other matters.

On June 29, therefore, and four days after the onset of hostilities, the British ambassador to Moscow, Sir David Kelly, met with a Soviet official from the British section and urged his government to use its influence in order to effect a peaceful settlement in Korea. The Soviet deputy foreign minister, Andrei Gromyko, responded to this message on July 6, requesting specific proposals from the British, a request that encouraged London to anticipate likely Soviet counterproposals. As the U.K. foreign minister, Ernest Bevin, relayed to the U.S. secretary of state, Dean Acheson, in his view the Soviet government was likely to raise the question of Taiwan and that of giving China's seat at the U.N. to the P.R.C., issues that were undermining international support for the U.S. position in Korea and that London believed could be traded in return for the restoration of the status quo on the peninsula.[1]

Concurrently with this activity, the Indian government was pursuing a similar course in Peking, Moscow, and Washington, suggesting that the Truman administration should support the P.R.C.'s admission into the Security Council, and that the council as newly constituted would then immediately move toward a ceasefire in Korea, to be accompanied by the withdrawal of North Korean forces to the 38th Parallel. The United Nations would then undertake the task of creating an independent, unified Korea.[2] The Indian prime minister, Jawaharlal Nehru, followed this suggestion with identical letters to Stalin and Acheson reiterating the necessity for seating the Peking government in the Security Council in order that it, Moscow, and Washington together could find a basis for ending the war. Stalin appeared receptive and in his reply suggested holding a five-power conference in order for the council to hear representatives of the Korean people from both sides of the dividing line.[3]

Though Soviet interest in the British and Indian mediation efforts intrigued Washington (the U.S. ambassador in Moscow describing it as "genuine"), any responses of a positive nature were far outweighed by considerations against negotiating at that stage of the conflict and with the Indo-British terms already having been aired publicly. Given Acheson's well-known belief that one could bargain with the Soviets only from a position of strength, the existing position of U.S./U.N. forces was simply too disadvantageous as a basis for discussion. Charles Bohlen, the Soviet expert, then minister at the U.S. embassy in Paris, argued that, although the Soviets seemed serious about negotiating and probably wished to find a way out of a "situation which obviously has taken a turn unanticipated by them," the quid pro quo for the withdrawal of North

Korean forces behind the 38th Parallel might involve the departure of U.S. troops, which "would clearly be unacceptable to us."[4] Little wonder, therefore, that the Truman administration should be dismayed by New Delhi's and London's offers to the Soviets of much larger concessions concerning policies toward China. As Acheson told Bevin, in a frank exchange on July 10, it was "imperative that (a) the aggressor not be militarily successful and (b) the Soviets not be paid any price whatever for calling off an attack which they should never have started."[5] The question of China's seat in the United Nations or the final disposition of Taiwan would simply have to wait on events in Korea.

Moreover, even if the arguments about the necessity for a balance of power between negotiating parties had not been enough to convince Truman and Acheson of the need to reject diplomatic bargaining at this stage of the conflict, domestic critics of the administration's Asian policy were enough to confirm the wisdom of a negative response. Senator Joseph McCarthy's attacks on the State Department had become irretrievably entwined with China-bloc criticisms that the Democratic administration had consistently failed to give Chiang Kai-shek its full support. Despite Truman's and Acheson's distrust of the Chinese Nationalist leader, they could not abandon him now and still hope to retain bipartisan support of their Korean policy and of the budgetary provisions—designed to support a global military containment policy—that it had set in train. Furthermore, New Delhi's and London's peace initiatives were viewed negatively as examples of appeasement, not only by certain members of Congress but also by news commentators and the wider American public.[6] Not surprisingly, therefore, when George Kennan, then head of the Policy Planning Staff, had argued in favor of exploring India's proposal, his views had been quickly stifled, John Foster Dulles (a Republican who had been brought into the administration to shore up bipartisan agreement) stating that such a course of action would confuse the American public and weaken its support for the administration's enhanced military spending program.[7]

Despite these setbacks to New Delhi's suggestions, however, the Indian government persisted in its efforts to solve a conflict that it saw as capable of becoming a general war. Sir Benegal Rau, the leader of India's delegation to the United Nations, next proposed on

August 11 that a Security Council commission—made up of non-permanent members of the council—be established to search for a "peaceful and honorable settlement of the Korean question" based on the premise that North Korean troops would withdraw and that there would be a ceasefire.

This suggestion, too, found little favor with Acheson since he feared that, instead of functioning as a committee designed to secure North Korean compliance with the U.N. resolutions of June 25 and June 27, the envisaged commission would undertake mediation during which the United States would not have the primary role.[8] As we shall see in later chapters, despite U.N. cover for American involvement in the Korean conflict, Washington would continually resist U.N. efforts designed to supplant its dominant position at the truce negotiations.

THE ATTRACTIONS OF "ROLL-BACK"

Concern about Indian activity was further heightened in the United States because the 38th Parallel was rapidly losing its sanctity as a possible ceasefire line. As Ernest Gross of the U.S. delegation to the United Nations revealed to his British counterpart, Gladwyn Jebb, on August 11, talk about a ceasefire bothered him because it "might be that we would want to advance well beyond the 38th parallel and not have our hands tied in any way by a commitment made at such an early stage."[9]

Gross, in fact, was referring indirectly to the discussions that had been taking place within the Truman administration since early July and that were weighted heavily in favor of U.S./U.N. troops crossing the parallel and rolling back the frontiers of the North Korean state. The R.O.K. president, Syngman Rhee, was responsible for bringing this matter to the forefront of international attention on July 13, when he argued that the North Korean attack had "obliterated" the parallel and warned that there would never be peace in Korea as long as the country remained divided. Many within the Truman administration supported this analysis; Dulles, for example, arguing that perpetuation of the boundary would simply give "asylum to the aggressor." Other members of the bureaucracy broadened the appeal of the proposal to move north, seeing in it the "first opportunity" for the United States to "displace part of the Soviet orbit" with incalculable strategic and psychological benefits to the "free world."[10]

Congress and the wider public also perceived these benefits to be worth the risk of a slightly longer war. As early as July 6, Senator Taft agreed that U.S./U.N. troops would have to "march right on over the 38th parallel and at least occupy the southern part of North Korea."[11] Newspaper editorials, and well-known columnists such as Walter Lippmann and Joseph Alsop, also argued for the line to be ignored. As U.S./U.N. fortunes improved still further, these ideas gained even wider currency and were more firmly supported. The success of the Inchon landing on September 15 made movement across the parallel virtually irresistible. At a cabinet meeting later that month, Acheson noted that the parallel was to be discounted and a commission would start the rehabilitation of Korea. Somewhat exultantly, he declared that the country would be "used as a stage to prove what Western Democracy can do to help the underprivileged countries of the world."[12] With the prospects of achieving roll-back rising daily, it is perhaps not surprising that the administration remained deaf to suggestions for a ceasefire during this period.

As U.S./U.N. forces approached North Korean territory, New Delhi, Moscow, and Peking (among others) embarked more urgently on attempts to restrain Washington from going beyond what had been the pattern: that of containing rather than reversing Communism. On September 30 India proposed that U.S./U.N. troops pause at the 38th Parallel, thereby allowing the North Korean Army a chance to lay down its arms. On October 5 the Netherlands' U.N. representative suggested something similar and proposed the suspension of all air, sea, and land operations north of the parallel until October 31, once again in the hope of providing that much-needed opportunity for the North Koreans to take stock of their position and agree that their objective of "liberating" the South had failed. The U.N. Secretariat also became active and drew up a plan for U.N.-supervised elections north of the parallel on the understanding that U.S./U.N. forces would not attempt to cross the line until these elections had been held.

Significantly, the Soviet government also came forward, both overtly and covertly, with certain formulae close to those that

Trygve Lie, the U.N. secretary general, had recently devised, and also designed to prevent the crossing of the meridian. On October 2 its U.N. delegation, together with those from the Ukraine, Byelorussia, Poland, and Czechoslovakia, submitted a draft resolution in the First Committee which called for the immediate cessation of hostilities, withdrawal of non-Korean troops from Korea, and the holding of all-Korean elections observed by a U.N. committee made up of representatives from states bordering Korea. A few days later the Soviet foreign minister, Andrey Vishinsky, authorized private talks between a Soviet member of the U.N. Secretariat, Vassili Kassaniev, and Hans Engen of the Norwegian delegation. Kassaniev told Engen that if General MacArthur agreed to stop his forces at the 38th Parallel, the "North Koreans would then lay down their arms, and, . . . a United Nations Commission would be allowed to go into North Korea to hold elections, et cetera."[13] On the surface at least, this appeared as a major retreat from Moscow's pre–Korean War position since for the first time the U.S.S.R. suggested it would accord the United Nations a significant role in the North.

While the Soviets were pursuing the possibility of negotiations, the Chinese government was becoming disillusioned with its efforts to signal interest in a settlement. Whereas on August 13 Peking had endorsed the Soviet proposal that it, alongside Pyongyang and Seoul, should attend U.N. discussions regarding the peninsula, by late September it was attempting to restrain the U.S. administration through the issuance of threats of intervention. Peking's most explicit warning came from Premier Chou En-lai on October 3, when he told the Indian ambassador in Peking, K. M. Panikkar, that if U.S. troops crossed into North Korea, Chinese units would enter the fighting. "The South Koreans did not matter," Chou explained, but American forces represented a danger that had to be resisted.[14]

The explanation for the discounting of these threats by senior members of the Truman administration need not detain us here, and have been discussed in full elsewhere.[15] What is important to note in the context of this analysis is the U.S. belief that stopping to negotiate at this juncture would incur greater risks than boldly marching forward. Halting the movement north, it was thought, would be equated with indecisiveness and timidity, and this fear of appearing weak was so potent that, even when it became clear that crossing the parallel had indeed led Chinese "volunteers" to enter into the fighting, the fear overrode doubts about the possible out-come of this changed military situation. Thus, when Keith Officer of Australia's U.N. delegation, Victor Belande of the Peruvian delega-tion, and, finally, Ernest Bevin (under pressure from the U.K. Chiefs of Staff) raised in early November the notion of establishing a demilitarized zone south of the Yalu River and a retreat by the rapidly advancing U.S./U.N. contingents to the neck of the penin-sula (roughly the 40th Parallel), powerful members of the Truman administration rejected the idea because of these fears of appearing flaccid. The U.N. commander, General MacArthur, portrayed the British proposal as appeasement of the kind found at Munich in 1938 and argued that to give up any portion of North Korea when victory was in sight "would be the greatest defeat of the free world in recent times." MacArthur's supporter in the army's Plans and Operations division in Washington, Maj.-Gen. Charles L. Bolté, agreed that such a suggestion was pusillanimous in the extreme. In his view, a "show of strength [would] discourage further aggression while weakness [would] encourage it." Furthermore, he stated, the establishment of such a zone would require negotiations with the Chinese Communists, an act that was "as fruitless as it [was] repul-sive."[16]

Though members of the State Department, notably John Paton Davies and Philip Jessup, were interested in the concept of a zone, and Acheson himself raised the idea at an NSC meeting on Novem-ber 10 and again on November 21 in discussion with officials from Defense, no one promoted the notion with any great vigor. At the meeting on November 21, Secretary of Defense George C. Mar-shall's view prevailed. He believed that MacArthur should push on with the "end the war" offensive (planned for November 24) and only when this had successfully been completed would the time have come for considering political proposals.[17] As a consequence of Marshall's intervention, Acheson informed Bevin on November 24 that adopting the British scheme, which would mean abandon-ing territory and population already fought for and won over, would have a catastrophic effect on the morale of U.S./U.N. troops and an adverse affect on American public opinion. Furthermore, the Chinese Communists would take such a proposal as "a starting point for negotiations to obtain something much more favorable to them and as an indication of the greatest weakness on our part." It would also imply recognition that China had a role to play in the settlement of Korea's future—a degree of importance which the United States was not, at this stage of the war, willing to grant the P.R.C.[18]

The Truman administration's rejection of establishing a buffer zone removed the last chance—slim though it might have been—of bringing the Korean conflict to a speedy conclusion. The Chinese had let it be known in mid-November, through the Polish delegation to the United Nations, that they were willing to consider demilitarization provided the zone was south of the Yalu only, and that it was accompanied by the withdrawal of the Seventh Fleet from the Taiwan Strait and by the removal of U.S. recognition for and aid to Chiang's regime. Under these circumstances, they might be willing to order their "volunteers" to return home.[19]

THE CHINESE OFFENSIVE

Harsh though these terms must have appeared to the U.S. administration, they were a strong hint that at that stage the Peking government's intervention in the fighting was primarily designed to enhance its security against the American presence in the region. Peking's leaked terms should have been considered alongside its other warnings that it was not prepared to stand idly by; instead, the failure to explore the Chinese position seriously, and the decision to push on with MacArthur's offensive, in part in order to probe Chinese intentions through military means, transformed the character of the Korean conflict once again. In this third phase of the fighting, U.S./U.N. forces were facing, as MacArthur put it, an "entirely new war" and, by early December, the prospect of defeat, as some 300,000 Chinese troops engaged them in fierce battle. By early January the Chinese and revitalized North Korean armies were south of the 38th Parallel and able to resurrect the war aim of liberating and unifying the entire peninsula.

With America now on the defensive and allied governments in disarray because of the speed of this transformation of fortunes, the U.N. community put still more energy into attempts to achieve a ceasefire. In recognition of the realities of this weakened political and military posture, Prime Minister Attlee rushed to Washington for talks with President Truman. He tried once again to persuade the United States to offer Peking what Britain believed was its due and something that would satisfy the P.R.C.'s international ambitions. In exchange for a ceasefire, Attlee suggested, Truman should consider giving Peking its seat in the United Nations and returning Taiwan to its jurisdiction, a suggestion that the U.S. president described negatively in his private diary as "fantastic."[20]

Other governments operating within the U.N. framework, led chiefly by India, were sympathetic to Britain's approach, and they tried to persuade the P.R.C. that, in exchange for a ceasefire at the 38th Parallel, Peking's interests would be taken fully into account. On December 12, therefore, Rau introduced two draft resolutions into the First Committee of the General Assembly. The first called on the president of the assembly to head a three-person group to determine the basis on which a ceasefire could be brought about, and the second called for a conference to settle "issues of concern in the Far East."[21]

Under American pressure, preference was given to the first resolution; but this meant that China's special delegation to the United Nations, led by General Wu Hsiu-chuan, which had arrived there the same day that MacArthur launched his offensive, treated the ceasefire group and its call for a cessation of hostilities with suspicion. In the Chinese view, such negotiations would be a trap as long as they excluded concrete assurances that other questions of vital importance to Peking would be discussed. Dismayed by this negative response but not yet willing to give up on its search for a settlement, the ceasefire group on January 11 introduced five principles that were to form the basis for negotiations subsequent to the establishment of a ceasefire. The principles promised Peking that, if a ceasefire with adequate safeguards could be arranged, representatives of the governments of the United Kingdom, the United States, the Soviet Union, and the People's Republic of China would convene a conference that would attempt to settle outstanding Far Eastern problems, "including, among others, those of Formosa (Taiwan) and representation of China in the United Nations."[22]

Again, the Chinese government rejected the terms, Chou En-lai on January 17 arguing that an initial ceasefire was simply "designed to give U.S. troops a breathing space." His government countered with a series of unrealistic proposals, calling for a seven-power

conference to be held in China, for the P.R.C. to be installed in the
United Nations from the start, for an agreement to the withdrawal
of all foreign forces from Korea, and for the subject matter of the
conference also to include the removal of American protective
power from Taiwan. It was a further indication, if any were needed,
of how intertwined the Korean and Taiwan problems were for
Peking.

Yet, despite the expansive nature of these objectives, it did not
mean that the Communist leaders as a result of their military successes were going to be totally inflexible. A few days later the
Chinese elaborated their position, confirming that the withdrawal
of foreign troops also applied to the Chinese units, and that there
would be a ceasefire for a limited period prior to the negotiations on
the larger issues. The Indians were interested in these Chinese
terms and their subsequent exposition since New Delhi believed
that for the first time the Taiwan issue had narrowed to the question
of American forces protecting the island, and that agreeing to a
ceasefire first was a genuine concession on Peking's part. Thus, on
January 25, New Delhi persuaded the Arab-Asian bloc to introduce
a new draft resolution requesting a seven-nation group to secure
"all necessary elucidation and amplification" of the Chinese response.[23]

Developments on the battlefield and on the domestic front within
the United States were rapidly overtaking these diplomatic actions,
however. In the uncertain and grim days of early December, with
U.S./U.N. casualities mounting, Washington established that, although a ceasefire at the 38th Parallel was probably the best military
option, politically it was totally unacceptable. As General Marshall
argued on December 1, to sue for peace then would "represent a
great weakness on the [United States'] part"; and Acheson foresaw
the likely Communist demands as a withdrawal of U.S./U.N. forces
from Korea, the removal of the Seventh Fleet from the Taiwan
Strait, a seat for the P.R.C. in the United Nations, and Peking's
participation in the conclusion of the Japanese Peace Treaty. It was a
"bitter choice" to be faced with, Acheson said; a political price that
was "too great," General Bradley agreed.[24]

Thus, at the time of Attlee's visit in early December, the Truman
administration had already decided that it should resist proposing
or accepting a ceasefire while its forces were in headlong retreat and

[30]

certainly would "not pay anything" for a truce if one was brought about. Indeed, U.S. forces would stop fighting only provided another state proposed the cessation of hostilities, that the termination of the conflict occurred at the 38th Parallel, that the truce had no political conditions associated with it, and that an orderly military retreat into the three beachheads at the Seoul-Inchon area, at Hamhung, and at Pusan preceded such a truce. If this proved impossible, and U.S./U.N. forces were forced off the peninsula, then retaliation against P.R.C. territory would probably be the next step.[25]

Nevertheless, although Washington found it distasteful to consider the need for a ceasefire, military developments forced it to do so. Moreover, the intense diplomatic activity at the United Nations directed toward terminating the conflict obliged the United States to consider in more detail what armistice arrangements it would find acceptable. In response to an NSC directive of December 11, the Joint Chiefs of Staff offered their terms. These included the establishment of a demilitarized zone across Korea, some 20 miles in width, with the southern limit at the 38th Parallel; the organization of a ceasefire commission with supervisory powers and powers of inspection entailing free and unlimited access to the whole of Korea, in order to ensure that there was no reinforcement of men or materiel; and the exchange of prisoners of war on a one-for-one basis until all U.N. Command men had been returned, to be followed by the return of those remaining in U.N. Command compounds.[26]

These terms deliberately emphasized only the military aspects of a ceasefire, and the discussions in early December similarly showed how reluctant the administration was to have any political conditions attached to a truce agreement. Thus, at first sight, it seems odd for the United States to have voted for the 13-power resolution with its promise, after a cessation of hostilities, of considering the settlement of other Far Eastern problems, including that of Taiwan. As Acheson stated later in his memoirs, the choice of whether to support or oppose the resolution "was a murderous one, threatening on one side the loss of the Koreans and the fury of Congress and the press and, on the other, the loss of our majority and support in the United Nations." And indeed, congressional critics of the administration did attack the State Department for reneging on its pledges not to reward the Chinese Communists and for offering them the opportunity to "shoot their way into the U.N." But as

Acheson fervently hoped and believed probable at that time, the Chinese did reject the 13-power resolution, for reasons outlined above. Moreover, even if Peking had accepted it, the United States would have attempted to confine the agenda of any conference to details about the Korean settlement, and would have tried to ensure that other Far Eastern questions were not linked to a Korean truce. But if other issues did intrude upon the agenda, this would be without any prior U.S. commitment to a particular position and might well have led to the inclusion of other items such as "Communist recognition and support of Ho Chi-minh, Tibet, treatment of US persons and property in China, etc."[27] In other words, the United States would not have entered into negotiations with the P.R.C. with the deliberate intention of exchanging a Korean armistice for the settlement of outstanding problems in Sino-American relations.

America's December decisions also make it unlikely that the discussions from January to May 1951 between C. B. Marshall of the State Department's Policy Planning Staff and the "Third Party" (a Chinese national identified with non-Communist elements in the Peking government) were primarily pursued in order to explore the basis for a possible settlement. Indeed, the tone of these discussions between Marshall and "Third Party" was distinctly threatening: Marshall on more than one occasion outlined the difficulties of constraining American emotions that dictated taking "naval and air action against the Chinese on the mainland." The United States had so far desisted from taking such action, the U.S. envoy said, but if reason were to be set aside, it would "lay waste their cities and destroy their industries." If such language—with its atomic dimension made clear—was not in itself enough to undermine the basis for negotiations, such contacts were also initiated against the background of administration efforts within the United Nations to obtain a resolution labeling China an aggressor in Korea—hardly an action conducive to the establishment of a modus vivendi between the two governments. As "Third Party" stated, once the resolution had passed, "several weeks" would be required before tempers would cool in Peking over this action.[28]

A number of factors caused the Truman administration to give priority to the aggressor resolution and made it unwilling to delay its passage any further, influences that undercut its desire to pursue

[32]

these elusive indirect contacts or to explore the elaborated Chinese counterproposals of January 22. Domestic criticism of the executive branch's dilatoriness was running at fever pitch. Acheson claimed in discussions with the British on January 18 that the delay occasioned by allied and U.N. opposition to the resolution and their preference for searching for the basis of a settlement had brought the administration "to the verge of destruction domestically."[29] And when the House and Senate adopted their own resolutions branding China an aggressor, it was apparent that the administration could no longer consider the sensibilities of other friendly states. With the passage of the U.N. resolution on February 1, the possibility of an early ceasefire reached a definite end.

Furthermore, the military crisis that had faced U.S./U.N. forces in early December and the heightening of fears that had occurred in early January as a result of a Chinese offensive that took their troops south of the 38th Parallel had abated considerably by the time of the resolution's passage—so much so that on February 2, Dean Rusk could confidently report to the ambassadors of countries cooperating with the U.N. effort that enemy forces were unable to carry out their "original intention [of driving] UN forces into the sea." He also reassured the ambassadors, in response to press speculation regarding the 38th Parallel, that the U.N. Command was not contemplating extensive ground action above that line because of the realization that its forces were not strong enough to "reliberate" all of the north.[30]

At this stage of the conflict the joint chiefs were in agreement that there should be no advance north of the parallel on the grounds that the troops were close to the limits of their capabilities; and even going beyond the Han River was then thought inadvisable since, as Gen. J. Lawton Collins argued, it "would put the Eighth Army in a position with an unfordable river at its back." However, with the continuing success of Eighth Army operations, then led by General Ridgway, the military's position hardened, and in consequence its territorial designs expanded. Rather than be restricted, as members of the State Department still seemed to prefer, to a line south of the Han, the joint chiefs began to consider an advance that could take them as far north as Wonsan on the east.[31] A compromise between the two departments was obviously urgently required; and with State overridingly concerned to maintain allied unity, and Defense

[33]

determined to ensure the best possible defensive line for its forces, it was agreed that U.S./U.N. forces would be permitted to wage an "aggressive-defense" and that this could require them to go up to 20 miles inside North Korea.

THE EMERGING MILITARY STALEMATE

A further development arising from the improvement in the military position of U.S./U.N. forces was that the president and his advisers became more receptive to allied and U.N. pressure to reconsider a ceasefire. A draft presidential statement, which had been discussed with the allies and was responsive to the January 13 resolution, was therefore prepared. It argued that there was now a basis for "restoring peace and security in the area which should be acceptable to all" since the aggressors had been "drawn back with heavy losses to the general vicinity from which the unlawful attack was first launched." The planned statement also suggested, deliberately vaguely, that a prompt settlement in Korea would "reduce international tension in the Far East and would open the way for the consideration of other problems in that area."

MacArthur's known distrust of the administration's China policy and his belief that his primary military objective should remain the unification of Korea probably prompted him to issue his own declaration to the Chinese Communists and North Koreans a few days after being informed of Truman's intended initiative. The tenor of the U.N. commander's statement was completely at odds with the president's and was reminiscent of the powerful Athenians' demands made to the Melians in the Peloponnesian War. In the general's text, he pointed to the failure of the enemy's military tactics and drew attention to its inability to provide the essentials for modern warfare. His statement also carried a warning that the United States might still decide to expand the war and force China's complete military collapse. Meanwhile, MacArthur suggested, with the Chinese and North Korean armies currently facing total defeat, there should be no reason why an accommodation on the Korean problem could not be reached "without being burdened by extraneous matters not directly related to Korea, such as Formosa and China's seat in the United Nations."[32]

[34]

The statement was the latest, if not the major, outrage in Mac-Arthur's chain of insubordinate actions over Asian policy and, as he undoubtedly desired, it completely scotched any chance of a U.S. peace initiative's being launched at this stage. The Chinese regarded his words as an insult; there was nothing in his statement that acknowledged their continuing strength in North Korea or that suggested that there might now be a mutuality of interest in seeking an end to the war.

In other, more indirect ways MacArthur was instrumental in damaging any early modus vivendi between Peking and Washington. True, options were limited anyway, as shown when John McCormack, the House majority leader, told a State Department official that an exchange of a ceasefire for U.S. recognition of the P.R.C. "would completely destroy all of the Democratic support for the administration" and that he would rather see a withdrawal from Korea than "such an act of 'appeasement'." But at the congressional hearings called to investigate General MacArthur's subsequent dismissal on April 11 from his Far Eastern and U.N. commands, General Marshall, under pressure from administration critics, publicly conceded that Taiwan would *never* be allowed to fall into the hands of the Communists; neither would the P.R.C. be permitted to assume the U.N. seat. Although Marshall's statement "reflected established policy, its publication stripped the diplomatic camouflage from U.S. support of the Five Principles," introduced by the ceasefire group in January. Over the same period of mid-May, Rusk and Dulles made similarly uncompromising public statements, Rusk seeming to rule out any future accommodation with the current Chinese leaders and effectively calling for the overthrow of this "colonial Russian government," this "Slavic Manchukuo on a large scale." Moreover, out in Hong Kong, C. B. Marshall, in private conversations with Eric Chow, the editor of the newspaper *Ta Kung Pao*—a paper that reflected thinking in Peking—warned that he did not know at what point the "American people and their government would say, 'To hell with it. Let's give the Chinese what they're asking for'." It would be wrong to assume that the U.S. determination "to withhold itself from indulgence of its emotional impulses was limitless."[33] At this stage, therefore, there was not much of a bargaining position with the Chinese left intact, and the Soviet route began to look more promising.

[35]

Admittedly, there was a distinct preference for dealing directly with Moscow anyway. George Kennan, for one, argued that the Russians were the only ones to do business with because they were "the greatest land power in that part of the world and have an obvious and legitimate interest in what goes on in Northern Korea." Could it also have been that there was a marked preference for dealing with Europeans of great-power status rather than with the "savage and arrogant" Chinese, as Kennan had recently described them? An approach to the Soviets would also have the additional and agreeable affect of serving to diminish Chinese Communist prestige by treating them almost as puppets of Moscow and not as an independent force in Korea. Conversations between Bohlen and Vladimir Semenov were further designed to bolster this notion of a mutuality of interest between the two superpowers but only elicited a short response from the Soviet official indicating that the time was not yet ripe: the Chinese still believed, he said, that they could be victorious in Korea and push American troops off the peninsula.[34]

Before further progress toward a truce could be made, therefore, Washington perceived it to be necessary to await the outcome of the latest Chinese offensive, launched on April 22. By the middle of May the hollowness of China's proud boast was plain, as some 17,000 Chinese troops surrendered—up to that time, it had been a rare occurrence—and their casualties steadily mounted. According to Peng Te-huai, who then led the Chinese "volunteers," food and general supply problems caused "great difficulties," and those troops who did make it back to Chinese lines were "exhausted." In consequence, the American and Soviet governments quickly moved into action. On May 31 and again on June 5, George Kennan and the Soviet ambassador to the United Nations, Jacob Malik, discussed the prospects for a ceasefire in Korea. Kennan offered the narrowest of terms and no additional inducements to the Chinese. The United States required, he said, a "termination of hostilities approximately in the region where they were now taking place" and the establishment of a control authority to oversee that both sides were adhering to the terms of the agreement.[35]

The Soviets had obviously been receptive to the idea of a ceasefire since the early spring of 1951, and, as Malik told Kennan in June, his government wanted a truce at the "earliest possible moment." However, since Soviet forces were not directly participating in the fighting, and because the government did not wish to be too closely linked with the events on the peninsula, these points made it difficult for Moscow to enter into the kinds of detailed discussions that would be necessary. Nevertheless, Moscow could intervene to the extent of circumscribing the general scope of the negotiations and could force their pace. Malik's radio address on June 23, when he called for a "ceasefire and an armistice providing for the mutual withdrawal of forces from the 38th parallel," accomplished this. In a further clarification of this statement Gromyko confirmed, to the Truman administration's satisfaction, that this was to be a strictly military armistice to be arranged by the opposing military commanders, with no provisions regarding political or territorial matters.[36]

The evidence indicates that neither the Chinese Communists nor the North Koreans were entirely enamored with Malik's peace proposal. Indeed, according to the counselor at the Indian embassy in Peking, from conversations he had had with the head of the Asian department of the Chinese ministry of foreign affairs, he had formed the impression that the Chinese had been apprised in general terms that a Soviet initiative was likely, but they had not known in advance about the intended broadcast.[37] The North Korean press and radio gave greater attention to the subsequent statement of General Ridgway (now U.N. commander) offering to begin negotiations than to Malik's proposal, which was the starting point for the U.N. commander's offer. The first direct Chinese broadcast of Malik's statement for the Peking Home Service was not made until June 29 and was accompanied by the details of Senator Edwin Johnson's peace proposal, made in May, which suggested a ceasefire along the 38th Parallel, together with the withdrawal of all non-Korean forces from Korea by December 31 and for a full exchange of prisoners. The repetition of these points was an important indication of China's future position at the truce negotiations.

The Chinese also linked Malik's June 23 offer with all other occasions when they or the Soviets had urged a peaceful settlement of the war; and they continually stressed that the Soviet proposal represented only a "first step" toward a peaceful settlement—the implication being that they were hoping for and expecting a widening of the terms of the discussion.[38] However, it was clearly going to be an uphill struggle for the Chinese and North Koreans to get

additional items onto the agenda now that the Soviets had aban-
doned unambiguous reference to the need to withdraw all foreign
troops from the country and to the provisions that were of direct
political and military interest to the P.R.C. concerning Taiwan.

On the eve of the formal armistice talks, therefore, one year after
the start of the Korean conflict, crucial decisions had been taken and
moves made that already were to shape the course of the forthcoming discussions. In certain respects the United States was in the
strongest position and, within the administration itself, had established a reasonably firm base of support for various armistice provisions. True, the demands of Western and Asian states such as
Britain, Canada, and India, who wanted a more conciliatory approach to be adopted toward the Chinese and a speedy end to this
dangerous phase of the Cold War, still constrained the administration. For Europeans, there was the additional motive of wanting the
United States to resume a wholly Europe-first orientation. Then, at
the other end of the spectrum, there were the South Koreans, who
unrealistically outlined their armistice requirements as the withdrawal of all Chinese forces from the peninsula, the complete disarmament of the North Koreans, U.N. guarantees that no third party
would render any financial or military support to the D.P.R.K., and
full participation for the R.O.K. in any international conference
considering any aspect of the Korean problem. In addition, the
Rhee government warned the U.S. ambassador in Seoul, John J.
Muccio, that South Korea would cooperate with the armistice only
provided no use was made of the 38th Parallel as a dividing line.[39]
Moreover, there were also domestic critics, such as Senators Taft
and Richard M. Nixon, ready to seize on any negotiating concessions as evidence of the administration's perfidy and already claiming that a truce at the 38th Parallel would be an "appeasement
peace." Anything less than "complete triumph" on the battlefield
was evidence, Taft argued, that "140,000 casualties and billions of
dollars" had been wasted.[40] And sentiments such as these could be
found within the administration also. Students of American foreign
policy have frequently commented on the Truman administration's
dislike of negotiating with its Communist adversaries, and, as has
been indicated, this applied to the Korean case also. More generally,
too, Washington was uncomfortable with the notion of mediation.

[38]

As C. B. Marshall noted at the time, the United States was reluctant to settle a problem when the tide was adverse because "that would involve the submission to unfavorable circumstances" but was equally reluctant to settle when the tide was favorable, "for that would involve missing an expansive opportunity." The temptation was thus to be uncompromising in moments of weakness and in moments of strength alike.[41]

This distaste for the mediatory process was further intensified in the circumstances of the Korean conflict because the likely outcome of truce discussions was seen as being the establishment of a military stalemate and not a permanent settlement of the Korean problem. Even the idea of stalemate created special strains for Americans, given their history of involvement in wars that had resulted in outright victory and the surrender of enemy forces. These broader and more diffuse reasons for the dislike of negotiation, explored in brief in the previous chapter and associated with the American political and military cultures, pointed to the difficulties that lay ahead.

Finally, a stalemate on the peninsula would make it difficult, if not impossible, to satisfy one of the central U.S. objectives outlined in NSC 48/5 of May 17, 1951: the deflation of Chinese Communist political and military strength and prestige. The pursuit of this objective militated against the goal of achieving a cessation of hostilities and worked in favor of the continuing punishment of the Chinese People's Volunteers.

The Truman administration entered the negotiations, therefore, against the background of this negative attitude toward mediation and of conflicting international and domestic pressures. Nevertheless, even as it remembered the abject days immediately after the Chinese intervention, it could now savor the remarkable turnaround in U.S./U.N. military fortunes, together with its arrival at a battle position—the so-called Kansas line—valued by the joint chiefs. Furthermore, though the Eighth Army commander (Gen. James A. Van Fleet) railed against the administration's decision not to pursue the weakened Chinese armies, the realization that a push into the North would shorten enemy supply lines, encourage greater enemy resistance, and result in greatly increased U.S./U.N. casualties tempered General Ridgway's enthusiasm for going far beyond the 38th Parallel.[42] On balance, therefore, while U.S. ca-

[39]

pabilities remained restricted and the threat of Chinese armies loomed large, a limited war and negotiated settlement had to remain the preferred outcome. In a final instruction, ten days before the opening of the talks, Ridgway would thus be given certain minimum objectives to pursue. These were to restrict the agenda to military questions; to refuse to enter into discussions of any final settlement for Korea or consider such topics as Taiwan or the China seat in the U.N.; to seek to establish a demilitarized zone across Korea 20 miles wide based generally on positions at the time the ceasefire was agreed upon; to establish a supervisory commission with powers of inspection to ensure that the armistice terms were being adhered to and that no reinforcements of personnel or materiel were entering the country; and, finally, to exchange prisoners of war on a one-for-one basis as expeditiously as possible, meanwhile allowing representatives of the International Red Cross to visit all POW camps.[43]

On balance, the Chinese and North Korean negotiators entered the talks in a somewhat less favorable military and political position when compared with that of the U.N. Command. Admittedly, their actual numerical strength in Korea remained impressive, their military position was improving as supply lines contracted on the enforced return north, and troop reinforcements were easier to obtain than for the U.N. side. Yet theirs, rather than the Americans', was the most recent military setback on the peninsula with the failure of the April–May offensives. And it was the Communists who most recently had been forced to admit a reversal of their stated objectives in the war of driving U.S./U.N. forces into the sea, claiming now that they sought a more modest aim of achieving a settlement at the old dividing line between the two Koreas.[44]

Much had led the Chinese and North Koreans to expect that the parallel would indeed form the demarcation line in any future armistice agreement, including the publicity surrounding Acheson's statement at the MacArthur hearings in which he stated that a truce on or around that line would be acceptable; the debates and discussions within the United Nations from July 1950, all of which had emphasized a return to the status quo ante; and finally Malik's statement of June 23, which had started the formal negotiating process. However, on June 24, U.S./U.N. forces were above that parallel, except at its western end, and were to prove difficult to dislodge anywhere along it, either militarily or through political persuasion.

The implication of Semenov's statement to Bohlen in April that the Chinese believed they could regain the military initiative, only for the P.R.C. to be proved horribly wrong a few days later, also suggested that Peking was at a disadvantage in its relations with Moscow at this time. Kim Il Sung probably was at a disadvantage as well as a result of his mistaken claim, apparently made in discussions with Stalin before the intervention, that the projected war could quickly be won, before the United States had time to intervene.[45] Perhaps it was the imprudence of these calculations that in part explains Moscow's failure to refer explicitly in the June 23 statement or in its elaboration to any of the Communist negotiating terms once thought immutable—namely, representation for the P.R.C. in the United Nations, the withdrawal of the Seventh Fleet from the Taiwan Strait, and the removal of all foreign forces from the Korean peninsula. Though Malik in his broadcast spoke of the ceasefire as the first step in the negotiating process, his failure to outline any subsequent moves weakened Peking's and Pyongyang's positions on the eve of the talks, and their ability to introduce wider objectives into the bargaining process.

[41]

[3]

The First Phase of the Negotiations:
July to November 1951

The armistice negotiations were begun at the city of Kaesong on July 10, between the lines of the opposing armies. They were led on the U.N. Command side by Vice Adm. Charles Turner Joy and on the Communist side by Gen. Nam Il of the Korean People's Army and Gen. Hsieh Fang of the Chinese People's Volunteers. Very quickly the talks ran into a variety of procedural and substantive difficulties. Indeed, before they had officially gotten underway, disputes over the site for the discussions, including access for the Western press and guarantees of security for the negotiators, immediately slowed progress. Determining the scope of the agenda and agreeing the level of specificity of the items placed on that list would also become issues, even before the two sides came to what then appeared to be the most crucial item on the table, the fixing of the ceasefire line.

Negotiating Positions and Tactics

On June 30 Gen. Matthew B. Ridgway, the U.N. commander, made the first direct move in response to the Malik broadcast, suggesting that the Communist commanders in the field meet with the U.N. Command negotiators aboard a Danish hospital ship in Wonsan harbor, there to determine the armistice arrangements for Korea. Ridgway tried to phrase his message in such a way as to confirm that the initiative for the peace talks had come from the Communist camp. He also took the opportunity to remind his opposing commanders that the discussions would be strictly confined to military matters. In their reply two days later the North Koreans and Chinese countered America's opening salvo by implying there existed a joint agreement to discuss wider questions, such as suspending military actions and holding "peace negotiations." Furthermore, they suggested that the talks be held at Kaesong, just below the 38th Parallel.[1]

The rejection of the hospital ship should neither have been surprising nor unexpected since Denmark, through the provision of medical units, was associated with the U.S./U.N. side. Moreover, U.S./U.N. forces dominated the waters around the peninsula, and communications on the ship presumably would have been under U.N. control. And though mention of Kaesong disturbed some within the Truman administration (the JIC described the site as having "definite political and psychological advantages to the enemy"),[2] others found it an acceptable suggestion. As Dean Rusk, assistant secretary of state for Far Eastern affairs, noted in his briefing to ambassadors of countries with forces in Korea, the administration, too, "had been thinking in terms of Kaesong as an alternative site for the meeting."[3] Kaesong, the ancient capital of Korea, appeared at that stage to be midway between the lines, and U.S./ U.N. forces had frequently visited the area in recent weeks without encountering enemy troops.

The old capital, however, quickly became a problem. As the JIC had stated, Kaesong did have enormous political and symbolic importance to the Communists, and its location became part of their bargaining tactics. As a *People's Daily* editorial put it on July 2, it was the former capital of the country and, more importantly, "as the 38th parallel will be the military demarcation line" and as Kaesong "is at the 38th parallel [it] would be the most suitable place" for discussions.[4] Communist troops were in fact present in the area in considerable numbers, and their commanders used the intervening period before the start of negotiations to move forces into the city. Thus, when the U.N. Command liaison party arrived there on July 8, enemy troops, journalists, and photographers surrounded it and depicted the group as suing for peace. This propaganda exercise, designed by the Communists for both external and internal consumption, was to prove costly in terms of the relations between the two delegations at the talks and therefore would prove detrimental to progress.

Though the U.N. Command was stuck with Kaesong (for a time

at least) and with all that might now imply for the ceasefire line, it was determined to establish satisfactory procedural arrangements for the conference. The talks suffered their first recess on July 12 over the issues of the demilitarization of the site, access for the press, and unrestricted communications for the U.N. Command delegation between its base and the conference area. The Communists agreed to the U.N. Command's terms on July 15, but in accepting them attempted to establish the principle of reciprocity as their "idea of justice"[5] on all future points. As their message of acceptance said: "We maintain the principle that all matters will be carried out with the agreement of both sides," believing such a principle to be "the most impartial" because it left "no room for argument or opposition."[6]

Through their actions at Kaesong on the eve of the talks, the Communists had been attempting to bolster their negotiating position. As noted in Chapter 2, in a number of respects they were in the weaker military position and had suffered the most recent military setbacks. It was they, too, who had recently publicly changed their objectives from the unification of Korea to the reestablishment of peace at the 38th Parallel. Through their propaganda and military moves, they had tried to compensate for these weaknesses before their domestic and foreign audiences. The North Korean press and radio, for example, gave prominence to Ridgway's message of June 30 but claimed it implied that the "imperialist aggressors" were suing for peace because their military adventure had failed.[7] And by moving forces into Kaesong, they could try to give substance to their claim that their troops were still south of the 38th Parallel in strength.

Notwithstanding these tactics, their claims to victory would soon be seen to be exaggerated as the discussions moved to the question of the framing of the agenda. The U.N. Command delegation came forward with a nine-point agenda, some points of which were related to others and others of which were statements rather than items for negotiation. The Communist five-point agenda did not contain any overlapping portions but did mingle specific points (such as the establishment of the 38th Parallel as the military demarcation line and the withdrawal of all armed forces of foreign countries from Korea) with more generalized ones, such as concrete arrangements for the realization of the ceasefire and arrangements

[44]

relating to prisoners of war.[8] It seems probable, and the U.N. Command delegation apparently believed, that the Communists thought their two specific points had already been agreed upon tacitly, before the formal start of the negotiations.[9] As the *People's Daily* put it on August 11 with regard to the 38th Parallel, Malik's proposal, which was the basis for the negotiations, called for a ceasefire at that point; the parallel had been crossed three times during the war and battle lines were still not stable; it had been the dividing line before the outbreak of the conflict; the crossing of it by U.S./U.N. forces had occasioned Chinese entry; and generals Marshall, Omar Bradley, Collins, and Secretary Acheson had all advocated a ceasefire on that line at the MacArthur hearings. One analyst has confirmed through interviews in Peking in the early 1980s that the Chinese had paid great attention to Acheson's words in particular.[10] The secretary of state had indeed said on June 2, in response to a question from Sen. H. Alexander Smith (Republican, New Jersey), that a settlement at or near the parallel "would accomplish the military purposes in Korea," and earlier in March, General Ridgway, when Eighth Army commander, had stated publicly that "it would be a tremendous victory for the United Nations" if the war ended on that line. Moreover, the U.N. secretary general, Trygve Lie, announced on June 1 that a ceasefire approximately along the parallel "would fulfil the main purposes of the United Nations."[11]

The hearings had also made it appear that the United States did not wish to waste its resources in Korea, an area of secondary strategic importance, and Acheson had stated at least three times in his testimony to the Senate that if a stabilized settlement emerged, all foreign troops could gradually be withdrawn.[12] Therefore, discussions about foreign troop withdrawal (including Chinese forces, as the North Korean chief negotiator, Nam Il, made clear)[13] should have been welcomed by the Americans, in the Communists' view. But both of these issues were far more complex than the responses at the MacArthur hearings implied, involving the undoubtedly violent reaction of the South Korean authorities to either move, and the difficulties of reengaging recently withdrawn U.S. forces should hostilities break out in the future. There was also the question of America's global position to consider: as Paul Nitze, the new head of the State Department's Policy Planning Staff wrote, a settlement at the 38th Parallel "would give the impression that the Chinese and

North Korean communists had been able to achieve somewhat more than an even military result against sixteen nations, including the U.S., U.K., Canada, and France." Nitze's political arguments reinforced the important objectives of the joint chiefs regarding the military security of U.N. Command forces. They regarded the new battle line (Kansas)—above the parallel except for a small section in the west—as far more defensible than the 38th Parallel, and they had no intention of returning to that old dividing line.[14] For a combination of political and military reasons, therefore, the Truman administration was determined to reject Communist arguments regarding the placement of the ceasefire line.

The Communist delegation was to have a rude awakening, then, when it became clear that the U.N. Command would not accept either of its two specific points as agenda items. Moreover, it quickly became apparent that the Chinese and North Koreans had made an error in being so open about their objectives at this stage of the negotiations. Thus began a Communist retreat on the phrasing of the agenda, which was hardly matched by the U.N. Command side's agreement to collapse a number of their overlapping points under a smaller number of headings. On July 16 the Communists agreed to eliminate the reference to the 38th Parallel and on July 25 removed direct reference to the withdrawal of foreign troops, subsuming it under a separate agenda item (item 5), which became "recommendations to governments of the countries concerned on both sides." This statement allowed the Communists to claim that the question of foreign troop withdrawal would be taken up later, but for the U.N. Command it meant that they had made no commitment at all on the matter.

Having established the agenda (after discussions of less than 22 hours, spread over 17 days on seven of which there had been no meetings, as the Chinese remarked),[15] the two delegations moved on to the detail of the armistice agreement: first, item 2, the fixing of a military demarcation line between the opposing forces and the establishment of a demilitarized zone (DMZ). At the initial meeting on this item, neither side wanted to be the first to make its position known. However, under U.N. Command pressure, the Communists did so and reverted to their earlier arguments for a demarcation line based on the 38th Parallel. The next day, however, the U.N. Command countered with a line running generally through Pyong-

yang and Wonsan, well north of the Kansas line, the latter being the
U.N. Command's minimum negotiating position. To support its
arguments for a line that was so favorable to the U.N. Command
side, Admiral Joy, chief U.N. Command negotiator, presented the
notion of the three zones of military significance: the air, sea, and
ground zones. Since the U.N. side maintained air superiority over
all of Korea and controlled the seas around the peninsula, it should
be awarded additional territory on the ground, he argued.[16]

No doubt Joy's team believed that, in going for such a high
opening position, one on which it would later compromise, it was
following a textbook-approved method of bargaining. However, it
has often been argued that successful negotiation requires the ad-
vancement of credible arguments, and that even in adversary negotiations some notion of equity is necessary. The line put forward
rejected any notion of reciprocity since it took territory away from
the Communists. Furthermore, the argument for more territory to
be awarded made little sense, since, as Gen. Nam Il said, "your
battlelines on the ground are the concentrated expression of the
military effectiveness of your land, air and sea forces."

Nam's arguments probably made a considerable impact on the
U.N. Command delegation because apparently the team was experiencing a "strong sense of guilt" in advocating a line so far north of
the battle area, and this had led the negotiators to put this proposal
forward in a somewhat ambiguous manner. Whether or not the
Communist delegation detected this lack of firmness is impossible
to say, but once advanced, this U.N. Command proposal contributed to a notable deterioration in language and atmosphere at the
talks. Nam Il described the argument as "naive and illogical" and
"not worthy of attention." His side's stand on the 38th Parallel, on
the other hand, was "righteous and immovable"; furthermore, he
believed Joy's statements on America's military power to be intim-
idating in tone.[17] On August 3 he repeated 14 times the claim that
the U.N. Command's proposed line cut deep into present Communist positions; and eight days later, the two sides sat in sullen
silence for two hours and 11 minutes, in total deadlock over this
question.[18]

Not until August 16 did progress begin to be made in breaking
this impasse when Nam Il accepted Joy's suggestion that item 2 be
discussed at subdelegation level. At these meetings the two sides

appeared to be much more relaxed, as they met at a round table only two feet in diameter. The U.N. Command reiterated the reasons for its original demilitarized zone and offered some "possible hypothetical adjustments" to it such as narrowing its size and adjusting its southern boundary. Three days later on August 20 the Communists suggested that they were considering substituting the line of contact for the 38th Parallel as the final demarcation line.[19]

Before either delegation could act on these promising positions, however, the Communists called off the talks as a result of the alleged bombing of the conference site. There had in fact been a number of alleged and proven violations of the neutral zone surrounding Kaesong throughout the period of the negotiations. In addition, on July 24, as the agenda was being established, the commander of the U.S. Far Eastern Air Force confirmed that seven aircraft had also "unintentionally" violated the Chinese border.[20] The Communists reported the first incident in the Kaesong area on July 16, claiming that U.S./U.N. soldiers had fired toward the town of Panmunjom. On August 4 Chinese troops, carrying small arms, marched past the U.N. Command's house at Kaesong, which evoked a harsh warning from Ridgway. Four days later the Communists again accused U.S./U.N. troops of having fired at Panmunjom and a day later claimed that Communist trucks had been fired upon. On August 19 a Chinese platoon leader was killed in the neutral zone, and three days later the Communists alleged that the conference site had been bombed and strafed by a U.N. plane.

It is difficult to ascertain why the Communists decided to break off the negotiations over this last incident and not over earlier ones, and whether in fact they fabricated the evidence of the bombing. The conclusion of the U.N. Command investigating officers was that the "incident was unquestionably staged by the Communists."[21] But Admiral Joy registered some doubts about this in his diary, stating that it was "debateable" if it had been manufactured, and that it could possibly have been an R.O.K. plane. (Indeed, the Fifth Air Force did pick up an unidentified aircraft on radar screens that night.)[22] R.O.K. forces and guerrilla units had been responsible for a number of the previous violations, and activity from this quarter could be expected to increase each time that the two delegations came close to agreement on any item (especially one as controversial for the South Koreans as the ceasefire line). According to the

[48]

U.S. daily intelligence bulletin for Korea, the ambush of the Chinese patrol that led to the death of a Chinese officer on August 19 was probably the "work of a politically-guided civilian group operating under instructions." The bulletin also confirmed that the general area of Kaesong had been, since early 1951, an area of R.O.K. guerrilla activity.[23] And, on August 28 Dean Rusk told the British ambassador in Washington that he feared that Syngman Rhee would eventually issue a statement claiming credit for having caused the breakdown of the talks.[24] The U.N. Command had been reluctant to take any responsibility for controlling the activities of these "unofficial" units, arguing that the agreement on neutralizing Kaesong "did not deprive the Communists of the means to suppress the hostile partisan activities in the area." But the Chinese and North Koreans apparently believed that the U.N. Command should take responsibility for irregulars who were "connected overtly or covertly with the headquarters of the South Korean troops," as they put it;[25] and it might have been that this disagreement, combined with the U.N. Command's outright dismissal of the bombing evidence, led to the Communist decision to choose that moment to make a stand on the issue.

The Truman administration advanced other explanations for the recess, however. Washington believed that the timing of the break was connected with the signature of the Japanese peace treaty, which was to take place at a ceremony in San Francisco in early September. In its view, the Communist camp was seeking to raise tensions on the eve of the treaty's signature. Ironically, the Communists argued the same thing, but in reverse: that the United States had encouraged the incidents at Kaesong in order to spin out the negotiations, increase tensions, and thereby "force the Japanese peace treaty down the throats of its satellites." *New China News Agency*, for example, described the events of August 19 and 22 at Kaesong as providing "just the sort of atmosphere needed to get their peace treaty signed at San Francisco."[26]

If, ultimately, the Japanese connection must remain uncertain, one other explanation should also be considered. As noted above, on the eve of the bombing incident the Communists had implied a readiness to concede on the demarcation line. They had attached so much importance to a ceasefire line at the 38th Parallel that they must have viewed this change of position as a concession of major proportions. It is possible that disputes within the North Korean government, or between the North Koreans and Chinese, forced a halt and a reconsideration of this projected move. It may even have been felt necessary to focus domestic opinion on the incidents at the conference site in order to divert attention away from the change of position at the talks; or, to bring in the Japanese connection again, it may have been regarded as unwise to retreat at Kaesong when a diplomatic failure for the Communist bloc also appeared imminent at San Francisco.

Whatever the actual reason for the recess (and the Communists intended only a temporary suspension),[27] the talks, once stopped, proved extremely difficult to restart. In early September, Ridgway requested of Washington that he be allowed to seek a new site for the negotiations (a policy position that will be discussed in detail below). He later asked that he be allowed to terminate the neutrality of Kaesong and refuse outright to go back there. The U.N. commander was most insistent on these matters, and he made such a public and private issue of the location that the administration's prestige became irrevocably tied to the demand. It was, though, a difficult issue for the Communists to concede: in the midst of their probable concession on the 38th Parallel, they were being required to relinquish the site they had originally chosen for the talks. Therefore, when they proposed a resumption of discussions on September 20, they stressed that these should again be held at Kaesong. In their view, the call for a new site was simply an American device to delay restarting the talks.[28]

Concurrently with the dispute on the issue of the site, Ridgway had been increasing military pressure on the enemy, both in the air and on the ground, to further strengthen the Kansas line. In Washington, too, the recess stimulated thinking about the necessary military courses of action to be taken in the event of a total breakdown of negotiations followed by the renewal of hostilities, or a breakdown followed by a de facto ceasefire. (Indeed, the "general impression in Britain" was that the United States "discount[ed] the prospects of an armistice and believe[d] that it [was] more realistic to plan action in the event of the armistice talks breaking down than to waste time considering what might be done if the armistice talks succeed.")[29] A consensus over these proposals had more or less been achieved between State and Defense by early September, points that included an advance to the neck of Korea, attacks on the Yalu River dams and power installations, and the enforcement of a total economic blockade of China.[30] In Tokyo if not in Washington, this concentration on military courses of action may have drawn attention and resources away from the development of proposals to bring about a resumption of discussions.

The administration's exasperation with the recess and generally slow pace of the talks also coincided with considerable optimism about the U.N. Command's military position in Korea. In late September, Gen. Omar Bradley, chairman of the U.S. Joint Chiefs of Staff, and Charles Bohlen, Soviet expert and now State Department counselor, visited Ridgway in Tokyo. Part of their brief was to discover the urgency of obtaining an armistice. They returned brimming with confidence about U.N. Command capabilities. As Bohlen put it in his report, both in Ridgway's headquarters, and "more particularly, in the Eighth Army and along the front we found complete confidence in the military capabilities and positions of the UN forces." There was also "confidence bordering on absolute certainty that any [major] offensive was doomed to bloody failure due to (1) the present defensive strength of the UN line, and (2) the measures which had been undertaken by the UN Command . . . in the matters of supply, fortifications, etc." Furthermore, the level of morale and training appeared to be "extremely high," and the troops were "well-supplied with essential winter clothing," unlike the Communists who, based on refugee reports, were said to be suffering from both lack of food and clothing. The only "dark spot" related to the future air situation as a consequence of the "steady build-up of MiGs" on the Manchurian airfields, and the continuation of U.N. Command casualties. Overall, however, Bohlen concluded, the U.S./U.N. was in an "extremely favorable" position, and there was "no great need to hurry the talks"; rather, there was much to "justify stringing them out" while avoiding a complete breakdown.[31]

It was plain that Bohlen had left this conclusion of his in the minds of the U.N. Command negotiators. As Joy wrote in his diary, in view of the favorable military position it was agreed with Bradley and Bohlen that "we would not be in a hurry to meet with Commies or to present our new UNC proposed zone. . . . Time and the approach of winter [was] working to our advantage. Therefore it

[was] better from our standpoint not to hurry a meeting of the delegations."[32] Ridgway and the U.N. Command team were therefore encouraged in their general obduracy and unwillingness to concede on the new site or on the demarcation line.

Just before the recess on August 23, Ridgway had in fact been in a more conciliatory frame of mind. Then, he had proposed to the joint chiefs that the DMZ be narrowed to four kilometers, in order to eliminate the problems of military and civil control that would occur in a zone 20 miles wide.[33] Though it was the U.N. commander who had initially suggested this position, it still took strong pressure from the joint chiefs in Washington to persuade him to introduce this proposal once the sessions had resumed at the new site of Panmunjom. Eventually, the adjusted position was put forward and was acknowledged as being "better" as far as the Communists were concerned, especially since it incorporated the idea of a reciprocal withdrawal from the line of two kilometers in order to form the demilitarized zone. However, the U.N. Command obviated potentially speedy agreement on this new line when the delegation demanded that the Communists withdraw from Kaesong and that the city be allowed to come into its hands. By the end of October, Kaesong had become the main item holding up agreement on the ceasefire line. In the Communists' view, they had agreed that the battle line should form the demarcation point between forces (as the U.N. Command had wanted all along), and that meant that they should retain Kaesong (even if they had obtained it by underhand means). Soviet reports saw in the proposal further indications of a U.S. intention to interrupt the negotiations. As far as the North Korean chief negotiator was concerned, it had become "the key point to the solution of our problems."[34]

The U.N. Command's proposal to retain Kaesong was popular neither within the conference tent nor outside it—in Washington, in the world's press, among foreign governments (with the exception of South Korea, of course). On November 4, therefore, and though indications were that they might have obtained a share of this area,[35] the U.N. Command delegation in Korea was instructed to give up the city. Perhaps realizing that their opposite numbers had slightly weakened their overall political position in maintaining for some days their demand for the retention of Kaesong, the Communists next proposed fixing the line of contact at that time, in order, as they put it, "to prevent the second item of the agenda from being procrastinated without end."[36] The U.N. Command team would not accept this proposal in the first instance, however, arguing that a ceasefire before other agenda items had been resolved would deprive U.S. forces of the ability to use military pressure to force agreement on the outstanding issues. Once again, Washington disagreed with its chief negotiators, though, and on November 17 Joy's delegation, under pressure from the joint chiefs, suggested that the existing line of contact could constitute a provisional military demarcation line, to become effective in any armistice agreement signed within 30 days.[37] It was the first substantial compromise that the Communists had obtained as a result of a proposal they had made. With this achievement, and the reciprocal nature of the demilitarized zone between forces confirmed, both sides worked to determine the actual location of battlefield forces. On November 26, item 2 was resolved.

A number of factors had influenced the pace and course of the negotiations in this first phase. Both sides had different expectations on the eve of the talks about the shape of the likely armistice agreement; U.S./U.N. forces were in possession of some territory north of the 38th Parallel and, whatever may have been said at the MacArthur hearings, were not about to be dislodged from a position that had daily been becoming stronger; and on a personal level there existed a distinct lack of trust between the adversaries, which had been exacerbated by initial Communist behavior at Kaesong. Broadly, over the five months the U.N. Command had shown a willingness to slow the pace of the talks in order to impose its position, and it seemed willing to compromise only over its weakest bargaining points. According to the RAND analyst that had been attached to Joy's negotiating team, U.S. negotiators were also slow to pick up Communist hints that they were about to concede on the ceasefire line, or were ready to return after the August 23 recess.[38] The Communists, however, having revealed their primary objectives as the withdrawal of foreign troops and securing the 38th Parallel as the ceasefire line, were forced into a series of difficult concessions.

In terms of negotiating styles, there were also indications that the two sides were following rather different approaches. The U.N. Command delegation started with a more combative negotiating

[53]

stance: opening with a high opening position and expecting to compromise. The Communists, on the other hand, seemed to expect a series of mutual concessions; thus, they would hold onto a position quite rigidly and eventually hint that a change of a certain kind was possible, in the expectation that this would be taken up and reciprocated.

However, these factors alone cannot explain the tortuous path of these early weeks, and it is necessary to return to a discussion of some of the cultural, structural, and psychological influences relevant to the U.S. policy-making process first discussed in Chapter 1.

FORMULATING THE U.S. NEGOTIATING POSITION

The Truman administration's relationships with its allies and with Congress, as well as its sensitivity to press reaction, all influenced the way in which policies for the truce talks were formulated. Within the administration itself, relations between the U.N. Command in Tokyo and military and State department officials in Washington also had a crucial impact on policy positions; and it would not be an exaggeration to say that, at times, there was a double set of negotiations in progress—between Washington and Tokyo as well as between the U.S. and Communist commanders.

On nearly every point at issue in this first phase of negotiations, for example, and perhaps because he wanted to add "to his reputation as a strong person,"[39] General Ridgway showed considerable reluctance to modify U.N. Command positions, even when his team in Korea had opened the bid well above the minimum position. To some degree in these first weeks, he had received support from Acheson, who had told the cabinet that the administration would maintain an "attitude of skepticism" toward the talks, and that Ridgway had been instructed to meet the Communists "head on" when they appeared obdurate.[40] Perhaps in response to this initial mood in Washington, as early as July 15 Ridgway informed the administration that he would be willing to recess the conference over the Communist agenda item concerning foreign troop withdrawal. On July 20 he went further and demanded complete U.S. and U.N. support for his decision to recess the negotiations unless the Communists accepted the four agenda items already agreed

[54]

upon, which excluded the issue of foreign forces. Moreover, his preference was for issuing this ultimatum publicly. Washington had to step in quickly and prevent this course of action. In the administration's view, it would raise the prestige factor to such a degree for the Communists as to make it even more difficult for them to concede on the point. In a response that indicated that maintaining Western allied unity had quickly become more important to the administration than appearing inflexible to the Communists, Washington informed Ridgway that "world opinion" would also not be supportive of a decision to break off the talks on this particular issue.[41]

Ridgway's deep-seated hostility toward negotiating with Asian Communists was displayed most markedly shortly after this in connection with the entry on August 4 of armed Chinese troops into the neutral zone. On August 7 the Communists acknowledged "the mistake" and ordered their guards "to obey strictly" the neutrality agreement worked out for the site so as to "guarantee that there will be no such violation" in the future. They hoped, they added, that later meetings would not be impeded by such "accidental, minor incidents." Ridgway objected to these final remarks, obtained two translations of the message, and found the Japanese version to be "insolent in tone and peremptory in tenor." This extreme sensitivity to the nuances of the phrasing unleashed a wave of hostility in Ridgway. The language of diplomacy was "inappropriate and ineffective" where these people were concerned, he claimed. The Communists considered "courtesy as concession and concession as weakness." He went on to describe them as "uninhibited in repudiating their own solemn obligations" and charged that they had "attained power through murderous conspiracy" and had remained "in power by that and other equally infamous practices." In short, he announced that he intended to "direct the UNC delegation to govern its utterances accordingly and while remaining, as they have, scrupulously factual and properly temperate in conduct and deed, to employ such language and methods as these treacherous savages cannot fail to understand."[42] The statement was almost MacArthurian in its level of vitriol, and such feelings would require the joint chiefs on this and future occasions to tone down the language of Ridgway's messages to the enemy commanders. Not always, however, would the general carry out their wishes to the letter: though the chiefs prevented Ridgway from replying to the message described above in the manner he desired, the U.N. commander did add a crucial final sentence to the joint chiefs' recommended reply, and those few words made further meetings conditional on Communist guarantees of site neutrality.[43]

Ridgway was also responsible for making the issue of the new location for the talks such a large stumbling block to the reopening of negotiations. On September 5 the U.N. commander requested that he be allowed to press for a new conference site; but although the joint chiefs were sympathetic to this suggestion, they were not enamored of the general's categorical refusal to have any further negotiations within the Kaesong area. When on September 20 the Communists proposed the resumption of discussions at Kaesong, Ridgway's intended reply was so angry in tone that an immediate redrafting exercise began in Washington. The U.N. commander was instructed to delete the "purple adjectives which give it a necessarily truculent tone," though the substance of his message remained untouched.[44] It remained, then, tough (if a little more courteously phrased), and still as unbending as Ridgway wished on an issue that Washington did not feel strongly about. As Bohlen said on September 26, in acknowledging that the administration had got itself tied up quite unnecessarily over the issue, now that the matter had been raised publicly, it was difficult for the U.N. Command to back down.[45]

It is possible that Ridgway had remained so adamant about returning to Kaesong because he was under pressure from Washington to modify his tactics on another item: the location of the demarcation line. The U.N. commander felt so strongly about the continuing disagreement with the Chinese and North Koreans on this issue that on August 11 he had told the chiefs that he was thinking of giving an ultimatum to the Communists, with 72 hours to think over the U.N. Command position, and if the notion of a ceasefire at the battle line continued to be rejected, he would break off the talks. Once again, the joint chiefs refused such a precipitous course of action, pointing out that it would take time for the Communists to amend their position on such an important item, one that they had expected to be settled on the basis of the old dividing line between the two Koreas.[46]

Nevertheless, despite these indications of different attitudes to-

ward the negotiations in Washington and Tokyo, Ridgway continued to ignore the signals and remained intransigent. When it
seemed that the talks would shortly resume, the general announced
that his delegation would be proposing a DMZ of 20 kilometers
north of the battle line; and only if the Communists dropped their
insistence on the 38th Parallel would he allow the delegation to offer
concessions. To do otherwise, he cautioned, would be taken as a
weakening of the U.S. position. As with his earlier suggestions, this
proposal initiated a debate in Washington. Officials there were of
the view that Ridgway's proposal took no account of the Communist concessions that were in the making on August 23; that the
southern boundary he was proposing took in some territory beyond
his present positions; and that he was not even proposing the line of
contact as the southern boundary of the DMZ. Even General Bolté
(an admirer of General MacArthur and his policies for ending the
war) was moved to remark that Ridgway was "resisting making
concessions." General Bradley agreed; his grim conclusion was that
the U.N. commander had "decided not to follow our views." As has
been suggested elsewhere, the qualities that made Ridgway a successful general were not proving helpful to the negotiations.[47]

This dispute over the ceasefire line, the DMZ, and the new location for the talks occasioned the Bradley-Bohlen trip to Korea referred to earlier. It was considered necessary because of the indications that "our thinking" might soon "get too far apart." On that
visit the two officials found Ridgway to be irretrievably committed
to the new site and of the view that a return to Kaesong would
amount "to a surrender." He was willing to concede on the DMZ,
but he wanted the two officials to realize that the negotiators in
Korea felt that they "had made steady concessions . . . on procedural matters," and the two were not able to dissuade the U.N.
commander from that opinion. If Bradley and Bohlen were unper-
suasive, however, Ridgway did manage to convince his visitors
that, because of the favorable military situation, there was "no great
urgency" to get on with the talks.[48] The visit, therefore, was of less
use than it might have been in moving Ridgway toward a greater
appreciation of how the war and the talks looked in Washington,
and at the United Nations. Undoubtedly, their responses to the
news of the excellent military position contributed to the delegation's willingness to delay resuming the negotiations and to the

bargaining that took place between the opposing liaison officers concerning, for example, the size of the neutral zone around the new conference site, and the restrictions on the number of flights over the conference area.

Not until October 25 did the talks restart, only to be stymied over the U.N. Command proposal to retain Kaesong. Once more, with Bradley and Bohlen again susceptible to Washington's influence, the joint chiefs reined Ridgway in. They warned him that he should not be inflexible and reminded him that it was the Kansas line that had been agreed as the most secure position for U.N. forces. Ridgway thought he had understood something different during his discussions with Bradley in late September, but when told his recollections were in error, he conceded the point.[49]

Perhaps the largest disagreement over tactics between Washington and Tokyo concerned the question of agreeing on a time limit for negotiating the remaining items on the agenda, while the demarcation line stayed fixed. Washington favored this idea in view of the recent concessions that the Chinese and North Koreans had made over the ceasefire line and the new site for the talks, and because of Western allied reactions to these recent agreements.[50] Ridgway definitely did not approve of this proposal, however. He argued fiercely against any acceptance of a de facto ceasefire, a position that angered Bradley, who reported that U.N. forces were "not going anywhere on the ground" anyway, and that the line the Communists were now putting forward was "better than the one we wanted in October in most respects." "I am damned if I understand why they refuse to put that [proposal] forward," Bradley added.[51] Hence, on November 13 the chiefs instructed Ridgway to press for an early settlement of item 2 and to suggest a time limit of one month during which the remainder of the agenda items would be tackled.

The U.N. commander beseeched the chiefs to reconsider this directive. In his view the U.N. Command should show "more steel and less silk, more forthright American insistence on the unchallengeable logic" of its position since only this would "yield the objectives for which we honorably contend." The course Washington was proposing would lead, he argued, "step by step to sacrifice of our basic principles and repudiation of the cause for which so many gallant men have laid down their lives." He ended with another MacArthurian flourish: "We have much to gain by standing firm. We have everything to lose through concession. With all my conscience I urge we stand firm."[52]

His plea fell on deaf ears, however. From the "broader viewpoint," the joint chiefs wrote, it was desirable to have an early agreement on item 2 because the line proposed was militarily sound, no major change on the ground was forecast in the next month—especially since Ridgway had already told the Eighth Army commander, General Van Fleet, to assume a posture of "active defense"—and military pressure in all possible ways would be maintained throughout the period. Ridgway thus reluctantly transmitted this directive to the delegation's headquarters in Korea and the subdelegation presented it at the talks on November 17.[53]

This debate between the U.N. commander and Washington officials demonstrated clearly the two contending strains in U.S. policy. On the one hand, there was the argument that the United States could best maintain its global objectives through the securing of a reasonable settlement in Korea and through a display of sensitivity to "world opinion" on the matters at issue in the talks. On the other hand, Ridgway, and those who agreed with him, tended to believe that a display of U.S. power, represented by inflexibility at the talks and military pressure, would better secure the U.S. global role and the optimum outcome for Korea. Indeed, as we have seen in Chapter 2, even before the start of the negotiations, C. B. Marshall, while exploring the possibility of opening discussions with Peking, had coupled his points with the threat of force (and possibly nuclear retribution) against the P.R.C. Though, as has been demonstrated, Washington in the autumn of 1951 had remained supportive of the approach preferred by its leading Western allies, the joint chiefs and other officials were somewhat sympathetic to Ridgway's viewpoint (and, as will be shown, became more so as time passed without final agreement) and thus were reluctant to educate him fully about thinking in the administration and in allied capitals. This reluctance contributed to the U.N. commander's intransigence and to the slow pace of the negotiations. And although they did rein Ridgway in on a number of occasions, the chiefs found it difficult to influence the day-to-day tone of the negotiations, a tone that helped undermine any mutuality of interest that existed between the two sides. Admiral Burke, for example, a member of the U.S. negotiating team in

Korea, in a letter to his wife on August 4 indicated something of the possible impact that language could have on the talks. They would all "have difficulty in the future, I imagine, in writing statements without superlative adjectives. Unjust, unfair, unreasonable are becoming standard usage in our vocabularies," he wrote.[54]

President Rhee also encouraged General Ridgway in his approach to the negotiations. If, as indicated earlier, forces loyal to Rhee were instrumental in causing a number of the incidents within the neutralized zone around Kaesong, the South Korean president was also responsible for stiffening the U.N. Command's position on the rejection of the 38th Parallel as the demarcation line; in addition, he encouraged Ridgway to hold onto Kaesong, even when the Communists had agreed to the battle line as the point of ceasefire. Even before negotiations had begun, on June 30, the R.O.K. government had insisted that they would cooperate with the talks only if a R.O.K. military officer participated and on the understanding that no use would be made of the 38th Parallel.[55] As agreement drew near on establishing the agenda, President Rhee wrote to General Ridgway urging that he seek the military unification of Korea and stressing his conviction that the "forces of freedom [were] not so weak as to be forced to bow before Sov[iet] menace." He also warned that, if the country were left divided, the despair of his people would be so great as to make the ground fertile for the acceptance of Communist ideas.[56]

It was not just Ridgway, of course, who had to take account of R.O.K. reaction. Washington was also alert to Rhee's position, and to a large degree the administration took the warning about the desperation of the South Korean people seriously. John Paton Davies of the Policy Planning Staff, for example, argued on August 3 that the 38th Parallel was a frontier "so deeply abhorrent to the people [that] a settlement on this line . . . would have incalculably explosive results in the ROK." The Kansas line, however, would be accepted, albeit with "some resentment and internal disorder."[57] On a number of occasions, therefore, it was necessary for the Truman administration to assure President Rhee that no use would indeed be made of the 38th Parallel. On August 3, after Rhee had threatened to withdraw his official from the negotiating team, President Truman wrote urging him not to take this course of action and pledging that Ridgway's instructions were to seek to achieve "an

armistice on lines approximating the present battle front." Only
after an armistice was agreed would there be any contemplation of
political discussions.[58]

Rhee was also able to make his mark on the negotiating position
regarding the retention of Kaesong. On September 20, the same day
that the Communists directly suggested the resumption of negotiations after the break on August 23, Rhee in a public statement
criticized the Communist acquisition of the city, which they had
"sneaked" into, he said. This public activity obviously affected the
negotiating team in Korea since, as Admiral Joy recorded in his
diary, the "real reason" the delegation had demanded the retention
of Kaesong had been as a "sop to the ROK government."[59]

Rhee, then, was instrumental in encouraging the U.N. Command in Tokyo to adopt a more inflexible stance at the talks in those
early months, and he reinforced the Truman administration's determination not to consider a ceasefire at the 38th Parallel. Moreover,
the South Korean leader could increase his influence with the administration because he also had allies within Congress at a time
when the executive branch was mindful of the signals emanating
from that quarter. The "Red Scare" centering on Senator McCarthy's indiscriminate charges was still a feature of domestic life in the
autumn of 1951; and, allowing for the growing public disillusionment with and increasing lack of interest in the truce negotiations,
there were still many critical speeches being made in Congress and
elsewhere about Truman's Asian policy. In Congress in early July,
for example, senators McCarthy and Irving M. Ives and Representative Walter H. Judd all claimed that the Communists had outwitted
the administration from the very start of the talks. "Let us remember," Senator Ives cautioned, "that the negotiations between our
forces and the Chinese Reds and North Koreans were initially carried on according to their terms, at their stipulated time, at their
picked location, and in their prescribed fashion." Even an "administration stalwart," Senator Paul Douglas, a Democrat from Illinois,
could write on the eve of the talks to the secretary of defense,
George C. Marshall, arguing against a truce on the 38th Parallel and
urging that U.N. forces move to the neck of Korea.[60]

By the autumn and after the recess in negotiations, the main
theme of the criticisms had become more or less fixed and centered
on two issues, one of which involved the supposed trickery of the

[61]

enemy, and the other of which probed the broader dislike of stalemate and compromise. The Communists had used this intervening period to build up their supplies and fortifications, it was argued, and the administration was enmeshed in a stalemate at the conference site and on the battlefield, a stalemate that could only be broken by the termination of the talks and by a bid for all-out military victory.[61]

Though Korea as a news item had lost center stage by the late autumn, the voices of these congressional critics were loud ones, and they reflected and reinforced a public sense of dissatisfaction with the talks, as well as the frustrations experienced within the military, especially those members of the branch in Korea. A fear of being accused of "doing nothing," of being called "appeasers," a perceived need to assuage these feelings of discontent, a recognition of the continuing potency of MacArthur's ideas for ending the war, and a keen desire to deflate the military prestige of the Chinese made the Truman administration reluctant to curb any of the military courses of action that Ridgway desired to undertake during these early months of the negotiations. On July 21, for example, Ridgway requested permission to make a major strike at Pyongyang, having first warned the civilian population of his intention. At first the joint chiefs demurred, "because to single out Pyongyang as the target for an all-out strike during the time we are holding conferences might in the eyes of the world appear as an attempt to break off negotiations." After Ridgway had explained the military benefits of the bombing, however, the joint chiefs changed their instructions and the raid was authorized, provided no warning would be given and on the understanding that it could be presented as a "normal operation against persistent enemy build-up." The raid was carried out on July 30 with the air force flying close to 450 fighter and fighter-bomber sorties.[62]

On August 1 the general asked for permission to bomb Najin (Rashin), a previously embargoed target after the advance of vigorous State Department arguments connected with the city's closeness to the Soviet border. On this occasion, and after consultations between the president and his trusted adviser the Secretary of Defense, permission was given on August 10. The attack in fact was not carried out until August 25 because of bad weather, but in the intervening period (August 14) Pyongyang was bombed once more.

[62]

At about this time, Ridgway also proposed a limited ground offensive—code named Operation Talons—in order to straighten out Eighth Army lines in central and eastern Korea. Although this was not thought to be "helpful" to the truce talks, it, too, was authorized (though, in the event, not carried out). Throughout the late summer and early autumn considerable ground action designed to give defense in depth to Kansas occurred. These were costly exercises, however, with 60,000 U.N. Command casualties between July and November, 22,000 of them American. According to General Collins, chief of staff of the U.S. Army, General Van Fleet's attack in mid-October to seize a triangular group of hills north of Kumhwa cost the U.N. Command 9,000 casualties in this one operation alone.[63] Communist casualties were estimated as being much higher throughout this period, of course (at approximately 234,000), and because of this, contemporary (and subsequent) reports of this activity tended to argue that the increased military action had a beneficial impact on the negotiations and had forced enemy concessions.[64]

Nevertheless, despite the certainty that began to grow in Tokyo and Washington at that time that military pressure was linked to Communist concessions, this now remains most difficult to demonstrate. As writers on coercive diplomacy have noted, attempts to convey a clear and appropriate meaning by military measures are fraught with difficulties. The attacks must be discriminatory in character, there must be strict coordination with political-diplomatic action, and there must be recognizable pauses in the military operations in order to allow the opponent time to reflect on the action.[65] When one examines the July and August bombing program, for example, the problems of coordination are immediately obvious. Ridgway, at a time when the talks were stalled over the framing of the agenda, called for the bombing of Pyongyang, but this was not carried out until July 30, four days after the agenda items had been agreed upon. Ridgway's request to bomb Najin and to launch Operation Talons at a time when the demarcation line had become an issue at the talks also cannot be deemed to have had a direct effect on the Communists' hint of a concession on the line: this indication of change came several days before Najin was bombed, and Talons was in fact never launched (for military reasons). The bombing of Pyongyang on August 14 may have influenced the Communist decision to concede on the line, but it is a difficult point to demonstrate one way or the other, and the raid in August was not as large as the one in July.

Similarly, ground operations could not be coordinated precisely with the discussions. On August 18, for example, just as Communist negotiators were hinting that they were about to concede on the ceasefire line, South Korean troops attacked a ridge south of Punchbowl, but, unexpectedly, it took until August 27 to clear it of North Korean forces. Bloody Ridge also came under fire on August 18, forcing a North Korean evacuation on September 4–5. (It was because of the extensive U.N. Command casualties sustained in this action that Operation Talons was canceled.) On September 13 an assault on Heartbreak Ridge began. After 30 days of hard fighting, and at the cost of some 3,700 American casualties (and many more South Korean), a "small sag in the line" was removed.[66] These actions and Van Fleet's operation in early to mid-October have been credited with influencing the Communist decision to restart the talks on October 25, but this argument neglects the point that the Chinese and North Koreans had not intended a long recess in the negotiations, that they had made a direct offer to resume discussions on September 20 and had agreed to the new site of Panmunjom on October 7 (the major sticking point). Indeed, the decision to resume talks on October 25 owed as much if not more to the difficulties of working out the neutralization details for the new site.

The Defense Department's reluctance to curb the military operations, in addition to deriving from the political considerations noted above, can also in part be explained by the American military's traditional belief that the commander in the field should have reasonable operational freedom. But the State Department's reluctance to press for changes in these military orders, despite its sense that these actions would undermine America's claims to its major allies that it seriously sought an end to the war in Korea, was born of a more complex set of motives and objectives, some of which have been indicated already. On the personal level, there was an unwillingness to challenge a Pentagon headed by the respected General Marshall. Dean Acheson's relationship with Marshall, and then with Marshall's successor in September 1951, Robert Lovett, was excellent. The secretary of state became much less combative than he had been when Louis Johnson was in control of Defense. Furthermore, and as stated earlier, all parts of the administration had agreed (and this was codified in NCS 48/5 of May 1951) with the need to deflate the political and military strength and prestige of the Chinese. Ridgway's actions promised at least the possibility of that.[67]

Nevertheless, the State Department did exercise some constraining influence over the U.N. Command in Tokyo in an attempt to maintain global support for U.S. actions in Korea. And in introducing this other level into the decision-making process, the department introduced views that, on the whole, encouraged compromise rather than intransigence at the talks. Allied views or "world opinion," as it was frequently termed, was passed on to Joy's negotiating team whenever necessary—the Australians, for example, believed Ridgway's tactics and communiqués to be "unnecessarily provocative"; the British hammered away at the point that the Communist concession on the demarcation line was a significant one[68]—and these thoughts and comments could help to curb Ridgway's more aggressive tendencies. For bureaucratic reasons, if for no other, it could be expected that in any diplomatic exercise involving the United States with other governments outside of its own hemisphere, the State Department would believe it necessary to introduce the allied perspective at the policy formulation stage. In the Korean case this was even more of a requirement, since the United Nations had authorized the action in Korea, and 16 nations had contributed forces to the effort. Moreover, the U.S. administration was keen to avoid the suggestion that responsibility for the negotiations should be taken away from it, a notion that might arise if other nations should become critical of U.S. efforts at the conference table. During the recess in negotiations in September 1951, for example, the Indian delegation to the United Nations had suggested that the foreign ministers of the major powers—the United States, Soviet Union, Britain, and France—should get together to discuss matters of disagreement between them, including Korea. In early November, at the General Assembly meeting in Paris, the Soviet Union had called for peace discussions in which the P.R.C. would be involved and that consideration should be given to a Korean armistice along the 38th Parallel.[69] It was these kinds of suggestions—which threatened to broaden the number of participants in the Korean negotiations, as well as the types of questions that might be considered—that the United States was anxious to avoid.

"World opinion" could, then, be a useful weapon in any internal administration argument designed to curb Ridgway's proposals. When the general suggested breaking off the talks in response to the impasse that had arisen over the fixing of the agenda, he was reminded that if and when a breakdown of negotiations came, "the onus for failure" had to "rest clearly and wholly upon the Communists." In addition, he was warned that "world opinion" would not support a break over this question. Similarly, when Ridgway contended to Bradley and Bohlen during their visit to his headquarters that the United States had been weak over procedural matters, Bohlen used the opportunity to try to convince him that other governments thought differently.[70] On more specific issues the Western allies (notably Britain) offered concrete proposals. Herbert Morrison, the new U.K. foreign minister appointed after the untimely death of Ernest Bevin, passed on the British Chiefs of Staff view on August 1 that it was time for the U.N. Command to indicate some flexibility over the DMZ. The ambassadors of countries with forces in Korea (apart from the R.O.K.) made sure the State Department realized that their governments were totally against breaking off the talks over the question of whether to return to Kaesong, leading Rusk to assure them that the United States would not make a major issue over this point.[71] When Joy's delegation announced its intention of retaining Kaesong on its side of the line, even though this proposal did not accord with the rest of its position on the line of contact, the British ambassador in Washington described the issue as confusing: "we had been struggling for the past several months to reach agreement on a line such as the Communists proposed," he argued. In one State Department official's view, the remaining differences between the two delegations in mid-November—over Kaesong, the demarcation point, the 30-day time limit—when viewed against the background of major Communist concessions, were "too subtle for general understanding."[72]

Allied positions on a possible expanded war in the event that negotiations broke down, or if there were a renewed Communist offensive, especially an air attack, were also instrumental in persuading Washington to push on with the negotiations. When in September, for example, Acheson and Morrison discussed the military operations that might be undertaken in the event of a break-down in the talks, the U.K. foreign minister reiterated the familiar British position: his government did not want a war with China, had no desire to further cement Peking's relationship with Moscow, and could not afford to allocate any more resources to the Far East. Britain had too many other things on its plate, including an urgent need to deal with the frailties of its economy, a requirement to respond to Egyptian demands over the Suez Canal, to devise a formula for the Iranian oil crisis, and to renegotiate its air base rights in Iraq. The Truman administration recognized that, without allied reinforcements, it lacked the necessary military capability at that time to ensure a decisive military outcome on the battlefield in Korea; thus, the reminder of Britain's desperate plight was timely.[73]

Editorial opinions, in the domestic as well as in the foreign press, often reinforced the Atlantic allies' perspectives during this period. In the first weeks of the talks reports in major U.S. newspapers, such as the *New York Times, New York Herald Tribune,* and *Christian Science Monitor,* had been based almost wholly on the information handed out at the official U.N. Command briefing; and *Time* Magazine on the basis of these handouts had been emphasizing U.N. Command successes in making the "Reds Yield" and "back down." Press censorship at the truce talks was "almost total," and this position encouraged Western journalists to turn to those newsmen in closest contact with the Communist delegation—Wilfred Burchett and Alan Winnington of *Ce Soir* and the *Daily Worker,* respectively—for alternative perspectives. As time wore on and Communist concessions on the agenda and the parallel became better understood, the East Coast press in America became more critical of the delegation's positions at the talks. When correspondents on the press train required Admiral Joy to explain the reason why the United States wanted to hold on to Kaesong, he found it too embarrassing to spell out that it had to do with Syngman Rhee. A *New York Times* editorial of November 11 stated that it could not understand why an impasse had been reached "over a seeming trifle" such as Kaesong, when "big issues" involving the ceasefire had already been decided. The next day a report in the same newspaper of the views of the men on the line recorded the troops' opinion that the Communists had "made important concessions, while the United Nations Command . . . continues to make more and more demands." As a result of this attitude, the joint chiefs informed Ridgway that press reaction made it clear that "it would be hard to make the people understand why negotiations [had] broke[n] down, if such should happen, over Kaesong in face of recent Communist concessions."[74] By November a consensus had emerged in Washington that the time was ripe for compromise.

The State Department's input into the development of negotiating positions was significant in other respects during these first five months, especially in its attempts at introducing consideration of the probable Communist reaction to the course of the discussions. On a number of occasions State informed Defense that they thought Ridgway's approach was making it difficult for the Communists to modify their positions on particular issues. When, for example, Ridgway proposed that he be allowed to issue an ultimatum to the Chinese and North Koreans over the dispute on the agenda, Dean Rusk argued that the U.N. commander's proposed use of an ultimatum would raise the "prestige factor" to such a degree that the Communists would find it even harder to concede the point. Rusk's intervention at this juncture was crucial because the joint chiefs were preparing to transmit a message to General Ridgway that basically approved of his intention. After Rusk had intervened, the message was suitably modified.[75]

It also became apparent that members of the State Department were unhappy with the harsh tone of a number of Ridgway's messages to the opposing commanders, many of which seemed to invite a negative response. On September 17 the general sent off a message to his opposite numbers that denied U.N. Command responsibility for violations of the neutral zone, except for an incident on September 10, and that reminded them that they were to blame for the suspension of negotiations. Acheson had drafted a message on the same matter, but it was never sent because Ridgway's had already been dispatched. The secretary of state's draft, written more in a sorrowful rather than in the angry tone of the U.N. commander's, acknowledged that there had been controversy over alleged violations of the neutral zone, proposed that the representatives should now meet to settle new arrangements or to renew discussions on the armistice terms, and promised that if the Communists would "affirm [their] determination to guarantee the neutrality of the neutral zone," the U.N. Command in turn would "repeat [its] guarantees that we will take every measure to insure

[68]

that no forces under control of the Unified Command violate our agreement with respect to the neutral zone."[76] The contrast between the two messages suggests how disturbed certain members of the State Department must have been at times with the way the negotiations were being conducted.

Acheson's draft message also demonstrated that he had come to appreciate how important the notion of reciprocity of action was to the Communist side. In arriving at this conclusion he had probably been influenced by Charles Bohlen, since it was Bohlen who forcefully argued for the adoption of this approach in the negotiations in late September at meetings between State officials and the joint chiefs. In his private papers he argued that the Communist suspension of the talks on August 23 "was in large measure motivated by the Communist desire to 'balance the books' on the subject of incidents in the neutral zone for reasons of prestige." At that time he inclined to the view that the Communists were ready for a settlement, that they were about to give up on the 38th Parallel, and that if they were offered a battle line and DMZ that required a reciprocal pull-back of forces, agreement would probably result. At the State–Joint Chiefs of Staff meeting the following day, Bohlen repeated his conviction that "reciprocity mean[t] a lot to those people," and that when the talks restarted, "they would come in with a concession and [would] expect one from us." He also tried to explain the basis of the mutuality of interest that existed between the two sides at the negotiations. When asked by General Bradley whether being forced to return to a new site for the talks was "too hard a pill for [the Communists] to swallow," Bohlen reminded him that it was not "quite black and white with these fellows. They probably see it much as we do. It [was] not just a question of whether they do or do not want an armistice. . . . Our attitude affects them as theirs does us."[77] His reply acknowledged that both sides were engaged in talks that were organic in form and interactive in nature, that each party was responding to the other, and that neither would accept a ceasefire at any price. He was clearly acting as an advocate for the "spiral model" of state behavior rather than the "deterrent model" (the former expects that "properly executed concessions will lead the other side to reciprocate," and the latter is based on the belief that concessions will lead an opponent to expect further retreats).[78]

During these same discussions Bohlen, Nitze, and Rusk took the

[69]

lead in pressing for Ridgway to modify his terms on the demarcation line and DMZ, and argued that as soon as talks resumed the U.N. Command delegation should be the first to present this new proposal.[79] In their view it was time for the United States to take the initiative and to compromise, if doors were to be kept open.

These officials believed, then, at this stage that offers and conciliation were likely to be reciprocated. But it was a difficult argument for them to maintain because relatively little effort had been put into understanding the objectives of these Communist states and even less time given to a consideration of their primary goals in the armistice negotiations.[80] The Communist position was never, of course, totally predictable and, as suggested earlier, was made more difficult to understand because of the joint Chinese and North Korean commands. Moreover, the Communist delegation tried to obscure the nature of the relationship between the two commands and to maintain the fiction that the Chinese, as guests in North Korea, were playing a secondary role. But over time, and especially as a result of the widespread use of subdelegation level meetings, Joy's officers detected that the Chinese were playing the dominant, although not necessarily the overriding, role. Chinese dominance did not mean, for example, that they were able to curb the North Koreans' more aggressive negotiating style; but, on occasion, dissimilarities in approach were noted. Joy, for example, found that the Chinese were more willing to "pour . . . oil when waters got troubled," and they were the first to give a slight indication of flexibility on the retention of the 38th Parallel as the ceasefire line. When the controversy arose at the start over the issue of access for the press, Nam Il, the chief North Korean negotiator, was adamant that journalists should not be admitted to the conference site until the agenda had been fixed. The Chinese representative, on the other hand, suggested a way out of the impasse that emphasized that mutuality of action would in future be a correct procedure for the two delegations to follow. "Both sides," he proposed, "must agree in respect to the delegations, including newsmen. We are prepared to discuss the matter of newsmen with your delegations on the basis of that principle." In October, when the North Korean delegate refused to accept a U.N. Command map and proposal connected with the new conference site at Panmunjom, the Chinese member of the team stepped forward and "with a conciliatory tone and manner" stated that he would be willing to take the papers. He then "courteously escorted" the U.S. negotiator to the door.[81]

This divergence in style may have been a reflection of different negotiating cultures in Korea and China but could also have been influenced by a greater Chinese willingness to concede on the issues at stake in these talks. As noted above, Joy had already picked up a hint on August 17 that the Chinese might be more flexible on the matter of the parallel, and on August 22 there seemed to be a clearer difference between Peking and Pyongyang on locating the ceasefire line. At that subdelegation meeting, U.S. negotiators reported, the North Korean continued to argue that no progress could be made unless the U.N. Command gave up its insistence that it be compensated on land for its air and sea dominance, and unless it overturned its proposal that a ceasefire line be based on the line of contact between forces. The Chinese delegate, on the other hand, referred only to the necessity of dropping the first proposal. Though Joy's delegation came to no definite conclusion as to whether there was a true divergence of view between the two Communist negotiators, it seems possible that there was a dispute, given that China and North Korea broke off the talks the next day, and given their careful use of language. Similarly, the Chinese seemed less obdurate over the matter of the retention of Kaesong behind U.N. Command lines: when the U.N. Command delegation dropped its demand for outright control of the city and moved toward a compromise in which the demarcation line would run through the middle of the town, the North Korean immediately opposed this solution whereas the Chinese "seemed less positive."[82]

Obviously, both of these issues would be of far greater moment to the North Korean government than to the government in Peking. Pyongyang had been forced to adjust its military objective from the unification of Korea to the restoration of the former boundaries of the North Korean state; now they were being required to give up yet more territory. This outcome would not, of course, be as painful for the Chinese to contemplate. Furthermore, the war in Korea had created controversy in the P.R.C. The decision to intervene in the fighting had been difficult for the Chinese leadership to take, and the financial and personal toll of the fighting in 1951 had been considerable. In a speech delivered in October 1951 Mao Tse-tung hinted at the divisions within the country that the war had caused but argued that the "great struggle to resist US aggression and aid Korea is going and must go on" until peace was restored. He also called on the people to "stiffen [its] efforts" and to "press on with this struggle, which is as necessary as it is just."[83] In late November L. H. Lamb, the British counselor at the embassy in Peking, had been informed in the strictest confidence by an intelligence source that Chou En-lai had stated in an address that the Chinese had had to take part in ceasefire negotiations because of the adverse effects of the war on the national economy. Chou reported that the Korean War "had already cost China more than the whole of the Japanese war had done." Moreover, signals that the Chinese had sent via the Indian chargé d'affaires in Peking indicated that there was a genuine opportunity to conclude an agreement at this time.[84] As noted in Chapter 2, the fighting, and especially the last campaign in May 1951, had led to huge casualties, and large numbers of Chinese troops had surrendered. Modern Soviet weapons had also been slow in arriving, and this further contributed to the demoralization of the troops as well as to tensions at intergovernmental level.[85]

For these reasons, therefore, the P.R.C. government was probably eager to conclude the fighting in 1951; indeed, it claimed that it had made large concessions during the first five months of the talks in order to secure a peace.[86] The U.N. Command team, however, was not receptive to these signals, nor did it know how to capitalize on any of the differences that might have emerged between the Chinese and North Koreans. It was, in a sense, more "straightforward" and more in keeping with general administration attitudes toward Communist and Asian powers to assume that they were intransigent and untrustworthy.

An examination of the decision-making structure on the U.S. side shows, then, a complex set of positions and influences. The formulation of a bureaucratic consensus between State and Defense, between Washington and Tokyo, between the administration and its allies in the West and in Asia, as well as a need to respond to domestic critics charging "appeasement" and the Eastern press demanding greater reciprocity had to be enmeshed with a procedure in Korea that to some extent had an existence of its own. Consideration of this complex structure is vital to an appreciation of the course of these negotiations.

By the time item 2 was agreed upon, certain attitudes toward the talks had already developed within the Truman administration, some of which encouraged flexibility and others of which encouraged intransigence. On the whole, people in Washington dealt with a wider range of influences than those charged with the task of negotiating in Korea. This narrowness of experience in part explains the harshness of approach adopted by Joy's negotiating team, which increasingly, on a personal level, found the process of bargaining tedious and distasteful. Moreover, the U.N. commander had developed a personal sense of outrage with regard to the Communist negotiators, which revealed itself in markedly stubborn behavior and a preference for issuing ultimatums. The U.N. commander's differences with Washington were further exacerbated during this first phase of the negotiations because the U.S. mediators believed that the administration had let them down, and that they had been forced to appear weaker than the military position demanded.

For the Communists' part, and here it is necessary to be far more tentative, they seemed to believe they had made the largest concessions, and that they had not as yet firmly established the principle of reciprocity. Moreover, they had revealed to their opponents certain dissimilarities in the respective objectives of the Chinese and North Korean governments which the U.N. side might at a later date attempt to exploit. Goodwill, trust, and confidence, long regarded as important assets in successful negotiation, were already in short supply.

[4]

Convergence:
November 1951 to April 1952

By the end of the first phase of negotiations two conflicting beliefs had emerged among American officials. Some, with the support of Western allied governments, believed that the Communists had been forced into a substantial concession with their agreement to a ceasefire line that took no account of the 38th Parallel. Others, however, and notably those charged with the task of negotiating, argued that, in accepting the 30-day time limit, the United States had given the Communists a major political and possibly a significant military advantage, too, in that the decision would result in a curtailment of ground action. The former position encouraged a sense of urgency about the talks and a greater willingness to be flexible, whereas the latter fed an attitude of disillusionment with the negotiations, and the suspicion that Peking and Pyongyang would now become even more intractable.

In a number of respects, in fact, the armistice negotiations now moved into their most productive period, with, at one point, three agenda items being considered simultaneously at subdelegation level. Slowly but discernibly positions began to converge: on item 3 (concrete arrangements for the realization of a ceasefire and armistice) the two delegations offered a series of matching concessions until by March only one major stumbling block remained; and item 5 was dealt with by the expedient of keeping its terms vague and broad. Even item 4 (arrangements relating to prisoners of war) looked capable of resolution, though this belief rested on the weak foundations of an inadequate U.N. Command estimate of the numbers of prisoners of war willing to return to their Communist homelands, and on abstruse language on the part of the Chinese and North Koreans, in an attempt to conceal their eventual concession on the policy position.

ITEM 5: RECOMMENDATIONS TO GOVERNMENTS

It quickly became obvious that both sides would prefer that item 5, having been broadly phrased as an agenda item, stay couched in general terms, a decision that helped to ensure relatively rapid agreement. General Ridgway gave Joy his initial position on the item on December 5: it should be recommended to governments that they should consider convening a conference of the political representatives of both sides "to discuss appropriate matters arising from but not resolved by the armistice agreement." On December 19 Washington refined this stance a little and authorized the U.N. commander to develop a position that would not commit the United States to holding a political conference, and to keep recommendations in general terms—for example, "early steps be taken to deal with [a political settlement in Korea] at a political level." However, this proved impossible to implement because mention of a political conference had already been made at Panmunjom in connection with item 3, and it was difficult to backtrack on that suggestion once the actual debate on item 5 got under way in early February.[1]

At that first meeting of the subdelegation dealing with this part of the agenda, the North Korean negotiator proposed that a peace conference be held 90 days after the conclusion of the armistice, to be made up of five delegates from each side. His delegation also wanted that conference to discuss the withdrawal of foreign troops from the peninsula, and "other questions related to the peace in Korea." The U.N. Command team quickly agreed to consider holding a post-truce conference, provided South Korea could be one of the participants, but countered with the suggestion that the conference, if held, should only consider "other Korean questions related to peace." Semantic bargaining continued until the Communists proposed that the conference should deal with the "peaceful settlement of the Korean question, etc." They made it clear that they would rather not define too closely what the "etc." formula meant, but Joy's team believed it should put on record—to assuage Chiang Kai-shek and his domestic supporters in America—that "etc." did not relate to matters outside of Korea. Ruffled by this clarification, negotiations temporarily stalled over this agenda item during which the problem was turned over to staff officers. But despite Nam Il's objections to the understandings that had now become attached to the formula for item 5, this agenda point was agreed on February 18, only 11 days after its formal introduction into the negotiations.[2]

Item 3: Formulating the Administration's Position

Item 5 could be dealt with swiftly because of the broad nature of Nam Il's suggested topics at the conference, because of the vagueness of the "etc." formula, and because the negotiators were only making recommendations to governments which they might well reject and certainly need not regard as binding. The U.S. administration, however, was not willing to take this broad-brush approach to item 3. There were two main elements to this part of the armistice agreement: the first concerned the degree of inspection necessary to prevent or forewarn of future violations of the truce, and the second involved prevention of the reinforcement of military units and their equipment, subject to certain agreed figures for rotation and resupply of worn-out items. Inspection was expected to be the most difficult issue, given the Communist bloc's past dislike of access to its territory. In 1946, for example, Moscow had rejected the Baruch plan on atomic weapons in part because that plan had required free inspection.[3] Yet considerable prestige had already become attached to the notion of an armistice commission's having unlimited inspection powers. As early as December 1950, General George C. Marshall, then secretary of defense, had described full access as "essential," though he recognized at that time that such a condition "might in fact result in the Communists refusing a ceasefire." In consequence, on the eve of negotiations Ridgway was instructed to press for the establishment of a military armistice commission with "free and unlimited access to the whole of Korea."[4] However, only when the administration moved closer to consideration of this agenda item did its true minimum position in all its required detail actually emerge.

Ridgway was first responsible for focusing attention on the problem. On October 4 he argued that the U.N. Command did not need unlimited inspection since this would not ensure security but would only "multiply serious causes for friction . . . with no comparable gain." Furthermore, the U.N. side would not want to reciprocate by opening its areas to Communist personnel. He therefore proposed that his initial position should be (1) observation by joint teams at ground, sea, and air ports of entry, (2) joint aerial observation and photo reconnaissance throughout Korea, and (3) complete joint observation of the DMZ. He believed, he added, that point (2) could be omitted if necessary in order to reach the Command's final position.[5] Dean Rusk provided further evidence for the basis of this concession when he stated to the British ambassador that the terrain in Korea lent itself to "bottleneck inspection," that is, inspection confined to a number of key roads, bridges, ports, and railway centers. And he admitted that, even in the unlikely event that the U.N. Command obtained unrestricted inspection, it would still confine itself to inspection at these key points.[6]

Nevertheless, despite these early indications of flexibility with respect to item 3, at first the joint chiefs were willing only to accept Ridgway's initial position but not his final terms. The U.N. commander's suggestion had, in fact, stimulated an intense debate in Washington over inspection and over the reinforcement of men and materiel, with both points taking on dimensions that had not previously been considered. The discussions demonstrated that inspection and prohibition on reinforcement were much less vital issues to the State Department than they were to the Defense Department, with the latter perhaps being influenced by Marshall's earlier attachment to the best possible inspection arrangements.

At the beginning of November officials from State's Office of North East Asian Affairs energetically applied themselves to the questions Ridgway had raised, recommending as a minimum position simply joint inspection of the DMZ. Their grounds were that even if there were a buildup of troops or supplies, the U.N. Command would be unlikely to take any action unless there was an "overt act of aggression." Furthermore, inspection in the South would impede U.S. attempts aimed at rebuilding South Korean forces and would facilitate intelligence-gathering operations. "We should be wary," the report concluded, of committing the United States to a course of action that could lead to numerous "embarrass-

ing incidents," that would prove difficult to enforce through renewed fighting, and whose "nonenforcement would adversely affect the prestige of the U.N." Inspection teams were not therefore
the "ultimate sanction against a renewal of aggression." Rather,
what was needed was the "clear likelihood that renewed fighting
cannot and will not be limited in scope as the present hostilities
have been."[7]

The points raised in this boldly worded paper were taken up in
earnest at a joint State–Joint Chiefs of Staff meeting on November
16. State officials were again active in eliciting the joint chiefs'
attitudes toward the minimum inspection considered militarily essential and for their views on any future North Korean attempts to
rebuild airfields, railroads, and roads in the postarmistice period.
The Pentagon's initial response was to register its disturbance at the
thought of giving much away in the area of inspection, and it also
wanted to prohibit both airfield and railroad repair. In that case,
Nitze argued, the United States would not get an armistice and,
moreover, would find it difficult to counter Pyongyang's claim that
the North needed to repair railroads to assist with general economic
rehabilitation. Reluctantly, the joint chiefs acknowledged that rail
repairs might have to be permitted, given that similar actions would
probably need to be undertaken in the South. But they would agree
to modify their position on inspection only if State could get allied
and, particularly, British agreement to a statement making it plain
that if the Communists violated the armistice, then retaliatory
action—specifically, bombing of northern China and blockading
the China coast—would be forthcoming. General Collins argued
that in the absence of such a firm agreement (and clearly the chiefs
doubted that one would be forthcoming), inspection at key points
outside the DMZ would have to become a breaking point at the
talks.[8]

While State explored what became known as the "Greater Sanction" idea, first with the U.K. government, the joint chiefs asked
Ridgway for his views on inspection, the rehabilitation of airfields,
and the Greater Sanction. It was apparent from Ridgway's reply
that he feared the abandonment of Washington's position on inspection was near, fateful in his opinion because it would weaken
the U.S. stance on this question elsewhere in the world. He considered it "unacceptable" therefore for the U.N. Command to adopt

anything less than the "final position" he had outlined on October 4.[9]

With the diplomatic branch having made most of the running in the development of this policy, the joint chiefs now tried to reinforce the U.N. commander's position. As Adm. William M. Fechteler, chief of staff for the Navy, put it (he was always the most solicitous of Ridgway's position, possibly because of his intense dislike of the Korean negotiations), the administration should "support the man in the field." But the State Department believed there was no need to be rigid on this matter, especially since, in Bohlen's view, the United States was asking "for something in Korea" on inspection that it did not have in "Berlin, Norway or Turkey."[10] In the light of this continuing controversy, Ridgway was authorized to start discussions on item 3 by first dealing with the problem of prohibiting reinforcements, and only after that examining inspection. The joint chiefs then offered the general one thing with one hand when they agreed to the final position he had outlined on October 4 while taking it away with the other when they suggested that modifications might have to be made to that final position as negotiations developed.[11]

With negotiations already under way on item 3 at Panmunjom at the end of November, it became imperative to establish the viability of the Greater Sanction plan. This took some time, however, since such a policy required numerous consultations with the allies. It was deemed important to get the British to accept the idea because it was assumed that U.K. acceptance would lead other governments to follow suit. Oliver Franks, the U.K. ambassador in Washington, was briefed on November 21, but the first substantive discussion of the proposal took place on November 28 in Rome, where Western allies had gathered for a NATO meeting. The major inducements offered to Anthony Eden, the new British foreign secretary, to encourage him to agree were the prospect of an armistice sooner rather than later and a willingness on Acheson's part to allow Eden to remain uncommitted to specific courses of action against China. Undoubtedly, the British foreign minister was lukewarm about the proposal, much as Admiral Fechteler had predicted, and would not countenance the idea of a blockade against the P.R.C. But he did indicate a willingness to consider a statement that carried a retaliatory message, and he revealed that bombing across the Yalu River would be a less difficult course of action for his government to contemplate than a naval blockade. His grounds were that a blockade would be ruinous to Hong Kong and would be ineffective unless it included Port Arthur and Dairen, at the risk of a direct clash with the Soviet Union; whereas if Manchuria were to be bombed, the U.S.S.R. would probably intervene only in a defensive way.[12]

By December 3, Eden was ready with a more detailed response, having had discussions with his cabinet colleagues. In the U.K. view, he stated, the United States should continue the search for an acceptable inspection system, perhaps involving joint inspection at key points, or, failing that, should establish a supervisory team composed of neutral states. Only if it became impossible to agree to these terms should the Greater Sanction statement come into operation, and then with more than just the British and American governments associated with it. This proposal did not go far enough in the U.S. administration's view; it now argued that, regardless of the extent of inspection, a statement carrying the threat of retaliation would be necessary to deter the Communists from renewing hostilities.[13] Faced with such determination and unwilling to jeopardize its relationship with its major ally, the United Kingdom acquiesced in the request to associate itself with the Greater Sanction statement. Nevertheless, though committed in principle, it still worked to soften the terminology that the U.S. administration initially wished to see adopted. Whereas the first American draft implied that in the event of renewed aggression the countries' responsible would receive full retribution without geographical limitation, the British wished to propose a weaker statement that read: "in the event of a renewal of aggression, it might not be possible to confine hostilities to Korea." A compromise was called for and found when the Truman administration countered with: "the consequences of such a breach of the armistice would be so grave that, in all probability, it would not be possible to confine hostilities within the frontiers of Korea." Despite the establishment of this compromise, the British government still remained uncommitted to taking any particular courses of action against China; but the U.S. government at least had an agreement in principle. Moreover, Washington had retained its own freedom of action should it wish to act unilaterally against P.R.C. territory.[14]

As predicted, other Western allies also acquiesced in the policy. The Canadian foreign minister, though similarly reluctant to institute a blockade and wishing also to redraft the original American statement along British lines, praised the administration for its "realistic" attitude toward inspection. Australia and South Africa announced their willingness to follow the British and American lead on the matter. Only the French were "holding up everything" in their efforts to get the Greater Sanction idea extended to cover Indochina. But the United States, under pressure to prevent the Korean issue from being discussed at the next session of the U.N. General Assembly and aware of the need to respond to the Communist negotiating position on item 3 (put forward in early December), would not allow French arguments to muddy the waters at such a delicate stage.[15]

As noted previously, it was considered crucial to get agreement to the Greater Sanction statement because it allowed for flexibility on the inspection issue and on matters related to that, such as rehabilitation and reinforcement. It had been something of a struggle to trade the question of unlimited inspection and repair of certain facilities for the sanction idea within the U.S. bureaucracy, including those members in Tokyo. The president, too, had at first been reluctant to consider compromise on the two issues and the apparent imminence of a concession on rehabilitation had so moved him that he had returned early from a vacation in Key West to discuss the question. In his view the negotiators in Korea "had been a little too conciliatory"; the Communists, he claimed, "had been making the demands and we the concessions." In an earlier message on December 8 he had asked for an explanation as to why the administration should allow the repair of roads and railways (though not airfields) when the United States had "expended lives, tons of bombs and a large amount of equipment to bring these people to terms." General Bradley invited him to consider that rehabilitation would be mutually advantageous, and he questioned what Washington would do if it could not later repair facilities in South Korea affected by weather, accidents, or guerrilla action. Furthermore, at a time when the United States and its British and French allies were in no position to force a showdown in Korea, the preferred alternative had to be an armistice. In the view of Frank Pace, the secretary of the army, a statement outlining what the United States would do in the event of a breach of the armistice would allow Washington to "yield on fundamentally minor questions but hold on the major ones." The president, with some reluctance, accepted the logic of this position, and he and his advisers even left the way open for the repair of airfields, if that should become the last obstacle to an armistice agreement.[16]

The military had therefore come to embrace the Greater Sanction proposal, a suggestion that originated in the State Department. Only Ridgway remained seriously disturbed by the policy since it meant nothing, he contended, unless nuclear weapons were to be used. As things stood at that time, the U.N. Command was incapable of "posing a threat to Communist China sufficient in itself to deter it from renewed aggression." Moreover, in his view, now that the airfield matter had become the "gravest question" posed in the negotiations, the time had come, he suggested, "to press the enemy to a point of ultimate decision and choice—an armistice or airfields." The joint chiefs demurred. Complete prohibition on the repair of airfields was impracticable; aerial observation was "desirable but not essential"; the major deterrent to renewed fighting was Communist realization that a "new war would bring upon China . . . full retribution." Every other safeguard was essentially illusory, they seemed to be implying.[17]

Negotiating Positions and Tactics on Item 3

The administration's willingness to be flexible at this stage of the talks owed much to the American public's growing impatience with the seemingly endless debates over what appeared to be minor points, and, particularly, to international influence: to allied pressure to show progress in light of the Communist concession over the 38th Parallel, and rumblings in the United Nations (often encouraged by Moscow) to have that body more closely associated with the negotiations. The Communist negotiators had also come forward with their opening position on item 3, and it was essential to respond to that, especially given the expectations the 30-day time limit had generated.

The first discussions between the two delegations on item 3 took place on November 27. The U.N. Command team did not start with the rehabilitation and reinforcement questions, as Washington had suggested, probably because instructions reached them too late. Instead, they began by setting out a list of measures designed to reduce the possibility of any resumption of fighting, and they argued for the establishment of a supervisory organization with joint observer teams.

For the Communists, on the other hand, item 3 boiled down to two main requirements: that all armed forces should be withdrawn to the correct side of the ceasefire line, and that foreign troops should be required to leave Korea, proposals that ignored completely the question of supervision and joint inspection. As discussions progressed, the North Korean negotiator, Nam Il, linked Joy's position on no reinforcement of men and materiel to his side's principle of foreign troop withdrawal. If forces withdrew, he said, "there [would] be no question of supplies, equipment and facilities exceeding those existing at the time of the signing" of the armistice agreement. Furthermore, in his view, free access for observer teams to the whole of Korea was "entirely unnecessary" and represented an unwarranted interference in internal affairs. When the U.N. Command countered with the contention that the question of troop withdrawal was beyond the scope of military negotiations, Nam Il queried the American team's authority to discuss limitations on forces and their equipment, given the delegation's apparent lack of authority to discuss decreases in the numbers of units—that is, troop withdrawal.[18]

Prohibiting the reinforcement of men and materiel and constraints on the repair of facilities had thus moved quickly to the center of the stage at the discussions. The Communists were quite open about their intention to reconstruct and rehabilitate facilities in the North, Nam Il informing Joy that it was the Korean people's right to undertake this activity. The Chinese press was even more explicit in explaining what the North intended, adding that Pyongyang had "every right to protect themselves against further indiscriminate bombing by strengthening all defences including repair and construction of airfields."[19] At this stage, however, the U.N. Command would not countenance such activity in the North.

Not until December 3 was there a major breakthrough on this agenda item, when Nam Il unexpectedly proposed limited behind-the-lines inspection by neutral nations at agreed ports of entry, and a prohibition on the introduction of military forces, ammunition, and weapons into Korea. Both these points represented considerable concessions since each involved "interference" in North Korea's internal affairs, although the latter point implied the slow reduction in the presence of military forces in Korea—a small step along the road of troop withdrawal. As one official history of this period has argued, the U.N. Command delegation was therefore thrown "on the defensive" since it was "unprepared for . . . the drastic restrictions upon all military forces and equipment."[20] The Communist proposals were an example of how policy formulation in Washington could be derailed by the unexpected happening at the bargaining table, one explanation, perhaps, of why the joint chiefs were reluctant to give Ridgway the final negotiating positions that he craved.

Following these propositions, Admiral Joy believed that the time had come to make it clear to the Communists where the U.N. Command stood on this agenda item, and he demonstrated that he, too, was prepared to be flexible. The admiral wanted to insist on rotation of troops and replenishment of supplies, to give up his side's claims to the control of islands north of the demarcation line (presently maintained as a bargaining ploy), and to remove restrictions against the rehabilitation of airfields, instead substituting restraints on new construction.[21] However, any new U.N. Command position was slow in coming because of the discussions that were taking place in Washington over the Greater Sanction statement, and the necessity of forging a consensus between State and Defense on the points contained in item 3.

The administration realized, however, that some momentum had to be kept up and that the concession on neutral inspection ought to be reciprocated quickly. It thus authorized the subdelegation to encourage the Communists to name those nations that might possibly make up the supervisory commission. The Communists suggested Czechoslovakia, Poland, Sweden, Switzerland, and Denmark as possibilities. The U.N. Command team found it difficult not to respond to this proposal and could only counter Communist charges of "stalling" by stating that it was still "studying [the] neutral nations concept." Not until December 12 were the U.S. negotiators finally authorized to accept neutral inspection, putting forward Switzerland, Sweden, and Norway as possible "pro-Western" members of the neutral commission. This movement of position generated another response, as two days later the Communists gave a little on the question of rotation of troops, offering a rotation figure of 5,000 per month, a figure that the Americans considered to be wholly inadequate.[22]

Despite these disputes over what might seem to be minor details, item 3 became so broken down into its constituent parts that concession/convergence bargaining, which could result in mutual benefit, now looked possible. The Communists therefore tried to trade on what for them seemed to be the most crucial issue and suggested that, if the U.N. Command removed its restrictions on airfields, they would give further consideration to the rotation figure of 5,000. Joy's team responded on December 22 by offering limited repair for civil air operations, provided this did not include the extension of runways. Though criticizing the continuing restrictions, the Communists still shifted their position a little, lifting their 5,000 limit on rotation and confirming that ports of entry designated for inspection purposes would include all the types the U.N. Command thought necessary—that is, sea, air, and ground. At the end of the month the U.N. delegation showed that it, too, could be flexible as it accepted the principle of a limitation on the number of troops for rotation, agreed to the Communists' request that the noncombatant inspection body should be practically independent of any military armistice commission, and gave up its demand for aerial observation.[23]

The repair of military airfields remained as a sticking point, but the joint chiefs, unwilling to neglect an opportunity to build on these promising discussions, instructed Ridgway to try to leave that question until later while dealing with more easily resolvable items, such as the figure for rotation and the number of ports of entry. At the end of January, therefore, the U.N. Command offered a rotation figure of 75,000 (artificially high because it included those on short rest leave in Japan and visits of inspecting personnel), and 12 ports of entry, proposals well above its then minimum position of 40,000 a month for rotation and six ports. In response, the Communist team raised their minimum to 25,000 and three ports of entry. By February 19 they had improved this offer to 30,000 and four ports, the U.N. Command insisting on 35,000 and six ports. The Communists accepted the 35,000 figure on February 23 but would not go above five ports of entry, a figure U.S. negotiators agreed to on March 7 without having received instruction on the matter from Washington.[24]

At this point, and as these issues were moving slowly toward resolution—it took several days for each concession to be matched—the Communists introduced the notion of having the Soviet Union as a representative on the neutral nations supervisory commission (NNSC). Why they should have done this at this time is difficult to ascertain. It could have been that, given the expectation that the POW question was also nearing resolution (see below), the airfield issue remained the sole outstanding problem, and they may have assumed that it could perhaps be traded for Soviet membership. (Certainly, John Hickerson, assistant secretary of state for U.N. affairs, believed this might be the case, and the Communists gave strong hints of this possible trade in early April.) Alternatively, it may have been that Peking and Pyongyang did not approve of the U.N. Command's nomination of Norway when the Communists previously had mentioned Sweden, Switzerland, and Denmark as possible members of the supervisory body. Indeed, the Chinese press raised a query about the Norwegian nomination since Oslo "had supported UN action in Korea." Joy's team also seemed to think that might be the explanation, as shown by its suggestion on February 25 that both Russia and Norway be dropped from membership of the supervisory commission.

Nevertheless, the Communists' introduction of such a controversial proposal into the negotiations at this late stage seriously disrupted proceedings and caused a deterioration in relations between the two negotiating teams. General Ridgway and Admiral Joy were adamant that the U.S. government should publicly denounce the notion of having Moscow on the NNSC, although at the talks the only explanation they were authorized to offer in support of their objection was Soviet proximity to Korea and its past role in deciding Korean questions. Interestingly, however, feeling ran much less strongly on the issue in Washington, with the notable and crucial exception of President Truman, who supported Ridgway on the matter. On March 12, for example, at a State–Joint Chiefs of Staff meeting, State Department members argued that there might even "be some advantage in having the Soviet Union on the inspection teams" provided such teams were not labeled as neutrals.[25] Even-

tually, however, and probably as a result of presidential preferences, officials in Washington decided not to force Ridgway to
accept Soviet membership on any kind of commission. Instead, the
outstanding problem was to be incorporated into a three-part package deal (see below), also to include the military airfield question
and the POW issue.

ITEM 4: FORMULATING THE POW POLICY

Indications are that the U.S. administration believed at the start
of the talks that items 2 and 3 were going to be the toughest to
resolve in the armistice negotiations, and that item 4 would be a
relatively straightforward matter. On the eve of the discussions
Ridgway had been told to argue initially for the exchange of prisoners of war on a one-for-one basis, until all U.S./U.N. prisoners
had been returned, after which he could hand over to the Communists those that remained in U.N. Command hands. He was also
authorized to insist that the International Committee of the Red
Cross (ICRC) should visit the camps to help with the process.
Although there was no formal consideration at that stage that any
prisoner of war might not wish to return, Rusk in his briefing to
ambassadors did point out the military implications of the issue:
that wholesale repatriation would virtually restore intact the North
Korean Army, hence the one-for-one formula. On July 4 the U.S.
ambassador to South Korea, John Muccio, brought up another point
for consideration: the question of the approximately 40,000 South
Koreans in U.N. Command camps who had been impressed into
the North Korean Army and then taken prisoner.[26]

Gen. Robert McClure, the army's chief of psychological warfare,
was the first to raise explicitly the issue of whether all prisoners of
war should be repatriated, pointing to both the humanitarian and
propaganda aspects involved. Many Chinese and North Koreans
would be "severely punished, sentenced to slave labor, or executed" on their return, as many Soviet citizens had been after World
War II, he argued. Furthermore, repatriation would have "seriously
adverse effects upon future U.S. psychological warfare operations."
The large numbers of Chinese prisoners who were claiming to have
been forced into Chinese Communist armies, if permitted to

[87]

choose, "would seek repatriation to Formosa," a useful boost to America's Asian policies. On General Collins's suggestion, the Joint Strategic Survey Committee (JSSC) took up McClure's points. It concluded that "it would be of great value to establish in the free world not only the reliability of the promises of the UNC but also the principle of UN asylum from terrorism."[27]

With initial support from the joint chiefs and Secretary of Defense Lovett for voluntary repatriation, the idea was next presented to Dean Acheson, who at that stage was unequivocal in his rejection of the policy. "The overriding consideration should be," he said, "the prompt return of all UN and ROK POWs." Furthermore, broader interests dictated "strict observance of the provisions of the Geneva Convention," article 118 of which stated that prisoners of war should be released and repatriated without delay once hostilities had ceased. This reaction may have surprised those who were aware of Acheson's vigorous role in 1945 when, as under secretary of state, he had argued for a revision of the U.S. position on forcible repatriation for Soviet refugees. However, when the Geneva Convention was being drawn up in 1949, a large majority of states, including America, had rejected an Austrian amendment that advocated exceptions to the repatriation rule, apparently accepting the argument of the Soviet delegate who "feared that a prisoner of war might not be able to express himself with complete freedom when he was in captivity. Furthermore," he had maintained, "this new provision might give rise to the exercise of undue pressure on the part of the Detaining Power." The United States at that time "shared that opinion." Perhaps remembering the shades of that debate in 1949, Acheson in 1951 would countenance exceptions only for those prisoners who had rendered outstanding assistance to the U.N. Command and for the South Koreans who had been forcibly impressed into the North Korean Army.[28]

This forthright response from Acheson led Lovett and the Joint Chiefs of Staff to think better of McClure's plan and to return to the former position of a one-for-one exchange and then return of the remainder who were in U.N. Command hands, a policy that those in Korea and Tokyo agreed with. Probably that would have remained the position if it had not been for President Truman's keen interest in the problem. On October 29, in discussions with Acting Secretary of State James Webb, Truman described an all-for-all exchange as "not an equitable basis. He [did] not wish to send back those prisoners who surrendered and have cooperated with us because he believes they [would] be immediately done away with." It seems likely that the president had in mind his experiences with the Soviet Union at the end of the war. As he recorded in his diary later in 1951, he demanded to know from Soviet leaders not only what had happened to South Koreans and Americans in 1950 and 1951, but what had become of the Germans and Japanese taken prisoner during World War II: "Are they murdered," he wrote, "or are they in slave labor camps?"[29]

In trying to educate the president on the matter, Webb pointed out that a "situation might come about in which all other matters might be settled," leaving only the exchange of prisoners. The president acknowledged the import of this statement, but said he would agree to an all-for-all exchange only if the administration had received "some major concession which could be obtained in no other way." It was a classic example of what has been described as the president's tendency for "premature cognitive closure," or impulsiveness. There was little indication that he was about to reflect on all the ramifications of this developing POW policy.[30]

Despite fears about holding some prisoners back, together with doubts about the legality of such a policy and about the precedent that might be established for future wars, the president's "strong personal interest" in the problem initiated and shaped a new and intense discussion of the matter, resulting in Acheson's reversal of his previous stand. As a result, and despite Ridgway's and Joy's strong preference for exchanging all prisoners as soon as hostilities were concluded, they were instructed on December 7 to go for one-for-one of those willing to return home, but allowing those "expressing a desire not to be exchanged . . . to remain under the jurisdiction of their captors." Teams from both sides would then screen these remaining prisoners of war to confirm their repatriation wishes.[31]

Ridgway immediately voiced serious doubts that the Communists "would agree to any formula which involves individual expression of opinion . . . because of extremely adverse effect that large scale defection would have on world-wide Commie prestige." But it was precisely this political aspect of the problem that appealed to so many within the Truman administration. As the Psychological Strategy Board noted, forcible repatriation would have serious effects on psychological warfare operations for years to come, as had U.S. actions between 1945 and 1948. Others agreed with this argument: at a meeting among U.S. Army, Central Intelligence Agency (CIA), and State Department officials in mid-January, they referred to the need to stand fast for voluntary repatriation, even though it might lead the Communists to break off the armistice talks. To give way "would undermine the whole basis of psychological warfare since neither soldiers or civilians would defect from Communist rule if they thought they would be returned."[32]

Nevertheless, at this stage, doubts were still being expressed and the policy had not finally solidified. Within the Department of Defense (with the exception of Lovett, his deputy, and the secretary of the air force, who were all uncertain about where they stood) generals Bradley, Hoyt S. Vandenberg, and John E. Hull and Admiral Fechteler were now disposed to return all prisoners, "including even, if necessary, the 44,000 ROK personnel who had been reclassified to civilian internee status, to achieve an armistice." The State Department, on the other hand, represented at that meeting by the secretary, Bohlen, Johnson, and H. Freeman Matthews, were more united in their opposition to this view.[33] Indeed, within State there was a remarkable degree of support for the policy, with the exceptions of Frank Stelle of the Policy Planning Staff, Edward G. Barrett of Public Opinion Affairs, and John Hickerson. Stelle argued against voluntary repatriation on the grounds that it violated the Geneva Convention, that the critical factors influencing statements of defection were all local in origin and thus would not necessarily apply to members of the Soviet bloc, and that he felt more attention should be lavished on America's own prisoners of war, rather than on the "thugs" among the prisoners that ran the U.N. Command camps. Barrett cautioned that the administration did not know the size of the problem, and that public opinion and "moral factors against leaving our own POWs in enemy hands indefinitely" had not been sufficiently taken into account. Neither had there been any consideration of the "thousands of additional casualties" that would be caused if negotiations broke down or were "prolonged 6–7 months." Hickerson cautioned the secretary to consider the possible reprisals that might be taken against U.N. prisoners if the

United States refused to return Communist prisoners who "would [otherwise] still be fighting UN Forces except for the accident of capture."[34]

But it was Acheson's view that counted most within the department, of course, and more crucially with the president; and the secretary of state was himself aware of the president's thoughts on the matter. The basis of the excellent working relationship between the president and Dean Acheson owed much, not only to the secretary's undoubted expertise, but also to his loyalty to Truman and willingness to be responsive to the president's ideas. Because of this relationship, he was ready to discount, it seems, the implications of memoranda from the likes of Stelle and Barrett, whose comments actually struck at the heart of the administration's case for voluntary repatriation. Instead, on February 8 Acheson set out the position for the president in a way that would have had maximum appeal to him. The secretary of state, though acknowledging that such a policy could hold up the armistice and lead to reprisals against U.S./U.N. troops in Communist compounds, argued that any agreement requiring force to return prisoners "would be repugnant to our most fundamental moral and humanitarian principles of the importance of the individual, and would seriously jeopardize the psychological warfare position of the United States in its opposition to Communist tyranny." (In 1947, when drawing up the Truman Doctrine, Acheson had ensured that the speech would highlight the "global struggle" between "freedom and totalitarianism" for similar emotional appeal.) A troubled Lovett remarked that State's position was very persuasive, that he had come to the meeting without a unanimous recommendation from his joint chiefs, but that nevertheless he hoped that the government would not become irrevocably committed to the idea of voluntary repatriation.[35]

Over the next two and a half weeks, however, there was a groundswell in support of this policy. This solidification in support coincided with the height of the Communists' accusations against the United States that it was engaging in bacteriological warfare in North Korea and Manchuria. The part that such a campaign might have played in fostering the acceptance among U.S. officials of the "moral and humanitarian" nonforcible repatriation policy is impossible to gauge, but it may have been an indirect, additional factor encouraging adherence to it. Whatever the psychological impact of that Communist propaganda campaign, at a meeting at the end of February attended by the president and major administration figures, all those present, except Admiral Fechteler, expressed themselves willing to reject any armistice agreement that required prisoners to be forced to return home. And even Fechteler hedged, acknowledging that he realized that the policy "involved larger issues" than the strictly military aspects of it that he had put forward.[36]

The presidential intervention and Acheson's reconsideration of his own position on the matter had forged the policy consensus. Support (or, more accurately in some cases, lack of opposition) from international and domestic quarters also helped to soothe any lingering nervousness about the policy. In a number of respects the Western allies displayed an approach to the question that had parallels with Lovett's. They lacked confidence in the terms of any opposing argument, and the intervention of a powerful individual in favor of the administration's position, in this case the U.K. prime minister, Winston Churchill, overcame their uncertainties about the policy. Skepticism about the policy was rife in the British Foreign Office, for example, which was not in favor of adding to the suffering of British prisoners of war just for the sake of building up Chiang Kai-shek's army, as one member put it. Another official bluntly remarked that he would rather see the liquidation of "a few North Korean prisoners than delay the liberation of our people." When the prime minister stepped in to ensure that his government was agreed that no prisoner should be handed back against his or her will, Eden reminded him that the humanitarian argument did not work only one way: British prisoners of war, he urged, should not be forgotten.[37]

But, undoubtedly, the British foreign secretary was torn in two directions by the policy. He seemed much more sympathetic to the plight of returning North Korean and Chinese prisoners than he had been in 1944 and 1945 when he had stuck grimly to the repatriation policy he had agreed with the Soviets. In 1952 his conscience troubled him more: though he voiced doubts in February about the legal basis of voluntary repatriation, that did not make him "like the idea of sending those poor devils back to death or worse."[38] The Canadian government, too, clearly had mixed feelings and had suggested a two-tier policy that involved repatriating all the Chinese but not the Koreans who were participating in what could be termed a civil war. The Australian government also had misgivings, though once again it showed a willingness to take the British and American lead. The U.S. ambassador in New Delhi set to work on the Indian government's doubts, reminding its foreign minister of the "heartrending scenes" of returning Russian prisoners of war at the end of World War II. Only Churchill, among Commonwealth leaders, seemed totally certain of the justness of the policy; and this certainty, in combination with that of President Truman, served to silence doubters. Matthews could therefore tell the president that not one of the key allies had "indicated any disagreement with our position on this question," though he could not actually report unbounded enthusiasm for it either.[39]

American opinion leaders also confirmed the sagacity of adopting the voluntary repatriation policy. All major newspapers supported the policy, the *New York Times* questioning as early as November 24, 1951, what would happen to those large numbers of Chinese and North Koreans who wanted to go to Taiwan and South Korea rather than to return home, an early indication of the political polarization that existed in the camps. Hanson Baldwin of that same newspaper claimed that reneging on the promise of freedom that the United States had always "meant to the world" would destroy its "moral birthright." More importantly, he added, "we will have done what the Communists do—subordinated the lives and freedoms and wishes of individuals to the expediency of the state." The State Department's public opinion files also recorded the "dominant view" as being that the United States and its allies "must not repeat their earlier mistake of turning over anti-Communists to almost certain death." Congress, too, voiced few doubts; on the contrary, the Truman administration was considerably exercised over a report in February that Senator William E. Jenner intended to introduce a resolution—which already had the support of 60 of his colleagues—calling for an inflexible position on voluntary repatriation. As has been noted, domestic politics did not dictate but it did smooth the way for the POW policy. "It was what Congress wanted, which confirmed the ideological and moral position of the president and his secretary of state."[40]

One other aspect of the question also gave heart to some of the doubters in the administration, and that was some of the optimistic estimates that were available on the low numbers of prisoners of war who would actually resist repatriation. It had been decided to send General Hull (vice chief of staff for the army) and U. Alexis Johnson (deputy assistant secretary of state for Far Eastern Affairs) to Korea for discussions on the best method of reclassifying those prisoners unlikely to elect to return home. During that trip the two were presented with a staff study enclosing an estimate that suggested that only 15,900 would violently resist repatriation out of the 132,194 held in the camps. The only dark spot in the estimate was the suggestion that as many as 11,500 Chinese would not return out of the nearly 21,000 held. Though the author of this estimate stressed that it had not been approved and had no authoritative status, Johnson and Hull returned with those figures and presented them at a meeting with the president on February 25, where they also acknowledged that "qualitatively as well as possibly quantitatively, the problem of CCF POWs and possible Communist reactions thereto was much more difficult than that of Korean POWs." They also reported Ridgway's view that the only way of handling those who would violently object to repatriation was "by an overt screening of all POWs" and not by simply paroling the objectors, as had been the previously preferred course of action in Washington. As Joy had said, a release in this manner would put U.S. prisoners of war in jeopardy and would be "a breach of faith."[41]

Nearly a month later, as the screening of the prisoners drew nearer, Ridgway concluded that perhaps as many as 73,000 might resist repatriation, a figure that caused General Vandenberg, for one, enormous concern. On receipt of this information, the chief of the U.S. Air Force, supported tentatively by Admiral Fechteler, wanted to reopen the whole question of "nonforcible repatriation," as it had come to be called, and stated his belief that the president had left that possibility open in the most recent discussions of the policy. State Department officials did not support Vandenberg, however, arguing that Truman had made his position clear.[42] The chief of the air force therefore did not take the opportunity to express his doubts to the chief executive; instead, U. Alexis Johnson, ignoring the reports he was getting from the political section of the embassy in Korea and from Ambassador Muccio indicating that for organizational and political reasons (see Chapter 5) it would not be possible to conduct an accurate poll in the camps,[43] the implications of which were that the number of nonrepatriates would probably be very large, repeated the estimates that had been prepared for him while in Korea. Moreover, he stated his view (or was it blind hope?) that the figure of 11,000 or so Chinese resisting return "might be high." This estimate and Johnson's convictions about its validity became the basis of the U.N. Command team's statement to the Communists on April 1 that some 116,000 of their prisoners of war would probably be returning home.[44]

NEGOTIATING POSITIONS AND TACTICS ON ITEM 4

As with the inspection issue, POW policy was far from being settled when it was first introduced into the Panmunjom discussions, which must have caused serious difficulties for the U.N. Command team. The Communist negotiators, having said on December 6 that they would not move onto item 4 unless there was greater progress on item 3, agreed to subdelegation meetings on POW exchange on December 10. At these meetings Joy was authorized to press for the exchange of POW data and for the immediate admission of ICRC representatives to the camps. Ridgway also instructed the team, in the event that the Chinese and North Koreans objected to ICRC involvement, to excoriate them "as lacking in every concept of honor of which those who through all ages have called themselves soldiers, are proud. I would tell them this in the most blistering language we can command in every session at every opportunity." Once again, the U.N. commander was overreacting to a policy position that was highly unlikely to prove acceptable to the Communists, since they did not regard the ICRC as neutral. At that time the organization was "dominated by a group of very conservative Swiss businessmen who [were] more strongly anti-Communist than most Americans." Moreover, it was recognized as a Western movement by origin and leadership, was underpinned philosophically by Western Christianity, and financially was supported by the Swiss, American, and other Western governments.[45] Not surprisingly, therefore, the Communists did reject ICRC involvement and opened on the POW issue with the straightforward statement that "both sides release all POWs held by them after the signing of the Armistice."

[95]

With the talks in deadlock over the question of POW data and over the basis of the prisoner exchange, the Communists next offered to trade POW information for an agreement to an all-for-all release, a suggestion that so angered Ridgway that he called once more for the issuing of an ultimatum to the effect that item 4 would not proceed further until the lists of prisoners of war and the locations of the camps were made available. The joint chiefs again denied Ridgway his ultimatum and, instead, on December 15 authorized the U.N. Command team to soften its position on ICRC access. This concession quickly elicited one from the other side, and on December 18 the North Korean negotiator offered the names of those held in Communist camps.[46]

Criticism of both sides' lists quickly ensued: the United States querying the fact that the Communists' contained only 25 percent of America's missing in action and a very small number of South Koreans; and the Communists asking for an accounting of the 37,000 recently reclassified as civilian internees that the U.N. Command had removed from its list. It was "not a question of where these persons lived," General Lee Sang Cho said, "but of what side they were fighting for." He also claimed that many of those taken prisoner had been released at the front and directed to return to their own lines—an argument that had little basis in fact because so few did return in this way.[47] Sparring on the missing names, and on interpretations of article 118 of the Geneva Convention, continued until the end of the year, with the U.S. negotiators doubtful that the Communists would ever accept one-for-one and the Communist side increasingly suspicious of what they interpreted as their enemy's attempts to retain prisoners. Not until January 2 were their suspicions confirmed when the U.N. Command policy of nonforcible repatriation was formally introduced, alongside the requirements that delegates of the ICRC would be present to assure that all repatriation was voluntary and that those refusing to return home would be released only on the condition that they did not bear arms in the Korean conflict again.[48]

Dismayed by these proposals, the Communists attacked them on three main grounds: that they violated the Geneva Convention, which called for the exchange of all prisoners of war immediately on the cessation of hostilities; that they were an attempt to retain the majority of prisoners in U.N. Command hands and through "force

[96]

and cruel mistreatment to deliver part of them to a certain friend in South Korea and part to a certain friend in Taiwan;" and that nonforcible repatriation was a political question and should not have been brought up at military negotiations at all.[49]

The Communists made much of the presence in the camps of Taiwanese instructors (quoting *Time* magazine and Associated Press reports to substantiate their claims), who they said were creating anti-Communist organizations and forcing prisoners to denounce their allegiance to the P.R.C. (see Chapter 5 for further details). On this point a number of such incidents and statements helped the Communists' case. Joy's team had foolishly said at one negotiating session that since there were two governments in Korea and two in China, this implied that all prisoners were being repatriated even if they went to Taiwan or stayed in the South of Korea. Not surprisingly, the Chinese delegate responded vehemently to this remark, stating that if anyone dared to hand over any Chinese to the "deadly enemy of the Chinese people, the Chinese people will never tolerate it and will fight to the end." Chiang Kai-shek's government was responsible for raising the temperature still further when it released a statement welcoming all Chinese prisoners of war to Taiwan, a contribution which the U.S. State Department asked its ambasssador in Taipei to try to prevent in the future. The increased Chinese Nationalist presence in South Korea, both in their embassy and in the camps, to help with the psychological warfare program (which led Joy to request their removal) also heightened tensions between the Chinese and U.N. commands. Riots in the POW camps on February 18 when the U.N. Command had rescreened the civilian internees and again on March 14 also gave credence to the Communists' argument that deciding whether to be repatriated or not was impossible in that kind of environment. The incident on February 18 left 69 dead and 142 prisoners injured, against one U.S. guard dead and four wounded, a casualty level indicating how tense the atmosphere was at this time.[50]

Nevertheless, there was some flexibility in the Communist position on nonforcible repatriation, at least as far as the North Korean prisoners of war were concerned. Admiral Libby, a member of the U.N. Command negotiating team, had told the Communists at the end of January that they had nothing to fear from his side's POW policy because most in the camps would elect to return home. On

March 19 the Chinese Communists, having made much of their hatred of the rulers on Taiwan, gave the first hint of a breakthrough on this issue as their staff officers indicated that they might be agreeable to working out new POW lists from which some of those not desiring repatriation could be eliminated. Communist press correspondents at the conference site also passed on the additional information that concessions might be more readily forthcoming if conference sessions were closed. The U.N. Command quickly acted upon this suggestion, and on March 21 at an executive session the Communists explained their most recent thoughts on repatriation, stating that although they were not giving up on the principle of unconditional return, they appreciated that "there may be certain special cases" of prisoners "who originally resided in the area of your side and has [sic] some particular situation as your side said before. We are now considering whether there is necessity to make some special arrangements for such special questions together with the special questions regarding those who are said to be reclassified by your side." In response, U.S. negotiators warned that even beyond these cases, "some additional adjustments" might have to be made, but that they would "make every effort to insure that any such additional adjustments will be reasonable."[51]

Joy understood the Communists' position to be that they would accept U.N. Command retention of the civilian internees, nonforcible repatriation for prisoners of R.O.K. origin and possibly of other Koreans, but no adjustments to the list of Chinese prisoners of war. However, rather than continue to argue over these matters, and having received information from the U.N. Command delegation on April 1 that 116,000 would probably be the number of prisoners who would agree to return, the Communist negotiators suggested being "realistic" and entering "immediately into the work of checking the lists." The "round figure" of those who would be available for exchange would then reflect the "principles and understandings" that both sides had been advancing, they suggested. As Ridgway told the Joint Chiefs of Staff, "the questions of the numbers and nationalities of the POWs to be returned rather than the principles involved appears to be the controlling issue" for the Communists.[52]

At that point the two sides must have felt an armistice agreement to be close at hand. It seemed then as though the rejection of Soviet membership of the supervisory commission was to be exchanged for airfield rehabilitation and that the POW problem was capable of resolution. Mutual concessions and a different, though masked, interpretation of the repatriation principle had brought them close to final agreement. Unfortunately, however, the 116,000 figure turned out to be wildly inaccurate, with only about 70,000 prisoners of war available for return, much as Ridgway had predicted in March.

These results shocked everyone within the Truman administration, and many outside it, because little thought had been given to the way in which conditions within the camps might affect the figures. Insufficient discussion had also taken place of the likely outcome for the talks if large numbers of Chinese refused repatriation. The only consoling voice at a meeting of State and the joint chiefs on April 14 was that of Bohlen, who remarked that the screening "merely shows the problem we would have faced if we had tried to return all of these POWs." Later that month General Bradley and Robert Lovett both voiced their fears about the effect this outcome would have on the armistice negotiations. When Admiral Joy in Korea was apprised of the results, his reaction was much more violent. He stated "emphatically that the POWs, particularly the Chinese, should be rescreened"; but, "just as emphatically," he was "overruled." It was not considered politic to admit, through immediate rescreening, that there might have been something amiss in the original poll of prisoners. A gloomy Ridgway believed that he could not delay in presenting these figures for long since the information would almost certainly leak out, but he did not relish passing on the numbers. As he and others predicted, the figures were to have a devastating effect: the chief Communist negotiator, "struggling to conceal his shock and outrage, immediately moved for a recess." The next day he charged the United States with a breach of faith: "You flagrantly repudiated what you said before," he said—that 116,000 would be willing to return.[53]

Chiang Kai-shek's domestic supporters in the United States moved quickly to ensure that there would be no administration wavering on the POW policy, a course they feared because of the recent preference for secret sessions at Panmunjom. Senator Knowland held up U.S. propaganda leaflets in the Senate that he claimed offered asylum to any surrendering enemy troops. "I hope," he intoned, "that the Government . . . is not going to consider turning over a single captive soldier . . . who has surrendered under those guarantees." He also quoted an AFL trade union committee declaration that urged the U.N. Command to stand fast on nonforcible repatriation and "to remember that the price of surrender at Panmunjom is the weakening of resistance forces . . . in all countries now enslaved by Communism." At a meeting between the State Department and the House's Far East Subcommittee on Korea, Walter Judd made it clear that he felt voluntary repatriation should have remained the administration's policy rather than the supposedly more restrictive nonforcible repatriation; and in the House, Judd (and others) went so far as to recommend that South Korean and Chinese Nationalist government representatives have free access to the prison camps.[54]

Though the administration was aware that it had not specifically offered asylum in the surrender leaflets, it knew, too, that it could not turn away from the nonforcible repatriation policy now, even though that policy threatened to obstruct for some considerable time a settlement in Korea: too much of America's prestige had been invested in it. Other governments, however, were far less identified with the policy, and they did consider compromise now that it had become clear that an armistice would probably be long delayed by Washington's position. The Australian government was the most forthright, its ambassador describing the poll of prisoners as "superficial" and charging that the questions asked of the prisoners "did not go to the heart of the problem." He could not believe, he said, that approximately 70,000 prisoners would "have their lives jeopardized if they [were] returned to the Chinese and North Koreans." In the U.K. Foreign Office similar sentiments abounded, and rumors picked up, expecially in Washington, were that London was about to suggest yielding on the repatriation policy rather than letting negotiations fail. Certainly, these rumors did have some substance to them. As one British official was claiming, it was debatable whether any prisoner of war would return to certain death or slavery, and he recalled that the Chinese Communists during the later months of the civil war "genuinely gave captured Nationalist soldiers a free option between enrolment in the Communist forces and return, with journey money provided, to their homes as civilians." In his view the majority of prisoners "might only be subjected to intensive reeducation."

Nevertheless, despite these internal discussions in London and the rumors that had emerged, Washington could still count on the staunch support of Winston Churchill for the nonforcible repatriation policy. The British prime minister even went to the absurd lengths of describing Air Vice-Marshal C. A. Bouchier's dismay over the poll results (Bouchier was a British officer attached to Ridgway's headquarters) as showing the "taint of pro-Communism" and as "an insult to the British . . . uniform." Given Churchill's unfailing support for the U.S. administration, Eden agreed that, in these difficult times for the U.N. Command, the U.K. government would give its public approval of the POW policy, an agreement that bore fruit on May 7 when Eden announced in the House of Commons that in his government's view "it would clearly be repugnant to the sense of values of the free world to send these men home by force." The U.K. government also agreed to recommend that other Commonwealth governments follow suit with similar statements of support.[55]

The Emergence of the Package Proposal

In order to solidify this allied position and thereby demonstrate that its national interests had a universal appeal, Washington realized that it would be required to do two things: to offer neutral rescreening of the nonrepatriate prisoners after the armistice, and to present the outstanding issues at the talks—Soviet membership, rehabilitation of airfields, and the POW policy—in the form of a package proposal. Bargaining theorists have argued that when issues can be grouped in a natural way that provides for balanced payoffs, they can be handled as a package.[56] The administration in Washington was attracted to this approach not so much for the reasons of balance but more because a package deal would draw attention away from the POW issue as the sole outstanding item. If the Communists rejected the whole package, comprising at least three items, it might make them appear to "world opinion" to be more intransigent than the U.N. Command. Furthermore, it would also suggest that the Truman administration had brought matters to a head "as everyone on the Hill was demanding," according to General Collins.

[101]

Although Ridgway desired to "adopt inflexible minimum positions on the basic [outstanding] issues," he was nevertheless still against the presentation of a three-point package proposal, because he felt that the Soviet issue should be cleared away first. He also thought it inappropriate to require the Communists to give way on two issues to the U.N. Command's one,[57] a remark that either showed he had learned how important mutual concessions were in Communist bargaining tactics or was a way of repaying State for lessons they had frequently given him.

Despite Ridgway's criticisms, however, Joy's team was instructed to present its package proposal at an executive session on April 28. This was not to be in the form of an ultimatum, as Ridgway wished, nor was it to be in open session, as Joy had requested. Having set out the three items, the U.N. Command delegation then offered to compromise on the rehabilitation of airfields "contingent upon your acceptance of our position regarding prisoners-of-war and the composition of the neutral nations supervisory commission." It was made clear that this was a "final offer." It would "not agree to any substantive change in this proposal, and . . . we are absolutely firm that this proposal must be considered as a whole." The North Korean delegate's response was blunt: "Our side fails to see how your proposal this morning can really be of help to an overall settlement of the remaining issues." It was not a true package proposal because each side already realized well before this meeting that the Communists were willing to forgo Soviet membership for an agreement on the rehabilitation of airfields. The Chinese and North Koreans further exposed this position when on May 2 they proposed an exchange on these two questions, leaving the POW problem uncovered as the main point at issue between the two protagonists. Truman tried to revive the package idea in a statement on May 7 when he presented the three points once more as a combined position to be considered only as "an entity."[58] Everyone realized, however, that it was the POW issue alone that had brought the talks to a deadlock.

Negotiating these three agenda items demonstrated how difficult it was to formulate detailed armistice provisions and how hard it was to strike a balance between defining the administration's minimum position while remaining responsive to new, unexpected offers by one's adversary. Ridgway's team wanted final positions that they could stick to rigidly, having first compromised from a higher opening bid (perhaps in order "to avoid the difficulties of negotiating," as the RAND analyst attached to the mediating team suggested).[59] Such rigidity did not allow for flexibility in the face of an innovative response. At the same time, many of the points raised in the discussions in Washington—which made Ridgway and his team feel uncertain as to what their objectives should be—should have been dealt with well before these items were near introduction or actually on the table at Panmunjom. Furthermore, the obvious differences in priorities between the State and Defense departments, and within the Defense Department itself, where the navy and air force were generally more responsive to Ridgway's positions, should have been explored much earlier. All these discussions inevitably served not only to prolong the negotiations but also to confuse the negotiators, and were indications of the administration's unwillingness to treat diplomacy as a subject of significance and intellectual difficulty.

This phase of the negotiations also demonstrated the power of the president to direct thinking along particular lines and to foreclose the full discussion of alternatives. This was particularly the case with the POW policy, on which Truman had strong opinions. He also couched these views in moralistic, humanitarian terms, choosing to stress individual choice and America's protective capacity, thus making it difficult for anyone to argue against his position. Such an approach to the issue was also designed to have maximum appeal both internationally and domestically and would serve to confirm America's moral right to lead the international community. Thus, even when it became clear, particularly to Johnson in the State Department, but also more widely than that, that it was not going to be possible for prisoners of war to make a genuine choice concerning repatriation, and Ridgway had furnished his estimate that as few as 73,000 prisoners might be willing to return home, only one member of the administration sought to reopen discussion of the nonforcible repatriation policy with the president. Moreover, even he was uncertain about taking that course of action, especially since he received little or no encouragement from others.

On item 3, however, a more prosaic item than the POW question,

[103]

the administration displayed greater flexibility. A willingness to treat inspection as a general problem between Western and Communist states, the realization that the international community believed that Communist concessions on the ceasefire line should be reciprocated, and the mutuality inherent in this item—in which each restriction against or permission given to the North (whether that involved inspection, rehabilitation, or improvement) would have to be matched in the South—encouraged a more concessionary approach.

Though the Chinese and North Koreans did not seem prepared for the kind of detailed discussion that the U.N. Command team thought necessary to achieve an agreement on these two points and preferred instead to try to get acceptance of straightforward, generalized principles, at least the emphasis at this stage of the negotiations on mutual concessions suited their negotiating style. Both sides were ready to make adjustments, therefore; and by late March it seemed to both teams that they were ready to make a final trade. With the POW issue about to be resolved—so it was thought then—Soviet membership of the neutral supervisory commission would be dropped as a requirement in exchange for the removal of prohibitions on airfield repair.

Nevertheless, despite the convergence toward agreed positions that took place during this period, many within the United States—in official policy-making circles and outside of them—still criticized the length of time the negotiations were taking and refused to acknowledge that lack of agreement within the bureaucracy had materially contributed to that situation. Admiral Joy, among others, blamed what he saw as slow progress on the U.N. Command's adoption of the 30-day time limit during which the demarcation line remained fixed while other items were debated, a proposal that had come into effect on November 27. In his view "it gave the Communists what they had been seeking—a 'de facto' ceasefire for 30 days which enabled them to dig in and stabilize their battle line." Admiral Arleigh Burke, also on the negotiating team in Korea and someone who perceived himself as the "strong man" on the delegation, agreed with his superior, believing that the Communists as a result of his offer of the time limit now regarded him as a pushover. Having been forced to agree to this negotiating position, he was, as a result, "no more use to the delegation," he stated. Such criticisms were readily seized upon since they provided a more palatable explanation for America's inability to prevail either on the battlefield or unequivocally in the talks. The press, alive to these feelings, therefore took up the issue and reported Ridgway's supposed orders to General Van Fleet in mid-November to curtail ground operations during this period. These reports in turn led to Senate calls for an investigation by its Armed Services Committee and prompted Truman's staunch denial at the end of November that any ceasefire had been authorized.[60]

The source of this furor in the press and in Congress was General Ridgway's order to Van Fleet on November 12 to assume the "active-defense," that is, to seize territory most suitable for defensive purposes. Van Fleet transmitted these orders to his troops but explained that any military operations should "clearly demonstrate a willingness to reach agreement," that his men should "avoid all casualties" and "avoid engaging the enemy unless he threatens our positions." But the 30-day time limit was not the origin of General Ridgway's order. This instruction related more to the casualties the U.N. Command had suffered between July and November. As noted in the previous chapter, preparations for Operation Talons had ceased on September 7 because mounting casualties had convinced the U.N. commander that the cost of ground operations was simply too great.[61]

Joy's other criticism, that the curtailing of ground operations allowed the Communists to dig in, is also belied by the chronology. The tunneling activity of the Chinese troops, designed to protect men and supplies, began well before the start of the 30-day period. General Peng Te-huai in his memoirs dates it from the period of the Chinese fourth and fifth campaigns, between February and May 1951, when a network of good underground fortifications was constructed. He also records that a defense-in-depth tunnel system took shape gradually along the 38th Parallel in the summer and autumn of 1951. American observers confirmed this at the time: as early as August 1951 there were reports of an impressive buildup of enemy supplies, including artillery and ammunition. Bohlen, after his visit to Korea in October 1951, also acknowledged that the Communist forces had already built up sufficient logistic support to sustain themselves, though he believed they were still short of food and clothing.[62]

Moreover, though both sides cut down on ground operations because of the onset of winter and a reluctance to take further casualties, U.S./U.N. air and naval bombardment did not cease. Between November 1951 and April 1952 "FEAF averaged over 9000 sorties a month on interdiction and armored reconnaissance missions, while close air support sorties varied from 339 to 2461 per month." Though Operation Strangle, designed to stop supplies moving and to cut road and rail communications to the front lines, was never very successful, the reasons for its lack of success also bear on Joy's claims. The air operations' poor results not only owed much to the adept and swift repair systems that North Korea's highway and railway recovery bureau had developed, but also to the tunnel systems that had already been built to conceal stockpiles of materiel.[63]

Alternatively, it could be argued that the 30-day time limit actually benefited the talks, though few of these critics would have considered this possibility because of their preference for believing that force not negotiation was the better method for obtaining results. Setting deadlines can "distort or interrupt the natural convergence of views"[64] that takes place in a negotiating process, but they can also be useful in encouraging flexibility, in generating a sense of urgency, and in focusing attention on agreement. Though the talks were long and difficult in the phase of the negotiations that began with the time limit, this perhaps can more readily be explained by the degree of detail involved, together with the fact that neither side was ready to deal with these issues in that degree of complexity, and as a result of the time that Washington required to determine its true minimum positions on items 3 and 4. Yet, in spite of this complexity, greater attempts were being made to reach agreement on all points during this period, even on item 4. As Joy had said regarding the POW problem, the Communists were "sincerely seeking to negotiate a solution," though not on the basis of the 70,000.[65] Both sides had agreed to have three subdelegations working simultaneously, and both had shown a greater willingness to trade points. There was no armistice in April 1952 because the two governments made critical errors when peace was in sight. The Chinese, in trying to conceal their compromise over the POW issue, did not make it sufficiently clear to their opponents that they did not intend this revised position to apply to any Chinese prisoners of war, and they took a considerable risk in accepting the U.N. Command estimate of the numbers of prisoners that would be available for exchange. The American side ignored many indications that they were not going to be able to return the 116,000 they had promised.[66] Neither did they explore the implications of the fact that it was the Chinese that were going to be the most difficult to return home. It was a "breach of faith" in the Communists' eyes, but in reality it was a U.S. unwillingness to face up to unpalatable information when victory on such an important ideological issue seemed near.

[5]

Victims of the Cold War:
The POW Issue

The U.S. administration's adoption of the nonforcible repatriation policy initiated a number of public statements designed to emphasize the human rights basis of that decision. In a press release on May 7, President Truman stated that any use of force to repatriate the prisoners in U.N. Command hands would be "repugnant to the fundamental moral and humanitarian principles which underlie our action in Korea." His government, he argued, would "not buy an armistice by turning over human beings for slaughter or slavery." The British foreign secretary, Anthony Eden, in a speech to the House of Commons, also on May 7, used similar language to indicate his government's support for that position: "It would . . . clearly be repugnant to the sense of values of the free world to send these men home by force."[1]

Though some administration officials, such as General McClure, had been attracted to nonforcible repatriation because its adoption might undermine Communist confidence in the dependability of their armies, most of the statements supporting the policy's adoption emphasized its ideological element. This policy stance did, of course, provide a welcome opportunity for the Truman administration to dwell on the presumed moral superiority of its human rights position, based on individual choice, compared with the supposedly inferior Communist bloc preference for maintaining collective rights. As C. B. Marshall of the Policy Planning Staff succinctly put it, the POW policy was very different from the other points at issue in the negotiations, such as the battle line and inspection of positions. This item, in contrast, got "at the heart of the contention between Communism and the tradition we live by. It bears on the rights of men to make choices and to claim protection." C. H. Peake of the Far Eastern division put it even more forcefully when he argued that the administration should emphasize to others that the policy rested on the "fundamental humanitarian principle of individual human rights," and that the West was engaged in a struggle to maintain that principle "against the totalitarian state and the assertion of the rulers of such states that the individual lives only to serve the state." In his view such an emphasis would serve to "universalize the struggle in Korea," making it one based not only on containment but also on the protection of "fundamental principles which respect human dignity and rights." The U.S. negotiators in Korea had also chosen to focus on this aspect, informing their opposite numbers that they would not accept a solution to the POW problem unless it respected human rights and fully considered "the dignity and worth of the human person."[2]

THE U.N. COMMAND CAMPS

In reality, however, consideration for human rights, maintenance of dignity, and U.N. Command protection were in very short supply in the U.N. camps. The unexpectedly large number of prisoners taken, all within a relatively short space of time, is part of the explanation for that: by October 1950, for example, the compounds contained more than 104,000 prisoners, and another 20,000 were added in the following two months. More than 15,000 Chinese were captured between April and June 1951, and by July some 85 percent of all Chinese taken over the course of the war were already under U.N. Command control. The compounds in which these prisoners were held were makeshift and crowded, with some holding five times the number they were designed to contain. Inadequate records were kept throughout the war, there were manpower shortages, and it was difficult to recruit U.S. personnel with the requisite language skills. With only one U.S. military policeman (MP) to every 188 prisoners, the majority of the guards had to be South Korean, compatriots who were hostile toward and contemptuous of the North Koreans. Dislike of the task meant that those U.S. and R.O.K. guards in closest contact with the prisoners were the worst of the regular recruits. They were ill trained and rarely disciplined for offenses that included confiscating prisoners' personal possessions and shooting them for relatively trivial offenses such as singing, shouting insults, and throwing stones. The quality of camp administration was also affected by the high turnover of American camp commanders.[3]

British, Dutch, U.S. governmental, and ICRC reports all referred to the unsatisfactory conditions in the camps—to the poor sanitary situation, the inadequate lodging and heating, and the great numbers of stomach and digestive diseases among the prisoners of war that became chronic for many when two-thirds of the rice ration was replaced by "inferior grains often indigestible for many POWs and requiring more fuel to prepare," as one State Department official put it in July 1952. Medical treatment was inadequate until late in the war, and dysentery, malaria, tuberculosis, and pneumonia were rife, contributing to the more than 6,000 deaths in U.N. Command camps by the end of December 1951. As late as May 1953 the ICRC, though acknowledging overall improvements in conditions, and especially in medical care, was still requesting that tuberculosis cases be separated from other prisoners.[4]

Overcrowding understandably made all these medical problems much more difficult to control, but it also allowed relatively easy communication between compounds. Some enclosures were so close, in fact, that prisoners could pass messages without having to raise their voices. As POW leaders emerged from among the inmates, further techniques were devised for sending instructions to other compounds, including the switching of individuals who were out on work details.[5]

U.S. and R.O.K. guards treated the prisoners with hostility, contempt, or indifference. One Australian member of the United Nations Commission for the Unification and Rehabilitation of Korea (UNCURK) recorded the frequent maltreatment by U.S. guards and the unwarranted shootings. A British officer on duty in Korea in September 1952 claimed that American warders treated the prisoners as cattle, thought little of withholding their mail for four months or more, and regularly addressed the heads of the camps as "you slant-eyed yellow bastards."[6] The South Korean army's appalling treatment of its captives was well known to the Americans from the beginning of the war, but R.O.K. guards hardly modified

their behavior when they came under U.S. jurisdiction and continued to treat particularly badly those inmates who chose to be
repatriated to North Korea. In May 1952 the ICRC recommended
that Rhee's units be withdrawn from their positions of control in the
camps, "their employment as guards of their compatriots constitut-
ing a continual risk of incidents," and in May 1953 it again brought
to the U.N. Command's attention the cruelty being inflicted on
prisoners who were on R.O.K.-directed work details or were being
searched or interrogated by R.O.K. guards. As the journalist James
Cameron reported when he discovered, right next to U.S. headquarters in Seoul, political prisoners held by the South Korean
government in "sensationally appalling condition," little more than
"skeletons," "puppets of skin with sinews for strings—their faces
. . . a terrible, translucent grey," cringing "like dogs," few in Washington were willing to acknowledge, let alone to do much about, the
South Korean methods or the cruelties being inflicted in the prisons. This same indifference was true for those in direct charge of the
U.N. Command compounds where, as Ambassador Muccio reported, the "camp authorities usually took stand POWs internal
discipline and control within compounds no concern of camp command unless personal safety UN personnel endangered or duties
interfered with."[7]

Before June 1951 factional struggle between pro- and anti-Communist groups in these camps was not much in evidence. During
this period most of the key leadership positions inside the compounds were taken by South Koreans who had been impressed into
the North Korean Army. (Some 6 percent to 15 percent of North
Korean Army units were made up of former R.O.K. troops during
the period May to September 1951, it was discovered.) However,
after the Chinese began to be captured in large numbers, and when
the prisoners of South Korean origin were segregated from the bulk
of the prisoners, unrest grew. Leadership positions in the camps
were valuable, and now proclaimed anti-Communist North Koreans came forward to take the place of the southerners. Though
reports acknowledge that the Chinese troops had shown good
discipline in the field and had been captured only "amid frantic
efforts to escape," once the men were in the camps, old political
allegiances among the Chinese began to resurface. The "volunteer"
units sent to Korea contained between 50 percent and 70 percent

former Nationalist soldiers (CNA). The civil war practice of breaking Nationalist army officers to privates and subjecting them to indoctrination and reeducation was not completed when the Korean conflict began; thus the People's Liberation Army was caught in "a state of transition" with "many more former CNA soldiers . . . taken in than could be readily assimilated." On arrival at the camps, the embittered ex-CNA officers among the prisoners set about establishing anti-Communist organizations and, with the acquiescence if not outright assistance of camp administrators, became POW trusties. As one State Department official reported, these trusties, made up of "(1) former CNA MP's mostly captured by the C[hinese] C[ommunist] F[orces] on Hainan Island in South China, and (2) company-grade officer graduates of CNA military academies, many of whom were demoted to enlisted status upon absorption into the CCF . . . exercise discriminatory control over food, clothing, fuel and access to medical treatment for the mass of Chinese prisoners." They intimidated fellow prisoners frequently, mainly through "beatings, torture and threats of punishment" and, according to another investigation, "removed rivals by informing authorities of alleged Commie plots, which were investigated superficially, if at all."[8]

The U.N. Command authorities also sanctioned quasi-official police organizations, which quickly began operating like private armies. Structure, training, and recruitment to these organizations were all handled by the prisoners themselves. One Chinese trustie, for example (a former Nationalist officer captured late in the civil war on Hainan Island in May 1950), exercised "a personal monarchy over eight thousand PWs, exacting subservience and personal privileges and indulging in personal violence on a scale not reported in any other compound." U.S. guards tolerated his role, indulgently nicknaming him "Little Caesar." At one point, this leader managed to send one of his henchmen and 500 anti-Communist Chinese from one compound to another in order to organize it along pro–Chiang Kai-shek lines.[9]

Such prisoners not only enjoyed their privileges and enforced their will through terroristic tactics with little interference from the authorities, but they were also able to maintain close communication with the South Korean and Chinese Nationalist governments. Rhee had set up a special section of his war ministry to advise his groups in the camps, and the Chinese trusties had contact with Chiang's government through the Taiwanese appointed in various guises to administer to the compounds (or "Gestapos," as Ambassador Muccio later described them).[10] U.N. Command partiality for those compounds dominated by pro-Rhee and pro-Chiang groups was shown in numerous ways: for example, anti-Communist prisoners of war frequently held demonstrations, celebrated national days, flew national flags with official agreement or at least tolerance. Similar activity by the pro–North Korean and pro–P.R.C. compounds was met with violence and shootings. In October 1952 Philip Manhard, the State Department officer on interrogation duty in the camps who tried so diligently to make it clear just how appalling these U.N. Command camps were, criticized the frequency of the attacks on the pro-Communist prisoners. One U.S. officer, Captain Joseph Brooks, was full of "vicious hatred" for the Communist Chinese, Manhard wrote, and these prisoners after arrival on the island of Cheju had been "worked over frequently with various 'riot control' techniques." In the previous months they had been tear-gassed "at least several times a week . . . sometimes in such heavy concentrations that some POWs had to be given medical treatment for fairly serious burns." Another State official (A. Sabin Chase) sent along with Manhard to investigate conditions among the Chinese and to ascertain why they had chosen not to be repatriated in such large numbers, was equally blunt in describing the U.N. Command's preferential treatment toward nonrepatriates. Chase confirmed American encouragement of Chinese Nationalist control inside the compounds, the anti-Communist nature of the U.S. "information and education" program, the anti–P.R.C. political "sermons" of the Protestant U.S. Army chaplain, and such "gratuitous signs" of U.S. support as the "flying of Nationalist and US flags on American Army trucks." The Nationalist flag, with U.N. Command blessing, had been flying both "literally and figuratively" over the Chinese compounds, he recorded.[11]

Pro-repatriates subsequently claimed that they had become active in the camps in response to this provocative behavior, and one authoritative study of camp life agreed that, in general, "the development and activities of the Communist PW organization in Korea were in part a response to the development of the anti-Communist organization and the conduct of PWs under anti-Communist leadership." The pro–North Korean trusties' rationale for beginning their own propaganda posters, demonstrations, and flag flying was the U.N. Command's failure to respond to a Communist petition that objected to the production of signs and placards proclaiming "Anti-Communists" and "Kick out the Communists." And as one Chinese Communist interviewee stated in conversation with those working on an official army study: "we told the U.N. authorities that if they didn't stop the rightist group from hanging up those flags we would hang up the flag of the People's Republic. . . . But the anti-Communists didn't take them down, so I could not help but start to put up our own propaganda posters and Communist flags in the compounds." Gen. Mark Clark made much of the Communist commissar system in the camps which, utilizing trained agents, infiltrated among the prisoners, published newspapers, fomented trouble, and organized the prisoners in the compounds. Violent, intimidatory tactics were part of their methods, too, though the use of force in the Communist-controlled camps has been described as "purposive and minimal in contrast to the vengeful brutality of the anti-Communist leaders."[12] In general, however, the Communists' consolidation of their control in the compounds continued to receive far more extensive publicity in Western capitals than the activities of the anti-Communists, despite the illogicalities of an argument that stressed the efficient pro-repatriate terror tactics yet recorded the existence of a large number of nonrepatriates.

The U.N. Command's civil information and education program also contributed to political polarization among the prisoners of war and was the source of considerable unrest. It had been agreed at the highest levels in the Truman administration in September 1950 that "the treatment of POW's, after their transfer to places of internment, shall be directed toward their exploitation, training and use for psychological warfare purposes." Hence, that month, the U.N. commander, General MacArthur, began a pilot project for 500 prisoners. The political objectives of the program were clearly spelled out from the beginning by the chief of the section: "We mean to provide an ideological orientation toward an orderly, responsible, progressive, peaceloving and democratic society"; or, more specifically, "we would like to see these people develop a conviction that they and their people will be better off socially, politically and economically under a democratic rather than a totalitarian regime."

[114]

The program began in earnest for all inmates from the spring of 1951, with the assistance of R.O.K. government officials, 23 linguists recruited from Taiwan and selected from Chiang's Ministry of Defense, and some 2,500 recruits from among the prisoners of war themselves. In February 1951, MacArthur requested an additional 55 instructors from Taiwan, despite a warning from an official in the Office of Chinese Affairs that they "would assuredly be in the service of the KMT secret police." MacArthur also sent a staff officer to Taipei to work out an appropriate program of study. Unfortunately, however, the effectiveness of the enterprise was undermined for some prisoners, Muccio recorded, by the "undemocratic methods self-appointed POW trusties while UNCIE [civil information and education program] promoting high principles of democratic life."[13]

Classes were held on six main topics, including the lives of people in the nations of the "free world," and democracy versus totalitarianism. Extensive use was made of radio broadcasting material from Voice of America, Voice of the U.N. Command, Radio Free Asia, and from R.O.K. broadcasting stations. Inmates also read weekly United States Information Service (USIS) translations of news releases and saw USIS film releases. Chinese prisoners also received Nationalist magazines. In addition, many Protestant and Roman Catholic services that, by all accounts, also included a strong political ingredient were held.[14] Since so much of the material had an avowedly anti-Communist content, it was the source of much tension, and the program led the ICRC to recommend the elimination of its political elements. The U.N. Command complied with this in the pro-repatriate compounds, but it was kept going in its original form in the nonrepatriate camps for the duration of the war.[15]

The official aim of the program was to return to their own societies significant numbers of persons who would work there to promote democratic ideals. The prisoners were to be "psychologically prepared so as to serve U.S. psychological objectives after their return to Communist jurisdiction."[16] However, the use of pro-Rhee and pro-Chiang instructors meant that the unofficial objective became the assurance that, when the official poll of prisoners was held, a major propaganda boost for America's allies in Asia and a catastrophic defeat for the Communist bloc would result as men in their thousands opted either for South Korea or Nationalist China.

The civil information and education program and discussion at the conference table about exchanging prisoners, together with the U.N. Command's utilization of some prisoners as political instructors (which made participants "apprehensive" that they had "actually signed their own death warrant"), brought the repatriation issue into sharper focus inside the compounds in the winter of 1951–52, causing POW leaders to tighten their grip. Just before the official screening of prisoners of war in April 1952, Philip Manhard (in the first of a series of memoranda that were never refuted) had reported, on the basis of observations made in the Chinese compounds between July and December 1951 and during the last week of February 1952, that the trustees had "for several months conducted a drive to collect petitions for transfer to Formosa," a "propaganda drive" that was reaching a climax in mid-March "with use of brutal force to obtain signatures." Manhard went on to record that POW leaders, in their explanation of the repatriation issue, had informed fellow inmates: "It has been officially decided that all who wish to do so will be guaranteed an opportunity to go to Formosa— those who do not wish to fight Communism will remain in the POW camps indefinitely."[17]

Admiral Joy's emphatic demand that the Chinese prisoners be rescreened immediately after the figures for nonrepatriates were made available was partly a consequence of reports on screening activities given him by two interpreters in the U.S. Army's employ—Lieutenants Wu and May. They confirmed that "the results of the screening were by no means indicative of the POWs real choice." The two told Joy of one mock screening that had taken place before the official poll of prisoners: "The leaders had asked those who wished to return to step forward. Those doing so were either beaten black and blue or killed . . . the majority of the POWs were too terrified to frankly express their real choice. All they could say in answer to the question was "Taiwan" repeated over and over again."[18]

The unexpected poll result and the particularly large number of Chinese prisoners of war who had opted not to return to the P.R.C. had prompted State Department officials to request that two officers be sent to interrogate the Chinese prisoners. Regrettably, this decision had not been made in order to ascertain whether the policy of nonforcible repatriation truly deserved the U.S. administration's backing; rather, it was designed to discover whether the poll results indicated a significant lack of support for the Chinese Communist regime. A. Sabin Chase, chief of the Division of Research for the Far East, and Philip Manhard were chosen to undertake this task, and their reports were conclusive in demonstrating that the main impetus behind the large numbers refusing repatriation was the violent tactics of the POW trusties before and during the screening process. Once again, Manhard described the methods used by leaders determined to ensure a large figure for those wanting to go to Taiwan, including an information blockade, which meant that "(1) . . . many POWs not sure polling directly connected with POW exchange, (2) partially successful deception by POW trusties that polling was only test to distinguish pro-Communists for later punishment and execution by UN authorities" and was not in any way connected with a possible return to the P.R.C., and "(3) physical terror including organised murders, beatings, threats, before and even during polling process." A few days later he repeated that the screening had been "superimposed on background of extreme coercion and intimidation over long period of both pro- and anti-Commie leaders Korean compounds, anti-Commie leaders Chinese compounds." He also pointed out the unpalatable fact that the physical safety of the prisoners immediately before and during the screening procedure could not be "guaranteed due lack internal control of compounds by UN guards." Furthermore, he believed that the "honest naivete [of] polling questions" had confused the prisoners; as a result, many repatriates and nonrepatriates were involuntary, their "choice being made in atmosphere of fear and uncertainty." Chase reported in a similar vein, claiming that in the months preceding the screening pro-Chiang trusties "with Chinese Nationalist and American encouragement and aid, had built up a police-state type of rule over the main Chinese POW compounds, which provided the foundation and means for powerfully influencing the screening against repatriation."[19] These two officials, therefore, had not found significant lack of support for the P.R.C. or People's Liberation Army among Chinese soldiers, many of whom were ex-Nationalist army troops; what they had found instead was that the conditions in the camps had severely compromised the policy of nonforcible repatriation.

The civil information and education program, as well as the

[117]

segregation of prisoners into the two opposing political groups (some of which, as indicated, took place before the official poll of prisoners), caused numerous incidents and riots in the camps, many of which resulted in the deaths of prisoners and their guards. The U.S. administration produced a report in January 1953 entitled "Communist War in the POW Camps" that argued that the trouble tended to parallel developments at the truce talks and that Communist negotiators could readily pass instructions as a consequence of the efficient communication system that had been established between their headquarters and the cadres inside the compounds.[20] However, investigation of a number of these incidents tends to show a rather more direct correlation between the behavior of the guards, together with the segregation operations, and the outbreaks of violence and unrest.

As the prisoner factions became more firmly established, inmate turned upon inmate. On August 15, 1951, for example, 15 prisoners were killed as each Korean side tried to celebrate the sixth anniversary of the victory over Japan. In addition, the announcement of the 30-day time limit at the end of November 1951 raised prospects of an early armistice and caused panic in the camps. Thus, with feelings running high when an early screening of the Korean civilian internees took place in December 1951—undertaken with some coercion and intimidation—this, too, resulted in unrest and the deaths of prisoners.[21]

The segregation of prisoners into those who wanted to remain in South Korea and those who wanted to return to the North was in fact the cause of some of the worst violence in the camps. On February 18, 1952, for example, camp authorities had decided to carry out a second screening of prisoners on Koje-do who had earlier been divided into those of South Korean and those of North Korean origin. When a number of southerners decided that they wished to be allowed to return to Pyongyang after all, the U.N. Command decided that it must step in to ascertain the facts of the matter. According to the ICRC report of the events, a spokesperson for the 6,000 prisoners said that the inmates opposed this new interrogation on the grounds that the first had involved pressure. However, in the early morning of February 18, at 4:00 A.M., a regiment of troops entered the compound without notice and with bayonets fixed. According to POW accounts, the inmates feared they were about to be killed and charged the troops in self-defense. Conversely, U.S. officers reported that the committed Communists within the camps had incited the prisoners to attack the troops with iron bars, stones, clubs, and home-made weapons including grenades. As a result of this action, 77 prisoners were killed and more than 140 wounded, against one American soldier killed and four injured.[22]

News of this incident was withheld until mid-May when the Associated Press obtained information on it, the U.S. administration fearing the impact such details would have on its claims of being able to protect prisoners and hold them in calm and reasonable circumstances.[23] Nevertheless, despite American attempts to blame Communist incitement for the incident, it did shake international confidence in the screening process. The timing of the leak also added a significant new perspective to the kidnapping on May 7 of the camp commander, Brig.-Gen. Francis T. Dodd.

Dodd was kidnapped when he went to one of the compounds to discuss complaints about the official screening process. In an effort to save Dodd's life, Brig. Gen. Charles F. Colson, who had assumed command of Koje-do, made a statement that acceded to most of the prisoners' demands; but, more important, though it was obtained under duress, it gave further legitimacy to the reports of brutality and intimidation that had surrounded the polling. Colson stated, "I do admit that there has been instances of bloodshed where many PW have been killed and wounded by UN Forces. I can assure in the future that PW can expect humane treatment in this camp according to the principles of International Law. I will do all within my power to eliminate further violence and bloodshed." He also promised that there would "be no more forcible screening or any rearming of PW in this camp." Dodd walked free, shortly to be demoted, along with General Colson, to the rank of colonel.[24]

Inevitably, the Communists used Colson's statement to great effect at the truce talks and in public reports, claiming that it demonstrated the hollowness of the U.N. Command's stand on nonforcible repatriation. But though each violent incident resulted in a further propaganda blow to the Americans, they could not prevent their occurrence. The brutality of the R.O.K. guards, reluctance to use better disciplined fighting men on the job of controlling prisoners, the partiality of those in control toward the nonrepatriates, and the increasing polarization and hatred between the pro- and nonrepatriates contributed to the large numbers of POW deaths in 1952 and 1953. A fresh incident occurred at Koje on March 14 when an anti-Communist work detail, accompanied by South Korean guards and singing R.O.K. marching songs, raised large South Korean flags and jeered at Communists in a nearby compound. The Communists threw rocks, some of which hit the guards, who opened fire, killing 12 and wounding 26 of the inmates. Another in April, resulting in more prisoner deaths, occurred during an attempt to remove a wounded prisoner from a compound. In the course of this, disturbances took place and U.S. troops opened fire, to be joined by R.O.K. soldiers. Yet, when a Korean anti-Communist youth association organized mass demonstrations against forcible repatriation—which spread to 20 compounds in all—these were not dealt with in such a summary manner.[25]

One of the most serious incidents occurred on October 1, 1952, the third anniversary of the establishment of the P.R.C. Some 52 Chinese prisoners were killed and 113 wounded when guards opened fire against prisoners who were "milling around," singing, and flying P.R.C. flags. According to the camp commander, now Col. Victor Cadwell, the demonstrations were a prelude to a mass breakout of prisoners. When he ordered his troops to subdue the most recalcitrant of the compounds, improvised weapons were pitted against rifles with the inevitable result.

Manhard, in his report on the disturbance, expressed extreme skepticism about the "mass breakout" idea, arguing that there was "no tangible proof of this assertion in public or in private" and that pictures of paper wreaths in the shape of the Communist star, produced by the prisoners, were "highly unlikely equipment to prepare for a mass breakout." He pointed out that some 11 percent of the inmates had been killed and 25 percent wounded during this operation, leading him to charge that it was "absolutely unbelievable that such methods are necessary to achieve adequate security controls." Moreover, he had worked for many weeks in June and July, often alone and always unarmed, with these same prisoners, and he "found it possible to accomplish all necessary objectives without the massive use of force."[26] Manhard's attitude and approach were, however, very different from those of the men in day-to-day charge of the inmates. These guards were also responding to

instructions from the U.N. commander which on August 16 included the message that "prisoners who throw or attempt to throw
rocks at guards should be shot while in the act . . . I will be much
more critical of your using less force than necessary than too much."
Later on, a "shoot to kill" recommendation was made, perhaps
accounting for the ICRC's continuing to recommend in May 1953
that the resort to force should be in proportion to the resistance
offered.[27]

THE COMMUNIST CAMPS

The policy of nonforcible repatriation had, then, been severely
compromised by the experiences of the prisoners while under U.N.
Command control and by the inadequately supervised polling procedure. The other victims of the policy were the U.N. Command
prisoners in Communist hands in the camps scattered around
North Korea. As official Western reports and numerous memoirs
published in the West have demonstrated, they, too, were to experience severe deprivation, maltreatment and, in some cases, appalling brutality. The impasse over the repatriation issue would mean
that many would either die or spend a total of two and a half years
in the Communist compounds.

As noted in the previous chapter, initial administration reluctance to consider voluntary repatriation had hinged largely on a
natural desire to see the speedy return of U.S./U.N. troops held
captive north of the 38th Parallel. Intelligence reports of atrocities
against a number of American prisoners and of the harsh conditions
in the camps, especially during the winter of 1950–51, were available to the U.S. administration. However, once the administration
was committed to allowing Communist prisoners a choice regarding repatriation, the fate of the U.N. Command troops in captivity
became secondary to this larger political objective.

Treatment varied for the men in Communist hands, depending
largely on the degree of "cooperation" they showed (though reports
indicated that the South Koreans invariably were badly treated).
Those who repeatedly tried to escape suffered brutal torture: Capt.
Anthony Farrar-Hockley, who absconded more than half a dozen
times, was, after one failed attempt, beaten, burned with cigarettes,

and half-drowned in an attempt to force him to reveal what had happened to his two fellow escapees. Those who continued to resist political indoctrination and thus the chance to "repent" were labeled "reactionaries" and suffered horribly as a result. The senior British officer, for example, spent 19 months in solitary confinement, which could mean being "made to stand or sit at attention (legs outstretched) and in complete silence from 04.30 hours to 23.00 hours daily." For those who endured solitary imprisonment, there were "no beds and no bedding. Shoes and clothing, except for underclothes, were often taken away, even in the middle of winter." Other punishments for "reactionaries" included confinement in boxes 5' × 3' × 2' for long periods, or worse still, being bound hand and foot with a rope passed over a beam and fixed as a noose around the neck. According to the official British report, the prisoner was "then hoisted up on his toes and the other end of the noose was tied to his ankles." If he slipped, no blame would attach to his captors, since it would be claimed that he had taken his own life.[28]

The hardest time for most of the less "recalcitrant" prisoners was in the early months of MacArthur's advance north. The North Korean Army's policy for prisoners was made "in the heat of battle." Some 50,000 South Koreans had earlier been speedily inducted into the North Korean Army. The remainder of non-Koreans taken were marched north, sometimes traveling about 20 miles a day, often without boots and in inadequate clothing. Many were sick with dysentery or diarrhea, but if they dropped behind, they risked being shot. The North Korean Army in defeat was bitter and resentful and took out that resentment on American soldiers in particular. When MacArthur's advancing army took Pyongyang, 100 U.S. prisoners of war in North Korean hands were taken from a train that was hidden in a railway tunnel just north of the city and shot, with their hands tied behind their backs. Farrar-Hockley recorded seeing another three Americans who had been shot in the back of the head, their hands still tied with telephone cable. Conditions at the hastily organized POW camps at first were little better than on the march itself, and on arrival it was every man for himself. Food was still poor and scarce—perhaps some 1,200 calories a day compared with the U.S. Army's daily combat ration of 3,500. There was little medical care and few drugs, and there was terrible overcrowding. Lines of authority and comradeship were broken down as men began to be segregated by race, nationality, and rank. The captives were induced to inform on the attitudes of their fellow prisoners, contributing further to the sense of isolation. Some 2,701 U.S. prisoners of war are estimated to have died in captivity out of 7,140 taken. A weakening of their physical condition led many of these young men to give up, as comrades neglected them and the squad bully took over.[29]

Once the Chinese People's Volunteers halted the U.N. Command advance and battle lines were pushed south once more, it became possible for the Chinese to introduce a more organized POW policy, based on experience gained during their recent civil war. The Chinese thought of it as the "lenient policy," which—except for the "die-hard reactionaries" who continued to receive appalling treatment—involved attempting to create an atmosphere of friendliness and trust between captor and captive while breaking down bonds between fellow prisoners. Prisoners were treated as "victims of the ruling classes," as "students who were to be educated and pointed towards the truth." One authoritative study conducted by a captain in the U.S. Army medical service corps, neuropsychology division, described the key elements in the Chinese indoctrination program as being the removal of the supports to the men's "beliefs, values and attitudes." This was effected through the removal of natural leaders, attendance at lectures for two to three hours a day (other reports indicate these went on much longer), the showing of Communist films, and the study of propaganda leaflets. More direct participation was an important part of the process, and prisoners were induced to sign peace petitions, make radio appeals and speeches to other inmates. When two U.S. Air Force officers, John Quinn and Kenneth Enoch, who had received some of the worst of the Chinese treatment, confessed to undertaking bacteriological warfare in Korea, and, especially when Lt. Quinn was sent around the camps to denounce his government's policy, this added enormously to the doubts that had been created in many men's minds. Group discussion of the lecture contents, interrogation, self-criticism sessions, and, more crudely, the bestowal of rewards and punishment to elicit collaboration were all attempted in order to produce men who on return to their own societies would work for change.[30]

[123]

Attendance at lectures, according to the official British report, was compulsory until late in 1951. After that, study groups became voluntary, with three types of prisoner continuing to attend: (1) those genuinely interested in Communism, (2) those who were bored and wanted something to do, and (3) those who believed, correctly, that regular participation would better their lot in terms of extra food, access to medicine, and the gaining of positions of authority.[31]

The large numbers of American prisoners of war who participated in this indoctrination program or who died seemingly from apathy rather than from any other more specific cause subsequently led to enormous anxiety in the United States, where conservatives saw that generation as having been affected by the "socialist" tendencies of 1930s America and where liberals saw it as one consequence of American materialism. The U.S. Defense Department was especially alarmed at the apparent effectiveness of the Chinese campaign in the camps, one that could result in detailed confessions from long-serving U.S. Air Force officers. Defense was "particularly concerned lest the Communists release a huge batch of prisoners who . . . would have to be allowed to go to their widely dispersed home towns, where, having been 'converted', they could do immeasurable harm."[32] Yet another unexpected feature of the nonforcible repatriation policy was to emerge, therefore: the anxieties about the lengthening of the period during which American prisoners could be turned into apostles of Communism.

Bureaucratic Channels of Information

As stated earlier, much was known in the U.S. administration about the conditions under which the U.N. Command prisoners were being held, and the realization that nonforcible repatriation would likely prolong their internment led to unease within the administration and in allied capitals, and to criticism from those families who knew their relatives to be in the Communist camps. Public criticism of the administration's repatriation policy, however, would have been far more extensive had there also been greater knowledge of the conditions in the U.N. Command camps before and during the official poll of Communist prisoners. Private awareness was, of course, quite extensive, with a number of high- and middle-ranking officials in State and Defense receiving reports and knowing, as an army-commissioned study concluded, that the "UNC had failed to create the conditions under which the individual PW could make an uncoerced, unintimidated, informed choice." As early as January 1952, more than a month before the nonforcible repatriation policy had finally been agreed upon, Frank Stelle of Policy Planning, in his memorandum to Paul Nitze in which he argued against the U.S. adoption of that policy, spoke of the "reign of terror" in the camps. We should not be "blind . . . to the fact that our prison camps for Chinese in Korea are violently totalitarian, and that the thugs who run them are the people, aside from our own U.S. prisoners, that are the actual objects of our concern in the POW issue," he contended. On February 2, Muccio passed on reports from departmental officers in Korea acknowledging that the signing of petitions in blood and tattooing of prisoners was not being under-taken voluntarily; rather, the Chinese Nationalist factions in leader-ship positions had "forced some prisoners [to] tattoo themselves and print petitions as part of effort to convince UN authorities most Chinese prefer to go [to] Formosa." As early as August 1951, in connection with the civil information and education program, Muccio had also written of the "undemocratic methods [of] self-appointed POW trusties."[33]

In March 1952, as the official screening drew near, the U.S. am-bassador in Korea forwarded Philip Manhard's findings directly to U. Alexis Johnson, reports that, as described earlier, indicated the power that the pro-Chiang trusties had over the other inmates. Manhard's assessments were also passed on to generals Paul F. Yount and Dodd, involved with camp administration, the former of whom agreed that there were "many unsatisfactory aspects to the situation on the island." Johnson, who was so centrally involved with the development of the repatriation policy, did little with this information, or so it seems. He only replied lamely to Muccio during the period of the screening: "All I can now do is to keep my fingers crossed and hope for the best. I do not feel that it would have been possible for us to have taken any other course." In his memoirs Johnson argued that "the military largely ignored [Man-hard's] reports, because they came from outside the chain of com-mand," adding that later he "was able to make good use" of them in "private talks with the Chiefs." He does not acknowledge that he had an opportunity in March to reopen the whole POW policy with the president on the basis of Manhard's evidence and Ridgway's new estimate that as many as 73,000 prisoners might resist repatriation. He would certainly have had the backing of General Vandenberg (and probably Admiral Fechteler), who, as noted earlier, expressed considerable alarm at Ridgway's latest figures. Furthermore, there is little to support Johnson's contention that the military were unaware of conditions within the camps. As a result of a State–Joint Chiefs of Staff meeting on March 19, the joint chiefs sent the U.N. commander the latest instructions for use at the truce negotiations, instructions that acknowledged that the "circumstances existing in [the] enclosures" would "inevitably influence [the] choice of many individuals."[34]

Immediately after the screening, knowledge of conditions within the camps became even more widely distributed. As noted earlier, lieutenants Wu and May had apprised Admiral Joy of the appalling scenes in the Chinese compounds, and Joy had urgently passed these reports onto Ridgway. On receipt of this information, the U.N. commander immediately ordered General Van Fleet to organize a rescreening, but, on investigation, Van Fleet reported that this would not be possible because of a lack of facilities and of U.S. MPs, and as a result of the bloodshed that would ensue.[35]

The head of the Policy Planning Staff, Paul Nitze, had earlier been made aware of the conditions within the camps through the stark warnings contained in Stelle's memorandum. However, it is clear that he and the secretary of state shortly had this information more deeply ingrained on their consciousness when Howland P. Sargeant, in a memorandum to Dean Acheson dated May 20 (and marked as having been seen by him), listed the "facts about which there is some doubt as to the full desirability of full public disclosure at this time," adding that Paul Nitze had "described these as the 'firecrackers under the table'." Such dubious details comprised: "(a) Chinese Nationalist influence prior to the screening of the Chinese POW's; [and] (b) Prisoner-to-prisoner brutality preceeding [sic] and during the course of the screening." At a time, therefore, when the U.N. Command negotiators were making their self-righteous statements at Panmunjom and the U.S. administration and its allies were emphasizing the morality of the stance they had chosen, it had become clear, up to the level of the secretary of state—there is no evidence that the president was made aware of these events—that the official poll of prisoners had been severely compromised.

There was, therefore, some information available to the administration before the final agreement to a policy of nonforcible repatriation that a genuine choice for the prisoners—especially for the Chinese among them—would be virtually impossible to make. Furthermore, these details became more widely known just before the official screening. This suggests that opportunities did exist for the administration to explore the implications of the information contained in Muccio's memoranda, in Stelle's reminder about the conditions for the Chinese prisoners of war, and in the estimate that Hull and Johnson brought back with them from Korea that stated that as many as 11,500 Chinese might refuse repatriation. Admittedly, more graphic descriptions of life in the camps were provided immediately after the poll, but the information was there before the administration's position had solidified and been made public.

Having become tied to the policy, however, administration officials saw no possibility of retreat and little room for compromise. Rather, it was decided that the psychological warfare aspects of the policy were to be developed to their fullest extent, since, crucially, the "refusal of some 80,000 Communist POW's to return except at rifle or bayonet point to Communist control hits them in a most sensitive and vulnerable spot."[36] Immediately on the conclusion of the armistice, therefore, a Department of State InfoGuide Bulletin was sent to American embassies advising them that in their comments they should stress the "honorable" nature of the armistice agreement arrived at, for not only did it register success in stopping aggression but it embodied the "fundamental principle, overwhelmingly approved by free men and nations of the world that men shall not be forced into slavery against their will." U.S. officials were also to stress that the U.N. resolution on prisoners of war passed in the autumn of 1952 (see Chapter 6 for further details) demonstrated "the overwhelming free world support for NFR." Additionally, they should emphasize how well the U.N. Command had treated its prisoners, the "patience, skill and determination of UNC in conducting negotiations . . . [and] our refusal [to] compromise on Communist demand for forcible repatriation, entailing many months of sacrifice, finally acknowledged by Communist

[127]

agreement to present terms." In the following months the Psychological Strategy Board and its successor, the Operations Coordination Board, developed further plans designed to demonstrate how humanely prisoners under U.N. Command control had been treated, compared with the forced confession, brainwashing, and other atrocities perpetrated by the Communists. At the United Nations in November 1953, the U.S. delegation showed films and presented material in order to "unmask Communist torture techniques," footage that was also released to Warner, Pathé, and Movietone news.[37] Domestically and internationally, as much capital was to be made out of the POW policy as possible.

One author has described the U.N. Command prisoners in the camps in North Korea as the "real victims of non-forcible repatriation . . . who had to endure another year in their grim camps along the Yalu." The humiliations and inhuman treatment that some of these men experienced made a mockery of Communist statements at Panmunjom that they were strictly abiding by the terms of the Geneva Convention, and showed that hypocrisy was not only present in Washington but was also alive and thriving in Peking and Pyongyang. But there were POW victims in both sides' camps, many paying with their lives for a policy that may originally have had a humanitarian content but that, in the course of its enactment, became another casualty of the Cold War. This failure in policy implementation could not have been made plainer when Manhard yet again recommended (among other things) that if there was to be a rescreening of Chinese prisoners, the U.N. Command guards this time must provide absolute security for both pro- and anti-repatriate groups at all times; that all POW-appointed trusties be suppressed and new camp elections held; that "all polit[ical] indoctrination activities . . . and polit[ical] sermons and other non religious activities by camp chaplains, whether American, Chinese or Korean" should cease, and that the polling procedure be "administered by US or other UN personnel qualified in Chi[nese] language (as in first polling)" but "excluding all US, Chi[nese] or Korean personnel who have previously participated in polit[ical] or 'reorientation' activities among POWs."[38]

This memorandum summed up virtually all that was wrong with the official screening of prisoners of war and represented an indictment of the methods by which the U.N. Command implemented the nonforcible repatriation policy. Its recommendations, however, were in the main, made too late, as only limited rescreening took place before the armistice was signed, and prisoners remained wedded to their announced political attachments. Only a few were able to find the means to reverse their political allegiance yet again, at enormous personal risk. General Eisenhower, when president, publicly described the POW repatriation policy as "a new principle of freedom," one that might "weigh more than any battle of our time." His secretary of state spoke of the unreliability of Soviet-bloc armies in any future East-West conflict, though he must have realized that few Communist troops surrendered after the defeats their divisions had suffered in May 1951. As C. H. Peake had written in December 1952, the number of persons surrendering in Korea that year had "been extremely small," and the "same situation" also existed in Indochina.[39] General Boatner, however, onetime commander of the POW camps, put a more telling question when he asked rhetorically: "Is it not crass hypocrisy for the United States to restrict immigration in times of peace when men are relatively free, yet take pride in the conversion of our erstwhile enemies to 'our side' by their 'free choice'? Especially when they were in fact in our prisons, subject to our indoctrination and therefore not free to make a 'free choice'."[40] What Boatner was overlooking, however, was that such a policy, if carefully presented, could be projected as a great "free world" triumph, one that went to the heart of the differences between the Communist and capitalist systems. This triumph was so desirable, especially in conditions of military stalemate, as to overcome any examination of the hypocrisy that lay at the root of it.

[6]

Panmunjom Bypassed:
May to December 1952

There were few indications that the Truman administration in the spring of 1952 realized that its adoption of the policy of nonforcible repatriation for prisoners of war would long delay the signature of an armistice agreement. In early April, Dean Acheson had made a "wild guess" at a settlement in a month or so. A State Department Office of Intelligence and Research report produced in March suggested why it was still reasonable to be optimistic. After all, it recorded, to date the Communists had made a number of significant concessions in agreeing to drop any reference to the 38th Parallel in the agenda, eventually accepting that the parallel would not form the ceasefire line, and in October 1951 acquiescing to the change in site for the negotiations.[1]

By May, however, with the approximate figure of nonrepatriate prisoners known, the prospects for an armistice had receded dramatically. Moreover, the unrest and killings in U.N. Command camps, and the capture of General Dodd, had revealed something of the incompetent manner in which the camps had been administered. As *Time* magazine recorded, it was an "all-but-incredible story of chaos and bloodshed . . . and of almost complete lack of U.N. control."[2] Continuing violence in the compounds and the Truman administration's inability to move closer to the signature of an armistice agreement further undermined domestic support for the Democratic administration, as the election result of 1952 revealed. Similarly, such events caused consternation in allied capitals, leading to calls for compromise and greater involvement by other countries in the negotiations. There was, then, a high cost attached to this POW policy.

When General Clark took over from Ridgway as U.N. commander in May 1952, he had little option but to make the establishment of order in the camps an item of priority. During the official poll of prisoners in early April, about 40,000 prisoners had resisted all attempts at screening, and their numbers had simply been added to those who had indicated that they wanted to return home, to make up the round figure of 70,000. Now, after the Dodd episode, those compounds that had been impossible to enter were to be brought under control and the occupants dispersed into smaller units. Using tanks, flamethrowers, and tear-gas grenades, the new camp commander, General Boatner, and his forces set about the task. As a consequence, another 41 prisoners met their deaths and 274 were wounded, but thereafter it was possible to complete the final phase of screening. Completed on June 27, figures showed that some 83,000 would be available for return to the Communists, a number that was sufficiently above the original figure of 70,000 to make the U.S. administration reluctant to reveal it. The fear was that its disclosure would either exacerbate doubts about the original poll or might appear to indicate that the U.N. Command team was willing to bargain on numbers. It was not until July 13, therefore, and after a repeated request from Clark that he be allowed to give the new information, that the details were proferred to the Chinese and North Koreans. It was still well short of the 110,000 that they had indicated would be an acceptable number to be returned and, more seriously, it included only about one-quarter of the Chinese.[3]

THE SEARCH FOR A SOLUTION

The May crisis stimulated State Department interest in finding a method of maintaining the principle of nonforcible repatriation while meeting some of the Communist and Western allied objections to the original poll of prisoners. Suggestions included re-screening by neutral nations, or accepting a de facto ceasefire, exchanging those inmates who wanted to return home, and leaving the rest for future negotiations. Some members of the department also envisaged a large role for India. One official, for example, suggested that New Delhi assume responsibility for the Chinese nonrepatriates, that the United States be no longer directly concerned with their fate, and that it rely on India's "known humanitarianism" to dispose of the question in a way that would be acceptable to American opinion. Still other members of the diplomatic branch proposed establishing indirect contact with Moscow and Peking to get away from the unfruitful atmosphere at Panmunjom. Even General McClure, the originator of the nonforcible repatriation policy, stated to U. Alexis Johnson that, since the POW question was political in nature, it should be left for the political negotiations that were to follow the armistice.[4]

Paul Nitze, director of the Policy Planning Staff, was one of the most energetic in promoting the view that despite the inelastic nature of the principle that force would not be used to return prisoners home, there was "still an area of possible negotiation in connection with the manner and timing of the rescreening of the POWs." He also favored the establishment of a de facto ceasefire in Korea, which, backed by the Greater Sanction statement, would allow the United States eventually to withdraw some of its forces from front-line positions. As regards the prisoners who wanted to go home, he advocated seizing any opportunity to effect an exchange, "with or without formal agreements."[5]

Nitze and others in State were making these recommendations in part because Dodd's capture had raised serious questions about the legitimacy of the original screening operation. The president was also aware of the need to reestablish U.S. credibility over the matter and thus had responded enthusiastically to Senator Richard Russell's suggestion (Democrat, Georgia) that military representatives from neutral nations investigate and report on conditions within U.N. Command compounds.[6] (Perhaps this was an indication that the president was unaware of the way the camps had been run.) But whereas Truman was putting the emphasis on recreating support for the POW policy, Nitze was trying to mask those aspects of nonforcible repatriation that were so difficult for the Communists to swallow—namely, the specter of several thousand Chinese prisoners noisily rejecting the newly established P.R.C. and marching into the embrace of the Peking government's hated enemy, Chiang Kai-shek.

Indeed, conversations between Indian officials and Premier Chou En-lai and discussions with Soviet officials at the United Nations indicated that it was this propaganda element of the issue that disturbed the Communists most of all. As Krishna Menon told

[132]

British officials, he believed that the Chinese really wanted an armistice and that if some way could be found of saving Chinese "honor," the deadlock might be broken.[7] In addition, America's delegate to the United Nations, Ernest Gross, was told by Constantin Zinchenko, the Soviet assistant secretary general of the United Nations, an armistice should be concluded on the basis of the Geneva Convention, and, afterward, "if some of the prisoners on either side do not want to be repatriated, this could be taken into account." To Israeli and Swedish officials, Zinchenko had mentioned that the National Red Cross societies of China, North Korea, and the United States might be left to deal with the nonrepatriates.[8]

The Chinese position, as outlined in conversations between Chou and the Indian ambassador in Peking, K. M. Panikkar, was more complex. If Panikkar's reports were to be believed (and, subsequently, strong doubts were expressed about their validity[9]), Chou had put forward two proposals. The first involved a straightforward settlement on the basis of the return of about 90,000 Koreans, but all 20,000 of the Chinese. The second alternative, however, was the one that sparked most interest in Western capitals, since it mirrored the Soviet suggestion in recommending acceptance of the Geneva Convention and agreement that all prisoners of war prima facie desired repatriation, but included an understanding that any who stated they did not wish to return home would be brought to a neutralized area, freed from military restraint, and there interviewed by representatives from the four neutral states designated to work on the armistice supervisory commission, and by Red Cross personnel from both sides. Under these conditions—and clearly the Chinese and North Koreans believed that, freed from restraint, many more would elect to be repatriated—the Communists would respect the views expressed at interview.[10]

Despite doubts about the reliability of Panikkar's reporting, on June 19 John D. Hickerson, the assistant secretary of state for U.N. affairs—originally not an enthusiast for nonforcible repatriation—agreed that the matter should be followed up "cautiously but promptly,"[11] not least because of its coincidence with Soviet ideas, but also because the United States had itself become committed to the notion of impartial rescreening in order to restore allied and public confidence in its POW policy. The Australian government, for example, was calling for a group consisting of representatives

[133]

from several countries to act as political advisers to General Clark. The Canadians were objecting to the U.N. Command's negotiating tone, especially to public descriptions of its package proposal as "final and absolute." Moreover, they also requested "frequent consultations on Korea as early as possible before proposals became decisions."[12]

The British had been especially vigorous in expressing the need for a new poll of prisoners. London was annoyed with Washington for causing it inadvertently to pass on false information to the House of Commons, to the effect that all prisoners of war had been interrogated, when in fact some 40,000 could not be approached until late June. More generally, the Churchill government seriously doubted—as a result of the riots, the Dodd incident, and the ICRC report—that "some 170,000 men" could have been "satisfactorily interrogated 'individually and in reasonable privacy'."[13]

Extensive correspondence on these issues appeared in leading British newspapers. Somewhat skeptical of the U.S. position was the historian V. G. Kiernan, who had reminded readers of what they had recently been told of the "fanatical courage, endurance, devotion and ability" of the Communist soldiers. Now they were being asked to believe that some 50 percent of those "fanatics" refused to go home. "Even *The Economist*," as the U.S. ambassador in London put it, "which normally leans backwards in favor United States said [on] May 24 that [a] strong case exists for review of screening results by impartial body." The *Times* maintained a similar position, arguing in its editorials that it was difficult to accept that some 60,000 prisoners would really be in danger of serious persecution if they were repatriated. In its view, the interrogation should be repeated "more carefully by an impartial commission."[14]

Criticisms of the American position voiced in Parliament, and the tabling of a motion by three Labour members of Parliament suggesting a repeat of the interviews with Communist participation, together with the press comment, persuaded the Churchill government to try to quiet these fears. It therefore sent Selwyn Lloyd, minister of state at the Foreign Office, and Lord Alexander, the minister of defense, to investigate conditions in the camps. They returned full of praise for the thoroughness of the original screening (especially that of the Chinese), and Lloyd also voiced his approval of the civil information and education program, which he had found had only "consisted of two voluntary one hour periods each week."[15]

The two British officials had obviously had a very selective guided tour, and any favorable impact that their report might have had was soon to be undermined. Their one suggestion for greater participation for the "small boys" in the negotiations and increased political advice for the U.N. commander who took many decisions with "substantial political content" was tactfully rejected, though they did manage to have a British deputy chief of staff assigned to U.N. Command headquarters. Moreover, new riots in the camps in October, when some 52 Chinese prisoners of war were killed, belied their statements about the "impressive job" of establishing discipline that had been accomplished within U.N. compounds. And more significantly still, especially for its impact on British support for U.S. policy, their visit to Washington after their return from Korea coincided with the U.N. Command's bombing of the Yalu River power installations. This event created yet another furor in the British Parliament, more so when it became known that London had not been consulted in advance of the operation.[16]

THE HARDENING OF THE ADMINISTRATION'S POSITION

The Defense Department had initially supported State's view that allied confidence in the U.S. administration's handling of the armistice negotiations had to be rebuilt. For this reason, in mid-May it had agreed that it would be a totally inopportune moment to suspend the talks, and that the time would be far better spent in capitalizing on America's psychological victory over the POW repatriation figures. The Pentagon did find more favor, however, in the U.N. commander's recommendation that the number of meetings between the two delegations be scaled down to one or two a week, in preparation for the day when talks might be completely suspended.[17]

By the end of the month opinions were shifting among the joint chiefs. In discussions with State about rescreening, General Collins remarked that he was unwilling to accept any Red Cross involvement in the light of their recent criticism of U.N. Command methods for restoring control over the camps, but he would accept a role for neutral nations. On the other hand, Admiral Fechteler, critical of the original decision not to have an all-for-all exchange of prisoners, was now much more inflexible than Collins and rejected the notion of any new interrogation at all, preferring instead to break off the talks and simply to wait for the Communists to agree to the U.S. position.[18]

As he had in the past, Fechteler was responding to the recommendations emanating from the U.N. commander and his negotiating team. Joy had once more asserted that the time for decisive action had come and, earlier in May, had requested suspension of the talks, a course of action that General Clark supported. In Joy's view, the U.N. Command "could not make a worse tactical error than to continue daily plenary sessions." A few days later, on May 21, the U.S. ambassador in Tokyo, Robert Murphy, additionally required to provide political advice to Clark, concurred with these sentiments but suggested the compromise course of postponing meetings from time to time. This was a position that the joint chiefs, still divided on the question of rescreening and on whether to continue with the negotiations, could accept.[19]

Though Clark did not receive the authorization he desired to suspend the talks at this time, nevertheless, he was remarkably successful in loosening the restrictions on the bombing of targets in North Korea. In April the Joint Strategic Survey Committee had produced a report that had recommended that, whenever the Joint Chiefs of Staff decided the Communists were protracting negotiations "merely to serve their own ends," the talks should be recessed and followed by increased military pressure. Selected items of value should be attacked, it suggested, including the North Korean hydroelectric installations.[20]

Perhaps connected with the publication of this study and certainly with the appointment of General Clark as the U.N. commander (Clark strongly believed that air pressure on the enemy had to be increased), "a significant change in combat operations policy" took place at about this time. On May 8 a supply depot at Suan was bombed in the "biggest single attack since the beginning of the Korean conflict." During the next two weeks vehicle repair and ammunition factories were destroyed. And between June 23 and 27 the North Korean power plants, including, on the express orders of the joint chiefs, the Suiho installation on the Yalu, came under attack, allegedly resulting in the destruction of 90 percent of North Korea's power potential.[21]

These attacks on the power plants were primarily undertaken, it seems, to "ginger up" the peace talks, as General Bradley put it. As a Pentagon officer informed a *Time* magazine reporter: "We now realize that the best chance of breaking the deadlock at Panmunjom is to hit the enemy with the forces at our command."[22] What these attacks may have done instead, however, was to undermine the Sino-Indian attempts to find a mutually acceptable solution to the POW problem. Indeed, the bombings came not only at the time when State had decided that Chou's formulae should be investigated "cautiously and promptly" but also during the period when Gross was having discussions with Zinchenko. Yet the State Department raised no objection on June 18 when the chiefs had asked for its opinion on the prospective operation; and by June 19 both that department and the president had given their assent to the air attack.

The Chinese press immediately criticized these bombings, describing them as politically motivated and deliberately intimidatory. At the United Nations, Zinchenko became elusive, preventing Gross from following up on their earlier conversation. On July 14, the P.R.C. government addressed a note to the Indian embassy in Peking, stating that it was no longer interested in negotiating on the basis of the second alternative and wished instead to reiterate that all Chinese prisoners of war must be repatriated. The bombing of Pyongyang on July 11, an operation that involved a "savage assault" against 30 designated targets in the city, may also have confirmed the wisdom of its hardened stance. Some 1,254 sorties were flown on the first day, and 23,000 gallons of napalm were dropped. Radio Pyongyang reported that the strikes had destroyed 1,500 buildings and inflicted 7,000 casualties. Subsequently, a U.S. Psychological Strategy Board report revealed that warnings to civilians in 78 towns and villages of raids of this kind were designed to "increase the pressure on the Communist negotiators at Panmunjom." But they led General Nam Il to state on July 18 that "in the face of such brutal bombings" the Korean and Chinese armies would "only fight more courageously and grow stronger." He also vowed that the U.N. Command would never obtain at the conference site what it could not gain on the battlefield. Shortly after that, the talks went into recess for a week.[23]

Little connection was made in Washington between the failure of the Soviet and Chinese indirect channels of communication and these bombing operations, though in New Delhi Nehru's view was that such tactics had undoubtedly "stiffened the Chinese attitude."[24] Instead, within the Truman administration, there was a tendency to view Peking's and Pyongyang's criticisms as indications that the tactics were working. As Lovett was to argue later in the year, the Communists "only changed [their position] under the application of military force" and "had even complained of military force in the course of the negotiations at the time that they were conceding points to us."[25]

Failure even to consider a possible link between the stopping of the political discussions in Peking and New York and the military operations in Korea possibly also stemmed from the popularity of the bombing program, not only in the Defense Department and among the commanders in Korea but also among the general public in the United States. A public opinion poll in June had recorded the disillusionment of the public, with some 30 percent of respondents having no faith in the negotiations, and 70 percent not foreseeing a settlement. State Department opinion reports found that in July 61 percent of respondents favored bombing across the Yalu, an increase of 7 percent over the March figure, and a rise in bellicosity that probably stemmed from the Yalu raids.[26]

The election-year atmosphere further enhanced preferences for a militant rather than a flexible stance at the armistice discussions. Senator Robert Taft, a leading member of the GOP and a presidential candidate, regularly spoke out against a negotiated settlement in Korea, leading the Democratic Senator Tom Connally to accuse him of subordinating truthfulness on the topic in order to get a "few slimy, filthy votes"—hardly a contribution likely to improve GOP-Democratic party relations during the campaign. But even Republican party moderates would attack the Truman administration's Korean policy. Henry Cabot Lodge, for example, described limited war as a shock to the "national sense of decency." John Foster Dulles, Acheson's prospective successor, in an early description of the doctrine of massive retaliation described Truman's containment policies as "negative . . . treadmill policies which at least might perhaps keep us in the same place until we drop exhausted."

These views, along with more plainly McCarthyist sentiment, were expressed in Republican party platform speeches that accused the Democrats of waging war with "no hope for victory" and of continuing to harbor Communists in government. At Republican rallies placards reading "No minks, no pinks" served to link the corruption issue that had tarnished the administration's reputation with McCarthy's charges. Dwight D. Eisenhower, eventually the party's nominee, became ever more closely associated with right-wing Republicans as the election campaign advanced. Appearing on a platform with Senator McCarthy, he declared that tolerance of Communism had "poisoned two whole decades of our national life." Before the American Legion Convention in August he called on the electorate to join him in "rolling back the Communist tide in a great moral crusade." Armed with the results from private polls that showed that Korea was a matter of grave concern to the voters, he increasingly focused on the war, describing the decision to enter into the negotiations as a "swindle" allowing the Communist military position to be repaired and to be made "half again as strong."[27]

Support for Truman's POW policy remained almost wholly intact, however, and both parties' nominees affirmed that they would never use force to return unwilling prisoners to their homes. Even if Adlai Stevenson had wanted to distinguish his stand on the matter from that of Truman, he would have found it was grist to the mill of Richard Nixon, who had already charged that the Democratic nominee was "soft on Communism" and a friend and defender of Alger Hiss. Indeed, in certain respects Stevenson seemed more uncompromising than General Eisenhower on Korean War policy. The Democrat depicted the conflict as a just war and a fight against tyranny that his administration would continue supporting for as long as it had to in order to secure "an honorable peace." Eisenhower, however, concentrated on assuring voters that he would bring the war not only to an honorable but also to a successful end, whatever the latter might have meant.[28]

With this degree of bipartisan support for the nonforcible repatriation policy, only isolated questions among congressmen and the general public were raised about it. The Dodd incident had sparked interest in the U.N. Command's administration of the

POW camps, but when Congress investigated conditions, it confined itself to condemning the roles of Generals Dodd and Colson in the affair and to applauding Clark for removing them from their commands. One congressman, J. Vaughan Gary, responding to ideas expressed in an editorial in the *Richmond News-Leader*, enquired why voluntary repatriation had suddenly become a "fundamental moral and humanitarian principle." Another House member received a letter from a constituent who had fought in Korea assailing the POW policy on the grounds that the South Koreans would soon "eradicate the entire group [of nonrepatriates] without hesitation." He also demanded to know if the United States was so hard up that it "must stoop to purloining prisoners of war for prospective converts to our way of life." His congressional representative, William R. Williams, was so affected by the trenchant views expressed in this letter that he passed copies of it on to the secretaries of defense and state.[29]

A few wives of American prisoners of war also began to get organized. In May, Walter Judd read into the House record the views of three women who had asked why the "lives of enemy POWs were being put before those of our own men." (Judd, well known as a staunch supporter of Chiang Kai-shek, also saw to it that a refutation of these views was incorporated.) I. F. Stone, writing in the *Daily Compass*, also focused on the fate of U.S. servicemen and asked "about the American boys who go on dying every week while the truce talks drag on." In August the administration had reportedly received some 2,100 petitions suggesting it should give in on the POW policy, and by the end of the year the deputy assistant secretary of state for public affairs would record a "constant under-current of privately circulating petitions demanding the return of our prisoners as a first concern," including one that was believed to bear about a quarter of a million signatures.[30]

Private State Department polls also showed that, although there was "virtually no sentiment in favour of making 'concessions'" at the armistice negotiations, when the public was "faced with the emotionally persuasive argument of returning all POWs for the sake of getting U.S. prisoners back," a July 1952 survey showed that 31 percent favored returning all Communist prisoners immediately; an additional 40 percent were in favor if it was needed to get U.S. men home, and only 20 percent said they would never return the nonrepatriate prisoners. Without an emotionallly persuasive argument, however, 58 percent approved the nonforcible repatriation policy.[31]

Such dissent as did exist about the POW policy, however, was never coordinated and always counteracted when possible by administration and congressional supporters of nonforcible repatriation. Moreover, since few Americans believed that the Communists had any intention of signing an armistice in the near future, the nonforcible repatriation policy was not seen as "the chief obstacle" to the return of American prisoners. Those against the war, whether radicals, pacifists, or pragmatists who believed that America should leave the peninsula rather than go on fighting a limited conflict, never combined their energies or found an appropriate channel for expressing their dissent. One senator (Ralph E. Flanders) who promoted a peace plan in August and September which involved establishing a neutral zone along the Yalu, free elections throughout Korea, and U.S. assistance in rebuilding the whole country, never touched on the POW issue at all. Those senators and congressmen who did refer to the prisoners frequently discussed the supposed "promises" that had been made in the U.N. Command's surrender leaflets (dropped over enemy territory in their millions), promises that could not be repudiated if the United States wished to maintain its moral standing in the world, it was argued. USIS press interviews with selected nonrepatriates were also distributed, and these emphasized the men's attachment to freedom and democracy. The State Department's response to Congressman Williams (quoted above) accentuated the broader questions involved in the POW policy, claiming it represented a "fundamental struggle developed out of the opposing attitudes of the free world and the Communist camp on personal rights and dignity." These men, the State reply said, who had risen up in a "spontaneous movement," could not be forced to return to "slavery and execution."[32]

The kind of letter the administration was more likely to publicize was not the type that Williams had received, but one of the kind that Capt. Charles E. Ewing—who had been stationed at Koje—had written to President Truman. In his letter Ewing reported on those prisoners in his care who had been brought to him "still bleeding from scratches from the barbed wires, some wounded by stones flung by strong Communists trying to hold them back, some wounded by birdshot from U.N. guards, but smiling and happy because they ha[d] fought their way through to a chance for permanent escape from a miserable life under the reds." Everything that Ewing had learnt about "life under the reds" had convinced him that the United States could not "force these poor devils to return to their enslaved homeland." With some alacrity, the State Department recommended that this letter and the president's intended reply be released to the press.[33]

FORGING THE POLICY CONSENSUS

Differences in approach between State and Defense as to the best method of achieving an armistice were obvious between May and August 1952. A national intelligence estimate (NIE) of July 1952 could also be used to support each side's case, since it argued that the Communists probably wished "to conclude an armistice," that "internal economic and political considerations [were] probably exerting pressure on the Chinese" to end the fighting, and that diplomatic moves indicated that Moscow and Peking "wanted to find a solution for the POW issue." At the same time, the NIE suggested that the Communists would "protract the negotiations so long as they consider that they can win advantages from the POW or any other issue."[34] Nevertheless, despite these contrary indications, election-year politics, the failure of the Soviet and Chinese channels, little questioning of the nonforcible repatriation policy by opinion formers in the press and in Congress, together with a growing if unsubstantiated belief that increased military pressure would bring forth the desired result: all these elements worked against the kinds of solutions members of the State Department had been considering. Against this unfavorable background, however, in August 1952 the diplomatic branch made a final attempt to negotiate rather than to impose a settlement on the Communists. A suggestion from Vincent Hallinan, the Progressive party nominee for president, sparked this initiative.

Hallinan suggested to the main parties' presidential candidates that an immediate ceasefire be concluded, leaving the question of the prisoners of war for resolution by civilian representatives from both sides in the period after the fighting had stopped. When George Kennan, now ambassador in Moscow, reported that both *Pravda* and *Izvestia* had carried reports of the Hallinan proposal, the State Department became interested in it as a possible negotiating avenue. State's conclusion was that a presidential statement should be made which referred to Hallinan's appeal and which in addition suggested that the U.N. Command would immediately return the 83,000 prisoners of war in its custody who wanted to go home in exchange for the 12,000 reputed to be in Communist hands. The nonrepatriates, it was agreed, could become the subject of subsequent negotiation.[35]

Though Kennan supported this idea enthusiastically, believing that increased military harassment of China should be combined with the search for negotiating opportunities,[36] the military were much more doubtful about it. Ambassador Murphy in Tokyo also voiced his concern, recommending instead the establishment of an impartial group of nations to determine the ultimate fate of the nonrepatriates within a specified time limit. Based on his recent World War II experiences in Austria, when he was involved with the repatriation of displaced persons, he believed it essential to dispose of the POW problem completely and that it was necessary to determine all administrative arrangements in considerable detail. The army, on the other hand, concentrated on the notion of a presidential statement, describing it as "unseemly" for the president "to dignify a proposal made in the Communist press by responding to it." Murphy agreed with these sentiments and replied in similar vein, cautioning against a display of "overeagerness . . . to an appeal from a discredited Commie sympathizer just released from prison."[37]

Clark and Murphy also argued that the military pressure the U.N. Command was exerting was beginning to produce results. According to one agent's report, General Clark said, it was having a "material effect on the civilian morale in North Korea." Murphy added that he was convinced the Hallinan proposal was the direct reflection of this heavy bombardment. Both of them agreed that it would be best for the United States to remain firm at the negotiations and await the outcome of this military activity.[38]

Despite this formidable opposition to State's proposal, it was unwilling to yield the point at this stage. On September 3, Nitze again recommended a presidential statement, but, in order to meet some of the criticism, suggested using the Mexican proposal—that all nonrepatriates be given immigration status in countries willing to receive them—as the pretext. He argued vigorously for these views at a State–Joint Chiefs of Staff meeting on September 8. At this meeting he, John M. Allison, and Johnson confirmed that they had no intention of reneging on the stand of nonforcible repatriation, reminded the joint chiefs that State's proposal, if accepted, would mean that the U.N. Command would get all its men back, and questioned what alternatives were available to the administration. Defense's response demonstrated how close thinking in Washington had come to the ideas that had long been expressed in Korea. In the chiefs' view, and especially in the opinion of Fechteler, the chief of naval operations, such a proposal represented a retreat from the package deal put forward on April 28; moreover, leaving an issue of this kind unresolved would give the Communists an additional pretext for violating the armistice.[39]

Neither of these points was very convincing. As Nitze argued, if the Communists did want to renew hostilities, "they could find plenty of other pretexts for doing so." Furthermore, as far as State could see, the package deal was a dead letter anyway by this stage since only the POW issue truly remained outstanding. The department also recorded its skepticism about the claims regarding the effectiveness of the bombing program. As the director of the Office of North East Asian Affairs put it, one "ancient report" from Clark's agent was hardly a "sufficient basis for evaluating the effect of civilian morale in North Korea."[40] But Clark repeated his arguments, stating that there were "increasing indications that the cumulative effects of our air operations are having increasingly severe results on the enemy." The United States would be disadvantaged if it tried to negotiate about the prisoners in a period when this heavy bombardment had been stopped.[41]

Passing over Clark's failure to provide detailed intelligence about these "cumulative effects," the joint chiefs adopted his arguments almost entirely. Moreover, in response to a presidential request to discuss these communications between State, Defense, and the U.N. commander, the Defense Department's views were put before the president. In the combined opinion of the Joint Chiefs of Staff, the three secretaries, his own views and those of his deputy, Lovett told Truman on September 15, any presidential offer at this stage would be considered a "sign of weakness" and in addition "would undo much of the advantage currently being gained by increased military pressure . . . since [Communist] judgment was influenced solely by force."[42]

These arguments, whether deliberately or not, were phrased in such a way as to have maximum appeal for a president who feared appearing weak or indecisive and who had himself recently stated in reference to Moscow's leaders that "only in the face of force [would] they talk and negotiate." Thus Truman quickly gave his support to the military's approach to the negotiations, even before he had heard the detailed views of the Department of State. In the light of this backing, the joint chiefs, at the next meeting with State, called to discuss the disputed proposals, could be much firmer in support of their position. Admiral Fechteler, the only one of the chiefs to attend, informed State that Lovett, the joint chiefs, and the service secretaries were against any presidential statement and were opposed to deferring the question of the nonrepatriates until after an armistice agreement had been signed. Instead, they favored allowing the U.N. Command negotiator to submit a final statement on the understanding that if this last offer was rejected, he would then propose an indefinite recess with no fixed date for the resumption of discussions. The admiral also repeated the argument—on behalf of the joint chiefs, he reminded his audience—that leaving elements of the POW question unsettled, and for postarmistice negotiation, would give the Communists a pretext for violating the ceasefire. It would be, in Fechteler's opinion, "a pseudo-armistice and the Communists would go ahead and build airfields and strengthen themselves."

Once again, Nitze and Johnson remained unconvinced. As the former official pointed out, "the question of withdrawal of foreign forces, claims of UN violations of airspace, claims that we were violating the rotation or build-up clauses of the armistice, or any one of a thousand other claims or pretexts" were available "if they really wanted to violate an armistice." But his arguments still made no headway. Positions between the two departments had polarized on this point, especially between Fechteler and Nitze, the former seeming to imply that State were advocating a retreat, the latter arguing that on the contrary his formulation, if accepted, would mean that the Communists had accepted nonforcible repatriation. Nitze added that the virtue of his proposal was that it gave the "maximum possibility that there might be Communist agreement to an armistice" at the same time as it convinced the allies that every possible opportunity for obtaining agreement had been exhausted. Fechteler stuck to his position of standing firm on the April 28 package deal, and, as he put it, walking "out of the [conference] tent", and piling on the military pressure. As Col. Jack B. Matthews of the Department of the Army explained, the problem with Nitze's proposal was that he was "thinking about our position with our friends," whereas Matthews thought the United States "should think about our position with the enemy."

Gen. Charles P. Cabell, from the air force, also supported this argument. In addition, he was reflecting the views of his superior, General Vandenberg, who had asserted at a meeting on September 2 that "the people in Michigan and Ohio and out there across the country" wanted something done, and that it was time for the administration to prepare for more drastic action. Thus, on September 16 Cabell argued for increased military pressure, stating that its expected favorable results were "merely a function of time," which was working in the U.N. Command's favor: "the longer our air raids last the more they are hurt, and now that the winter is coming up the foliage will disappear and the need for shelter will increase and our targets will be easier to find." What the military seemed to be implying, as Nitze discerned it, was that the "continuation of hostilities [did] more harm to the Communists" than it did to the United States, whereas he had been working on the assumption that the administration wanted an armistice "both to stop casualties and improve the pattern of deployment of our forces."[43]

This was a most revealing discussion and one that represented a new turning point in the war and in presidential relations with the two executive departments. The military had clearly become wedded, on very little evidence, to the notion that the bombing policy was generating results, and apparently they had convinced the president of the validity of that argument. Once the efficacy of military pressure was decided upon, it was a very short step to the lifting of restrictions on targets. Hence August, September, and October saw a further increase in air force activity, with Pyongyang being hit again on August 29. The timing of this raid was designed

[146]

to coincide with Chou En-lai's visit to Moscow, in the hope that it might induce the P.R.C. to request additional supplies from an already overstrained Soviet economy. The U.N. Command therefore launched its heaviest bombing campaign of the war against the North Korean capital, making 1,403 sorties and dropping 700 tons of bombs. According to Clark, the "relentless continuation of [the] program of destruction" was "frightening" the Chinese, as their radio broadcasts indicated.[44] A few days later, on September 1, permission was given to bomb an oil refinery at Aoji, a significant authorization because Aoji was only eight miles from the Soviet border and four miles from Manchuria. At the end of the month a chemical plant right on the Yalu was destroyed, Washington having "accepted the probability that a few bombs may fall on the other side of the Yalu River." According to the official U.S. Air Force history of the war, "almost every night in September Fifth Air Force light-bombers continued their fire raids against North Korean communications centers." October was no better for the inhabitants of the North as ten days of intensified air operations were launched in connection with a hoax amphibious operation at Kojo, near Wonsan, that took place on October 15.[45]

Whatever the U.N. commander and the joint chiefs believed, there was little direct evidence to show that the Communists were ready to concede on the nonforcible repatriation question as a result of this bombing. Indeed, in October they stepped up military action on the ground—in one day firing 93,000 artillery and mortar shells—in part, it has been argued, to coincide with the final stages of the American election campaign, but perhaps also to show their contempt for the U.N. Command's bombing policy. Both sides sustained very heavy casualties during this ground action, which illustrated that, despite the relentless air attacks, for the armies at least the war was still at a stalemate.

The Department of State did not capitalize as much as it might have done on this weak element in Defense's case—that heavy bombing was yielding the desired results. Acheson, for example, revealed his skepticism about these claims and reported on the increase in Communist mortar fire, but did not go on from there and forthrightly push his department's case of concluding a ceasefire and deferring the nonrepatriate issue for later negotiations. At the meeting between the departments of Defense (represented by

Lovett and Fechteler) and State (attended by the secretary and U. Alexis Johnson) on September 17 to discuss their disagreements, Acheson reiterated those arguments that Nitze had earlier expressed: that State was not convinced the military pressure was having much effect; that there were many other pretexts the Communists could use for violating the armistice; that the Greater Sanction statement would be in operation to cover the contingency of a renewal of hostilities; and, finally, that since under State's scheme the United States would retain the nonrepatriate prisoners in its custody, it would be "under no compulsion to obtain Communist agreement on the remaining POWs." In fact, the administration would be in a position simply to release them at any time that it believed the Communists were not negotiating seriously about their future.[46]

Despite the competent manner in which Acheson presented his department's position, as a Defense Department report of the meeting disclosed, he did not pursue all parts of that case and agreed to military recommendations that the diplomatic branch had recently rejected. For example, Acheson finally assented to Clark's request that he be allowed to adjourn meetings at Panmunjom without proposing a time for the next gathering. The secretary of state also failed to promote the idea of issuing a presidential appeal based upon the Mexican proposal. And furthermore, he apparently gave Defense the impression that he had become more receptive to the military arguments they had been putting forward.[47]

Acheson's lack of conviction may have been because he entered the meeting with certain doubts in his mind about his own department's proposal. As he had confided in a private memorandum in which he had noted that "the preponderance of military opinion" was against the political advice of his department, he himself doubted that the Chinese would accept the idea that nonrepatriates be sent to other countries—essentially the Mexican proposal. And if that was so, the U.N. Command could not hold these men for a "long and protracted period" since many would then decide they had waited long enough and return home, an outcome that "would undermine and destroy the very great psychological advantage which we have in offering refuge to Communist soldiers who give themselves up."[48]

In the light of these arguments (and more especially because

Acheson probably knew of presidential preferences expressed in the meeting with Lovett and the joint chiefs on September 15), when these matters were brought before Truman again on September 24, Acheson pushed neither for the presidential statement nor for leaving the nonrepatriates to future political discussions. Instead, he argued that the main question before the meeting was "whether the time [had] come to recess the armistice negotiations." The relieved ranking Defense member at that meeting described Acheson's remarks as a "fine summary." The secretary of state had certainly tilted the argument in favor of attempts to increase the military pressure and toward recessing the discussions for an indefinite period. Acheson's instincts regarding presidential wishes served him well once again as Truman, in response to these points, made it plain that he would not "do anything in the world to get an armistice." The president also believed that unless the United States "wipe[d] the slate clean," an armistice would "do no good." These comments finally secured the joint chiefs' policy: Gen. William K. Harrison, Joy's successor at Panmunjom, would present three reformulations of the U.S. stand on the POW issue, all of which required that no force would be used to return prisoners home, and would then give the Communists ten days to accept or reject one of those reformulations. In the event that they rejected all three, the U.S. administration would then be prepared to "do such other things as may be necessary."[49]

Two days later Clark received a personal message from the president which authorized General Harrison to put forward three variations of the nonforcible repatriation policy at the talks on September 28 "with the utmost firmness and without subsequent debate, and with insistence that the Communists' reply be given at a meeting to be held on or about 8 October." It was also essential, Truman said, that Clark's command maintain the military pressure that he believed had so effectively been applied. On September 28 the three positions were presented, Harrison stating that they represented "the only remaining avenues of approach on which our side can agree to an Armistice." The three were (1) all prisoners of war to be taken to the DMZ, and there identified and checked; if at this stage any prisoner stated that he wished to return to the side who had escorted him there, he would be allowed to do so; (2) the immediate exchange of the 83,000 for the 12,000, all remaining prisoners to go to the DMZ to be interviewed about their repatriation wishes by representatives from mutually agreed countries; and, finally, (3) the exchange of those willing to return home, followed by delivery of the nonrepatriates to the DMZ, where they would simply be freed and without interview be able to go to whichever side they chose.

The Communists' immediate response was that they could not find anything in the proposals that met "the reasonable require-ments of both sides." The talks then went into recess for ten days, after which the Communist negotiators described the U.N. Com-mand's position as "unacceptable" and instead recommended that all prisoners be sent to the DMZ, there to be helped by joint Red Cross teams to return home to lead peaceful lives. As ordered, the U.S. negotiators recessed the talks, leaving only the liaison officers in contact. At a press conference on October 8 Acheson reiterated that the United States would "not compromise on the principle that a prisoner should not be forced to return against his will." Any weakening of resolve, he said, would "constitute an abandonment of the principles fundamental to this country and the United Na-tions. We shall not trade in the lives of men. We shall not forcibly deliver human beings into Communist hands." With this public statement Acheson had tied the prestige and integrity of the Tru-man administration to the September 28 formulae. The door was now firmly shut.[50]

The policy consensus that had been arrived at in late September, which recommended inflexibility at the talks and enhanced military pressure, especially bombing action, was reached for a combination of personal, political, bureaucratic, and ideological reasons. The election-year atmosphere had contributed to the hardening of the stance and to fears that a compromise of the kind Nitze had been advocating would be seized upon by the GOP as a further example of the Democrats' "softness" toward Communism. On the bureau-cratic level, though Acheson must have been encouraging lower-level officials to search for areas of compromise in the POW policy, he himself remained doubtful about the solutions advocated. On the other hand, the military branch, led forcefully by Admiral Fech-teler, was much more united. Though General Collins and General Bradley were not forthcoming in this debate over future tactics at Panmunjom (probably because additional ground operations were not the main focus of the military plan), any misgivings they may have had about Fechteler's position were rarely expressed. The navy chief of staff was thus able and willing to put the joint chiefs' case forthrightly, in such a way, in fact, that would have appealed to Truman, a man who "throughout his career" had "followed a 'give 'em hell' script," thus allowing him "to conceal his diffidence and insecurity under a facade of 'tough talk'."[51]

The joint chiefs' proposition was also simpler than the one that State officials were putting forward. As Fechteler put it in response to Nitze's ideas: "What do you think of telling [the Communists] to take it or leave it on the present basis, calling off the negotiations, putting on military pressure, and then making them come up with a proposal?"[52] Undoubtedly, this straightforward approach touched a chord in many—including the president—who had never had much enthusiasm for the idea of negotiation.

Finally, there was a broader structural argument underlying all this which related to differing views about the best means for the United States to maintain its hegemonic position in the international system. It involved consideration of whether Washington should remain responsive to Western allied opinion in order to persuade the allies that America had "exhausted every possible scheme for securing an armistice" or should give priority to Communist perceptions of America's position, demonstrating to the enemy a determination to prevail, especially on an issue that gave the United States an advantage in its struggle against "Communist tyranny." Consideration of all these factors led the administration to rule out the formulations that some State Department officials had been advancing.

General Clark was soon made aware that at last Washington had begun to look at the conflict from his perspective. On September 23 the joint chiefs had requested his comments on the courses of military action that might follow any removal of all restrictions currently in force, except those involving direct attacks on the Soviet Union and the use of atomic or chemical weapons "other than as now authorized." The U.N. commander had been ready to respond to this sort of message for some time and on September 29 presented his interim plan for ending the war. In his view the real reason for failing to achieve an armistice had nothing to do with opposing views on repatriation but everything to do with the U.S. failure to exert "suf[ficient] mil[itary] pressure to impose . . . an armistice on the enemy." What was needed, he argued, was an extension of the air war to "suitable targets beyond the Yalu," followed by a major ground offensive and amphibious assault capable of being carried all the way to the Yalu, if the expanded air war did not lead to a successful outcome in the conference tent. The general also announced that he would be sending a team of staff officers to Washington to present his detailed plan.[53] Time was running out for the Truman administration, however, and such a proposal, requiring a considerable augmentation of U.S./U.N. forces, could not be dealt with, much less implemented, at a time when the Democrats had been arguing that they had been fighting this war at an appropriate level designed to achieve an "honorable" armistice. Thus, with diplomatic measures virtually ruled out, and the September 28 proposals representing the final word of the U.N. Command team, Truman's and Clark's legacies to the next administration were, respectively, a diplomatic and military stalemate or a military option that required a vast increase in capabilities and involved a wider and more dangerous phase of the Korean conflict.

THE GENERAL ASSEMBLY'S CONTRIBUTION

Though the Truman administration had left itself with almost no negotiating leeway, other governments believed there were possible solutions still to be found to the only issue that remained outstanding in the negotiations. Acheson had realized that these beliefs would generate action of some kind at the United Nations in the autumn and had at one time—before the policy consensus had been forged at the end of September—used this point in support of issuing the presidential appeal based on the Mexican proposal. As the secretary of state had said to his Defense Department colleagues on September 17, the "Mexican proposal had been made, and was the subject of wide discussion." If the United States wished to maintain the support of other U.N. members and to demonstrate that it really desired peace in Korea, he argued, it was essential to show that it "had exhausted every reasonable effort to obtain an armistice."[54] Acheson's predictions about other governments' attitudes were to prove accurate.

When the State Department had first considered its plan for

deferring the nonrepatriates for later negotiation, many governments, including the British, Australian, and Canadian, had been
favorably disposed to the idea. By contrast, another State proposal
for tabling a resolution in the U.N. General Assembly that (1) would
endorse the U.N. Command's stand at the talks and would include
the possibility that the Additional Measures Committee would recommend additional force contributions to the UNC, (2) would suggest the severance of or refusal to enter into diplomatic relations
with the P.R.C. and D.P.R.K., and (3) would require a tightened
economic embargo against the two states fell on deaf ears. Discussions with Commonwealth governments about this proposal revealed widespread objections. As the Australians put it, the United
States would do better to search for greater unity with other governments, and especially with the Asian nations. Canberra also believed that the cutting of diplomatic links would be unacceptable
and that a call for an embargo would never receive the necessary
two-thirds majority.[55]

In the light of this negative response, the administration realized
that it would have to curtail its aspirations. But it was still faced with
the need to take some kind of initiative in order to avoid the un-
desirable consequences of having the negotiations transferred from
Panmunjom to the General Assembly, where many governments
had already made it known that they wanted an immediate armistice, leaving the question of the nonrepatriates for later determination.[56]

An American initiative was made even more urgent because of
the large number of draft resolutions that other nations were drawing up ready for presentation to the General Assembly. By early
November, for example, the U.S.S.R. had produced a draft that
called for the establishment of an 11-nation commission that would
work out a settlement of the Korean question. There was the Mexican proposal already referred to, and a Peruvian resolution that
called for a commission to work out methods for dealing with the
nonrepatriate prisoners. Other proposals, not formally introduced
at that stage, included an Iraqi draft calling for the transfer of the
unwilling prisoners to a neutral nation, a Cuban suggestion to refer
the matter to the International Court of Justice, and an Indonesian
proposal envisaging a commission to negotiate an armistice and a
committee to supervise the prisoners of war who were unwilling to

return home. Finally, there was an Indian suggestion of establishing a commission that would interview and supervise the prisoners. In the U.S. delegation's summary of this activity, it reported that the idea of a POW commission had now come from "so many sources" that it would be "virtually impossible" for the United States to oppose the notion.[57]

The U.S. initiative—known as the 21-power resolution and introduced at the United Nations on October 24—called on the Assembly to support and commend the U.N. Command's efforts at Panmunjom together with its policy of nonforcible repatriation, and requested the North Koreans and Chinese to agree to an armistice based on that principle. Its basic aim was "to secure as many votes as possible in the General Assembly from the nonaligned countries and to demonstrate western solidarity and resolve." However, toward the end of the month, Krishna Menon of the Indian delegation had made it known that he was considering a resolution that embodied the proposal that prisoners be dealt with by a repatriation commission, made up of those four countries that had already been designated to serve on the armistice supervisory commission (Sweden, Switzerland, Poland, and Czechoslovakia). As Menon's thoughts became more widely discussed, enthusiasm for the 21-power resolution faded.[58]

New Delhi and Washington approached their initiatives from totally different standpoints. Menon's early thoughts were that his resolution should be "somewhat vague," whereas the United States was determined "to make it absolutely clear that the principle of no forcible return was in effect." America's allies increasingly came out on the Indian side of this particular argument, not only because the Asian resolution would gain wider support in the United Nations but also because it held out greater hope that an armistice would actually be achieved. Furthermore, unlike the United States, Nehru's officials were in direct contact with Peking about the matter, and that government had already begun to show some signs of flexibility on the nonrepatriates when Chou En-lai admitted that some of Chiang Kai-shek's agents in the U.N. Command camps might not want to return to the mainland.[59] Finally, the Indian resolution at this stage seemed to bear some resemblance to one of the formulae that Chou had allegedly put forward to Panikkar in June.

[154]

As originally envisaged, Menon's resolution was "vague" about nonforcible repatriation and did not explicitly mention it in the text. But under great pressure from Acheson, the Indian delegate agreed to insert a reference to the non-use of force in the preamble. Though other Commonwealth governments saw this amendment as a considerable achievement—especially the British, who had fought hard to maintain preferential treatment for the Indian resolution above the 21-power draft—a mention in the preamble was not enough for Acheson. He and the U.S. delegation wanted the body of the resolution to include a statement on nonforcible repatriation, and they also required that it spell out that prisoners would not be held indefinitely, but after a specified and limited period of time would be freed from the control of the commission.[60]

Acheson tried various methods to solidify allied support behind the 21-power resolution in preference to Menon's effort. The new Republican administration, he told Eden and Lloyd, would not take kindly to Britain's lack of support for the United States on this matter, and London would therefore have damaged its chances of "restraining the new administration from a 'get tough' policy with China." (In fact, Eden found Eisenhower "non-committal" but relatively sympathetic to the Menon plan, though the British foreign minister may have been indulging in some wishful thinking here.) The U.S. secretary of state also argued that support for collective security arrangements, including NATO, would diminish in America. In addition, he called the secretary of defense and the chairman of the Joint Chiefs of Staff to New York to explain their objections to Menon's approach. The two reiterated the points Acheson had already made concerning the need for an unequivocal statement on the non-use of force and for precision in the terms of the resolution. But they also hinted at future difficulties of various kinds if the United States did not get what it wanted: trouble with Syngman Rhee, who would exploit a foggy resolution for his own ends, and conflict of a more alarming nature when Lovett threatened that if the United States did not obtain an "honorable armistice," he saw a strong probability that it would seek a military conclusion to the war.[61] Threats rather than promises were the basis of all these attempts at persuasion.

The determined pressure of Acheson and the more sympathetic coaxing of Lloyd and Eden served to move Menon quite a distance from his original intention of preventing the use of force against prisoners while glossing over the specifics. By November 24 he had placed a reference to the non-use of force in the body of his resolution, had provided for an umpire to act as chair of the repatriation commission, and had agreed that at the end of 90 days any prisoners remaining in the commission's hands would be referred to the political conference. After 60 days (still too long a period, in Acheson's view) the conference would refer any remaining prisoners to the care of the United Nations. With Acheson having lost some considerable support for the 21-power draft as well as considerable respect as a result of the crudity of his attacks on Eden, Lloyd, and Pearson, he finally agreed that with further minor amendments the U.S. administration would give the resolution its support.[62]

However, before the United States could table these further minor amendments (concerning the time period that prisoners would be dealt with by the political conference), Andrey Vyshinsky stepped in and rejected the Menon resolution on the grounds that it had become the "camouflage for horrible American policy" and was now "nothing but a slightly veiled American draft." Vyshinsky was probably referring to the explicit references to nonforcible repatriation contained in the Indian text. In case the Chinese had overlooked this explicit endorsement that force would not be used, Acheson, in his speech later that day supporting the Indian draft, referred some eight times or more to the Indian resolution's endorsement of that principle. Soon after, the Chinese told the Indians that they agreed with Moscow that the resolution was unacceptable.[63]

Though Indian diplomats believed that the Chinese had been subjected to Soviet pressure and that if they had been left to themselves would have endorsed the Menon resolution, later Indian analyses might be nearer the mark. As Nehru's biographer has written, both Moscow and Peking were interested in the Indian resolution in early November but saw the final version as the product of a "subtle American move, through Britain, to use India against China."[64]

Acheson's brusqueness at the United Nations in the autumn probably arose from a combination of political, personal, and bureaucratic factors. Shortly to hand over power, after the election

result of November 4, he would not have wished his final international act to be one that would saddle him with the accusation that
he had compromised what he had so recently described as a fundamental American principle. Moreover, Truman's earlier endorsement of the Defense Department's preferred approach for dealing
with the POW issue, for the combined reasons enunciated earlier,
meant that the loyal Acheson would do his utmost to carry out the
final wishes of the president.

The secretary looked back on these events at the General Assembly with considerable distaste mingled with strong resentment
about allied behavior. Yet in many ways, with an endorsement of
54–5 of the U.S.-modified Indian resolution, Washington had
achieved a lot of what it had desired. Indeed, parts of the U.S.
administration, notably those concerned with matters of psychological warfare, were pleased with the outcome. In the view of the
Psychological Strategy Board, Moscow's "violent rejection" of the
Indian resolution, together with "the recognition by the United
States of the leadership of India in this matter produced favorable
consequences in the subcontinent and elsewhere." Gladwyn Jebb of
the U.K. delegation put the autumn's deliberations more bluntly to
Ernest Gross when he stated that clearly the "Americans thought a
tough, firm policy would be the best means of obtaining an armistice," whereas the British and other governments did not object to
taking measures that would "save Commie faces."[65] The resolution
certainly did not do the latter, showing that the American approach
had been imposed on its Western allies, though at some cost to its
standing with them.

During this period of the Korean conflict the Pentagon's frustrations with limited war and with the protracted armistice negotiations had become more difficult to contain. Frank Stelle of the Policy
Planning Staff had asked a key question in a memorandum to Nitze
in November 1952, but it was one that actually had been answered
some two months earlier. Stelle enquired whether the United States
wanted a resolution of the POW issue "in a way which leaves no
shadow of doubt in any one's mind that our will has been imposed
upon the enemy." If that was so, then the administration was
"obviously making avoidance of defeat for the U.S. correspond
exactly with clear-cut victory over the Communists." But if some-

thing less than this was acceptable, he argued: that is, that no U.S. principle had been sacrificed but doubt remained as to whether Washington had actually imposed its will, then that dictated a more flexible approach to the armistice negotiations.[66] Denied the opportunity to inflict a clear-cut military victory over Communist armies, the Defense Department, and especially those members of it in Korea and Tokyo, wanted to inflict military punishment on the enemy to the limit of America's capabilities in that region. Similarly denied, President Truman also wanted a decisive victory on what he saw as a worthy moral principle, one that embodied the essence of the difference between the two sides in the Cold War, and one that indicated the many months of sacrifice a nation like America would be willing to bear. His secretary of state more clearly wished to remain inflexible on the POW policy in order to retain the U.S. psychological advantage in the long-term ideological struggle with the Communist enemy.

Sensitivity to public attitudes, to congressional attacks, and to electoral charges that the Democratic administration had been led into a negotiating trap by its "cunning" enemies, all reinforced the administration's preference for standing firm rather than compromising. The State Department, between May and August, had pressed its arguments for flexibility on the POW issue but ultimately did little to build support, either internationally or domestically, for its position. Though it was clear from State Department polls that mass public attitudes, and possibly some congressional ones, too, could have been changed if the nonforcible repatriation policy had been reformulated in such a way as to stress the plight of captured U.S. servicemen, the administration did its best to ensure that such a reformulation never took place. Neither did the members of State who favored a compromise hold up for close inspection the proclaimed morality of the U.S. position on the prisoners or the contention that the alternative to compromise—more bombing— did not itself raise moral questions. Too many factors of a bureaucratic, ideological, and cultural kind were weighted against any compromise solution that might obscure the full impact of the victory obtained on this issue.

[7]

Breaking the Stalemate:
January to July 1953

President Eisenhower may have owed his electoral success in part to the voters' belief that he could handle the Korean conflict better than Adlai Stevenson, but he, too, would shortly face those same contradictory influences that Truman had encountered when dealing with the armistice negotiations. The military stalemate on the ground was still a fact of life; and the need to strike a balance between North Atlantic allies, who sought signs of greater U.S. flexibility at the talks, and Syngman Rhee, who continued to demand that an attempt at all-out victory be made, continued to require considerable diplomatic dexterity. Moreover, there was also the matter of an expectant domestic audience who wanted substance to be given to Eisenhower's promise of finding an "honorable and successful" end to Korean hostilities.

Eisenhower also seemed to have inherited the Truman administration's belief that additional military and political pressures rather than greater diplomatic pliability were essential to bringing the war to a close. In this, he seemed to be in accord with his designated secretary of state, John Foster Dulles, who argued in December 1952 in notes prepared for discussions on board the USS *Helena*, the Soviets *"expect* the Republican administration to be tougher and if it is *not* tougher, they will enlarge their estimate of what they can get away with." The president-elect hinted that he would shortly fulfill these expectations when, on his return to the United States and in reference to the Korean conflict, he stated: "We face an enemy whom we cannot hope to impress by words, however eloquent, but only by deeds—executed under circumstances of our own choosing."[1]

Precisely what those deeds should comprise was more difficult to determine, however. The British prime minister, on a private visit to Washington in early January 1953, concluded that the new administration had no plan at all at that stage "apart from doing something or other." U. Alexis Johnson subsequently revealed in his memoirs, "instead of the finely crafted plan for ending the war the Republicans had intimated they possessed, both the President and Secretary were clearly groping their way." Another analyst has observed that the new administration had "no coherent strategy" for ending the conflict and "thrashed about for four months" before coming to any decision.[2]

A new and popular president did enjoy the confidence of the public regarding any choice he might make for terminating the war, a confidence that reflected on his subordinates, too. A public opinion poll claimed that whereas only 30 percent of U.S. citizens in September 1952 had approved of the State Department's handling of foreign affairs, in February 1953 the approval rating was 71 percent. Similar majorities of 70 percent testified to the public's confidence in the president's handling of foreign matters, and especially the Korean problem. Confirming the administration's freedom of maneuver, Walter Robertson told the president on March 31 that the American people wanted an armistice, but if the talks were to drag on for a few more months, then the public would quickly agree to the need for an all-out effort.[3] With Republicans now dominating both houses of Congress, Eisenhower began his term of office with legislative support, too. This did not mean, of course, that those who had been most critical of Truman's policy—such as senators Taft and Knowland and congressmen Dewey Short and Joseph Martin, who all came to positions of prominence—would now be silent on Korean policy. However, the new president and his secretary of state were determined to try to reestablish bipartisanship in foreign policy and, at the least, to work closely with the Republican leadership in determining policy toward Korea. At an early cabinet meeting the president said that he intended to have weekly meetings with congressional leaders; in his view the "great responsibility of Congress" had to be recognized.[4]

In the first few months, in fact, the participants at these meetings concentrated on other controversial matters, such as the budget, the Bricker amendment, and the nomination of Charles Bohlen as ambassador to Moscow; at this stage, the Korean problem was rarely raised. Senator Flanders did continue to promote his plan to unify Korea, including the establishment of a neutral zone along the Yalu to be inspected by a commission made up of neutrals, U.N. agreement to the rehabilitation of all of Korea, and elections under U.N. auspices. Only Senator Wayne Morse, the independent Republican, raised the question of whether flexibility at the truce talks might be the way to end the fighting; he also suggested that negotiations could be taken out of the hands of the military and placed in those of an international tribunal or conference of foreign ministers,[5] not a suggestion that was taken up by others, however.

FORMULATING THE ADMINISTRATION'S POSITION

Preinaugural strategy meetings revealed the dilemma the new administration had to face. Dulles informed Eisenhower that he believed there were definite advantages for the Soviet Union in the continuance of the Korean War, but he also realized that it was difficult for the United States to shed the nonforcible repatriation policy and to end the conflict. Moreover, he suggested that adherence to that POW policy might have distinct advantages since it might well encourage defections elsewhere in the Communist bloc, thus making Soviet leaders cautious about sending their troops into other countries. He also revealed his basic dissatisfaction with the ceasefire arrangements presently arrived at, stating that U.S. objectives should have been to extend the "effective control of the ROK up to the so-called 'waist-line'" (often referred to as the "neck" of Korea).[6] During Eisenhower's trip to Korea in December, however, General Clark had not been encouraged to discuss in detail his military plan for ending the war through expanded hostilities. The president-elect had remained similarly reserved in discussions with General MacArthur that same month, when he, too, advocated certain military and political courses of action (though Eisenhower later stated in his memoirs that these discussions had influenced his thinking with respect to the role of nuclear weapons in the war).[7]

At this stage the nuclear question seemed to represent the central area of interest when Eisenhower deliberated upon the conflict. During the course of a number of discussions undertaken by the newly strengthened NSC, the president appeared to be searching for a role for these new weapons—either they should be used tactically, he suggested, such as on the deneutralized area of Kaesong, or in strikes against Chinese airfields. The nuclear dimension was attractive, first, because of these weapons' potential capacity to inflict a devastating blow on enemy forces, second, because Eisenhower and Dulles both believed that the United States had to be prepared to use those weapons in which it enjoyed a military edge, and, finally, because a nuclear blow would be less costly than an increase in conventional fighting, both in terms of U.S. casualties and economically. In the light of this reasoning, at an NSC meeting on March 31 the president and his secretary of state "were in complete agreement that somehow or other the tabu which surrounds the use of atomic weapons would have to be destroyed." On May 6, Eisenhower announced that it was time for the United States "to consider the atomic bomb as simply another weapon in our arsenal."[8]

Nevertheless, though now free to envisage the atomic bomb "as just another weapon," members of the administration remained divided in the spring of 1953 as to the objectives they sought in connection with its possible use. In discussions with Robert Cutler, the assistant for national security matters, for example, the president requested a study be made of what it would cost to do the "maximum damage to the Chinese forces" and to "reach and hold firmly the waist of Korea." Ten days later he repeated that it would be "worth the cost" if through using nuclear weapons the United States could "(1) achieve a substantial victory over the Communist forces and (2) get to a line at the waist of Korea."

Dulles and C. D. Jackson (the president's special assistant in charge of psychological warfare operations), on the other hand, were concentrating on trying to prevent acceptance of the terms of the armistice already agreed, Jackson because he did not want any forward movement before the president could deliver his "Chance for Peace" address scheduled for April 16, and Dulles because he had no wish to be "sucked into" an agreement of this kind. As he said at an NSC meeting on April 8, he did not see why the United States "should feel bound by the other provisions in the armistice which we had agreed earlier." The president, more circumspect in his response on this occasion, thought it "impossible to call off the armistice now and go to war in Korea. The American people would never stand for such a move," he argued. Despite this statement, Dulles continued to press for any future agreement to be over-turned, if a political settlement in Korea leading to a unified, demo-cratic country did not follow hard on the heels of the armistice, a recommendation that was included in the conclusions of that NSC meeting.[9]

A lack of clarity as to the objectives sought in connection with Korea—that is, whether primacy was to be given to achieving a victory over China's forces in Korea or to creating the conditions for agreement at the truce talks based on the current or a better cease-fire line—was compounded by divisions among the joint chiefs as to the effectiveness of nuclear strikes in any future, expanded war. The Truman administration had three times engaged in atomic diplomacy during its period of dealing with the Korean conflict, and its senior officials had finally become reluctant to consider the bomb's use. Now, with the requirement to consider an expansion of the war along with the use of the atomic arsenal, the joint chiefs were about to rehearse or rethink their earlier positions. Differences were therefore bound to come to the fore. Collins, for example, was skeptical about the tactical use of atomic weapons against enemy forces that were well protected in defensive systems underground. Bradley and Vandenberg, on the other hand, favored their use against strategic targets, the former because this would reduce casualties on the U.S. side and the latter because such action would provide the long-desired opportunity of destroying air bases in Manchuria and North China. Eisenhower tried to counter Collins's objections by enquiring about the effectiveness of "a penetration type of atomic weapon . . . against the dugouts which honey-combed the hills."[10]

The expression of these views and specific requests for the joint chiefs to brief the NSC on future courses of action eventually led, if not to a clarification of U.S. objectives, at least to a consensus on them, and, for the time being at least, resolved the debate over using nuclear weapons. In March the Joint Strategic Plans Commit-tee (JSPC) had sent a report to the Joint Chiefs of Staff which listed six possible courses that needed to be considered in order to reach a settlement of the Korean conflict. By April the NSC Planning Board had taken up the report which, for ease of comprehension, listed the six proposals in order of increasing severity. Three of these propositions (courses D, E, and F) required action outside the Korean peninsula and against P.R.C. territory, involving air and naval power and, in the most severe case, coordinated with a large-scale offensive in Korea itself. In the chiefs' view, none of these courses of action could be successfully carried out without the use of atomic weapons, and they would have "to be used in considerable numbers in order to be truly effective."[11]

Required to make a firm recommendation and unable to resolve interservice differences, the joint chiefs finally chose on May 19 a combination of these three military courses of action, a combination that served to encompass Collins's belief that nuclear weapons alone would not be sufficient to gain victory. If carried out successfully, these courses held out the possibility of a U.N. Command seizure of a position at the waist (or neck) of Korea, the destruction of effective Communist military power in Korea, and a reduction not only of China's future aggressive capabilities in Korea but also in the Far East generally. An expanded conflict, it was argued, would also increase the chances of an armistice being signed on U.S./U.N. terms and make it possible for the R.O.K. to assume increasing responsibility for the military operations in its country. Agreement at Panmunjom had thus become one of a number of larger objectives.

Notwithstanding the expressed concerns about possible Soviet retaliation against "the almost defenseless population centers of Japan" or more local retaliation against U.S./U.N. forces in Pusan and Inchon, coupled with the "disinclination" of U.S. allies to accept such a military proposal, the NSC on the president's instructions recorded on May 20 that "if conditions arise requiring more positive action in Korea, the course of action recommended by the Joint Chiefs should be adopted as a general guide." As has been acknowledged, this "was not a commitment"—for one thing, it would take until May 1954 before all would be ready to mount such a blow, and it was to be preceded by a number of conventional military and political actions—"but it was as close to a final decision as a President can come, short of the moment of execution." In the meantime, the allies were to be informed indirectly, and as in a nonalarming fashion as possible, of the way the administration's collective mind was working.[12]

Undoubtedly, in view of the fears the president had expressed with respect to Soviet retaliation against Japan and allied reactions to a nuclear expansion of the war, there would have been considerable reluctance to implement a decision of this kind. Hence, in the intervening period, other means were also introduced in order to induce an armistice agreement. A number of signals designed to ensure that the Communists realized that the U.N. Command negotiators had reached the end of the road accompanied this atomic contingency planning. Gen. William K. Harrison, was presented with his final instructions and on May 25 was authorized to indicate to his opposite number that this was indeed his last word. Dulles, on a trip at this time to the Indian subcontinent, informed Prime Minister Nehru, assuming that it would be relayed to Peking, that "if armistice negotiations collapse, the United States would probably make a stronger rather than a lesser military exertion and that this might well extend the area of conflict." It has been argued that the primary motive for these discussions with Nehru was to obtain India's support for the administration's negotiating terms, but it was this statement regarding a "stronger exertion" that impressed Nehru the most. As the Indian foreign minister relayed to the British high commissioner in New Delhi, Dulles had informed his government that if the negotiating terms were rejected, the United States would "break off the negotiations and have recourse to dramatic action."[13]

A similar combination of eliciting cooperation but making it clear that the U.N. Command had reached the end of the road was tried in Moscow. The U.S. ambassador, Charles Bohlen, was instructed to "emphasize" to the Soviet foreign minister the "extreme importance and seriousness of latest UNC proposals, pointing out lengths to which UNC has gone to bridge existing gap and making it clear these represent the limit to which we can go." In addition, Bohlen was to make it apparent that any failure to reach agreement on the U.N. Command's final terms "would create a situation which U.S. Government seeking most earnestly to avoid." Finally, General Clark was to send a letter to the Communist commanders reinforcing Harrison's May 25 statement. The text of the letter concluded with a warning: "It is our earnest hope that you will give urgent and most serious consideration to our delegation's alternative proposals regarding the sole issue on which an armistice still depends. If your

Governments' stated desire for an armistice is in good faith, you are urged to take advantage of the present opportunity."[14]

In other ways, too, the Eisenhower administration raised the level of tension on the Korean peninsula. In February ten American B-29s dropped 100 tons of high explosives on Communist front-line positions, only hours before President Eisenhower announced in his State of the Union message that the Seventh Fleet would "no longer be employed to shield Communist China." In the middle of the month the Suiho power installation was hit again. Later in February Sabre pilots were reported to be breaking the rules and engaging in "hot pursuit" of MiGs across the Yalu for short distances. (Although there are no indications that this was officially sanctioned, Eisenhower made it clear on more than one occasion that he did not understand why Truman had prohibited "hot pursuit.") In May another target system came under attack when Clark was given permission to bomb the irrigation dams in North Korea. This policy, aimed at washing out enemy lines of communication, such as railways and roads, and at destroying the rice crop in order to cause famine and unrest in the countryside, was allegedly "as effective as weeks of rail interdiction." Beginning on May 13, 59 F-84 Thunderjets set out to destroy first the Toksan irrigation dam, which had a three-square-mile lake behind it. When the weakened dam finally succumbed, the flood waters left a trail of havoc in the countryside. Photographs available the next morning showed a "scene of total devastation." Two more dams were attacked on May 15, and again railway lines and rice fields were inundated. One North Korean statement that described the destruction of Toksan reported that 70 villages had been submerged, 800 people were dead or missing, large numbers of domestic animals had been lost, and there was "enormous damage to the farms in the locality." It was estimated that it would take "200,000 man days of labour" to rebuild the dam.[15]

THE RESUMPTION OF NEGOTIATIONS

During the course of this military planning, the conventional bombing, and the calculated signaling, there were also developments affecting events at Panmunjom, changes that were of sufficient interest in April to slow down consideration of future courses of military action and the nature of an expanded war. During this period, sick and wounded prisoners on both sides began to be exchanged.

The timing of such an exchange arose primarily out of political motivations. In December 1952 the League of Red Cross Societies had passed a resolution calling for the two protagonists to exchange their wounded. Reluctant to allow another U.N. member—such as Britain—to suggest this at the forthcoming session of the U.N. General Assembly in late February 1953, the U.N. commander recommended that he be allowed to renew an earlier call he had made to exchange the sick and wounded. He had little expectation that it would be agreed to, he said, but there would be "obvious wide psychological and publicity advantages." Clark put forward this suggestion on February 22, but not until March 28 and after Chou's return from Stalin's funeral (see below) did the Communists respond positively, adding that such an exchange "should be made to lead to the smooth settlement of the entire question of POWs, thereby achieving an armistice in Korea for which people throughout the world are longing."[16]

The Communist commanders also proposed the speedy resumption of full negotiations, a suggestion that did not immediately appeal to Eisenhower because his trusted adviser, C. D. Jackson, had suggested that, unless the exchange was an "accomplished fact *before* we actually began negotiations on the wider issue, we would encounter the same kind of frustrations that have always characterized our negotiations." Dulles tried to follow this policy of delay and later told Ambassador Murphy, who had recently been appointed the official political adviser to Clark, that there was a widespread feeling within the administration that these negotiations would soon "prove to be a booby trap, enabling increased communist build-up to our disadvantage."[17] This perception of probable Communist bad faith may have been reinforced by the production of a new intelligence estimate, published on April 3 but agreed on March 26, which was far less equivocal than the one of July 1952, and which argued that internal political and economic conditions were not exerting compelling pressure on the Communists to conclude an armistice; furthermore, since the suspension of the negotiations in October 1952, the Communists had "not indicated any

[167]

readiness to compromise on their demand for 'total repatriation' of POWs."[18]

Chou En-lai's statement on March 30, however, which held out the promise of breaking the logjam on the nonrepatriates, had made the impetus toward restarting the negotiations most difficult to resist and rather undermined the central argument of the intelligence estimate. In this statement Chou proposed exchanging those prisoners of war who wished to be exchanged and handing over the remainder "to a neutral state so as to ensure a just solution to the question of their repatriation." The Chinese premier claimed that these prisoners were "filled with apprehensions and are afraid to return home," and he believed that once they were outside the control of the detaining power and had received explanations regarding their repatriation rights, they would want to return after all. Nevertheless, despite this continuing refusal to acknowledge that there were large numbers of genuine nonrepatriates, Chou's statement represented a major concession because it accepted for the first time, publicly, that there were two separate groups of prisoners, one of which at this stage did not wish to be repatriated. The British, Canadians, Australians, and Indians recognized this as an important distinction and argued that it was an offer that should be followed up speedily. In London's view the Communists "really mean business this time." General Clark agreed and suggested that the United States could not long delay the full resumption of negotiations, especially since on April 9 the Communists had set out their position formally in a letter. Though this communication for the record reaffirmed the Communist interpretation of the Geneva Convention, it also suggested that concessions could be made "as to the steps, time, and procedure of the repatriation of the POWs."[19]

Between April 20 and May 4 the Communists handed over 684 sick and wounded in exchange for 6,670 from the U.N. Command. It had taken only three days to arrange the details of this transfer, a fact that also encouraged those eager to resume discussions. In order to give more concrete form to the Communists' April proposal, Harrison's team notified its opposite number that Switzerland would be acceptable as the impartial state, that 60 days for persuasion seemed a reasonable length of time, and that those not already directly repatriated would be handed over to neutral custody in Korea. The naming of the neutral state, the time period for custody in the hands of that state, and the physical location at which the nonrepatriates would be handed over formed the three main elements in the discussion in the next few weeks.

The Eisenhower administration preferred Switzerland or Sweden and disliked the notion of India's being the custodian because of its perceived brand of neutralism, its supposed fear of the P.R.C., and its antipathy for Chiang Kai-shek's regime. At a pinch, Washington would accept Pakistan and would be willing to agree to three months' custody for the nonrepatriate prisoners but would not permit them to be transferred out of Korea to receive "explanations" concerning their repatriation rights. There was, then, some room for maneuver within these procedural points, and the Communists responded to these openings by proposing an Asian neutral as custodian in close geographical proximity to Korea, suggesting six months for persuasion, but still accepting that the time limit was negotiable. On May 5 they indicated some movement on the question of transporting the nonrepatriates out of Korea to the territory of the neutral state when they enquired as to the form that neutral custody in Korea would take. It was clear, therefore, that all three issues were capable of resolution.[20]

Further significant progress in this phase of the negotiations was made on May 7 when General Nam Il put forward an eight-point plan, the most important components of which were that prisoners would not be moved out of Korea to receive their "explanations"; that the period for persuasion should last not six months but four; and that a five-nation Neutral Nations Repatriation Commission (NNRC) be established consisting of Czechoslovakia, Poland, Sweden, Switzerland, and India. Nam Il also recommended that the future of any prisoners remaining after this time would be discussed at the political conference on Korea already established as part of the armistice agreement.[21]

Certain Eisenhower administration officials admitted that these proposals seemed "to represent a significant shift in their position and appear[ed] to offer a basis for negotiation of an acceptable agreement." However, the administration required some changes to be made to the eight-point plan including: unanimity in the voting provisions for the NNRC; India to provide all the troops needed to control the prisoners so as to avoid the presence of Polish and Czech forces behind U.N. Command lines; and a time limit of only three months for NNRC custody of the prisoners, followed by no more than 30 days during which the future of any remaining prisoners would be considered at the political conference. Most controversially of all, the U.S. negotiators were instructed at Clark's suggestion to propose that Korean nonrepatriates under U.N. Command control should not be handed over to the repatriation commission at all, but should be released in the south of the country as soon as the armistice agreement had been initialed.[22]

Not surprisingly, the Communist response to this latest counterproposal made on May 13 was harsh. The demands were "absolutely unacceptable" and the Communist side "resolutely" rejected them. A *People's Daily* editorial of May 16 explained why: in its view the unanimity rule would paralyze the work of the NNRC, and neither the Chinese nor North Koreans would accept that their prisoners should be treated differently. Peking felt so strongly about this that Chou En-lai informed Nehru that his government was intending to withdraw all the concessions they had recently put forward. Concurrently with this reaction, the Eisenhower administration was moving nearer to its May 20 decision to expand the war if the stalemate at the talks were not shortly broken. It was, then, a most critical phase of the armistice negotiations, one in which further concessions were required from both sides in order to avoid a new and more dangerous phase of hostilities.[23]

A combination of external and domestic factors had caused the administration to introduce these fresh requirements and had also confirmed the wisdom of its decision to leave the nonrepatriates in Korea. The R.O.K. government was central to the May 13 decision. From early April there had been regular reports from Clark of R.O.K. opposition to the resumption of negotiations and explicit threats that Rhee might soon order the withdrawal of R.O.K. army units from U.N. Command control in order that his forces could prosecute the war on their own. Rhee's claimed armistice objectives were extreme and unrealistic: he wanted the withdrawal of Chinese forces from the country, the disarmament of the North Korean army, and the prevention of any third-party assistance to Pyongyang. In order to impress Washington with the seriousness of his demands, he was even willing to countenance a demonstration and attempted break-in at the U.S. embassy in Pusan, and although Washington did not satisfy his more excessive claims, the South

Korean president's blackmail tactics did have an impact—hence Clark's recommendation regarding the Korean nonrepatriates. As Frank Stelle of the Policy Planning Staff later reflected, it was an "unhappy fact of international existence"—the "control which an intransigent small partner can have over the policies of a great power" when such a junior partner was vital to the prosecution of big-power interests.[24]

Furthermore, even if in spite of this disruptive activity there should be an armistice agreement, Rhee—supported by some members of the Eisenhower administration and certain members of Congress—found distasteful the idea of India's assuming the pivotal role in the NNRC, alleging that too often it favored the Chinese position. In Senator Knowland's view, for example, unanimity in the voting procedure for the NNRC was the only way to ensure that the "pro-Western" members of the commission would be in a position to veto any decision that did not seem to guarantee the principle of nonforcible repatriation for prisoners of war.[25]

If it had been these arguments, then, that had been responsible for the U.S. administration's decision to put forward its May 13 counterproposal, equally loud voices emanating from the North Atlantic allies were to be heard on the other side of the argument, advocating the rescinding of the latest U.N. Command negotiating demand. These governments argued strenuously that the United States should return to a position closer to the Indian U.N. resolution of December 1952. Only with "great difficulty," for example, was the Canadian foreign minister, Lester Pearson, restrained from "making a public denunciation of the UNC stand," the ambassador reported informally. In Ottawa's view the eight-point proposal went "a long way to meet the objections to [the Communists'] previous proposals." Peking and Pyongyang had made "an important concession in no longer insisting that the prisoners who do not wish to be returned home should be physically removed from Korea." In Pearson's opinion, therefore, there was "already adequate agreement by both sides on the principles which should govern a solution of the prisoners-of-war question, to provide a reasonable basis for the armistice." The U.K. government concurred with this analysis. In its view, though it was still willing to stick to the principle of nonforcible repatriation, there was "no other issue which need be a breaking point or even give grounds for indefinite adjournment." In Parliament, Winston Churchill crit-icized the U.S. truce negotiators for dragging their feet and berated Washington for its unwillingness to meet face-to-face with the new Soviet leadership. During a foreign affairs debate in the House of Commons on May 12, the opposition leader, Clement Attlee, que-ried whether Senator McCarthy was dictating Eisenhower's policy and thus preventing reasonable flexibility at the talks. In France the prestigious *Le Monde* newspaper also suggested that the senator was the real force behind the administration. The Dutch govern-ment additionally was moved to remark that although nonforcible repatriation was fundamental, the other questions were essentially "secondary and should not become obstacles to an agreement." In The Hague's view, "it would be difficult for world opinion to under-stand why armistice negotiations should break down on these sec-ondary issues."[26]

Western allies were being, then, unusually blunt and outspoken in their criticisms of U.S. actions in May 1953. On May 18, Ward P. Allen of the European desk in the State Department summarized the strength of this anxiety and concern, expressed not only by the Netherlands, Britain, and Canada but also by Australia, Belgium, New Zealand, and "even Italy," along with neutrals such as Burma and India. A Psychological Strategy Board report confirmed that there had been a "disappointing deterioration" in Western Euro-pean press and public support for U.S. foreign policy, policy which was seen as reflecting "anti-Communist 'hysteria'." Ambassador Murphy, now in his official position as adviser to Clark, weighed in to support these criticisms. The proposal to release North Korean prisoners immediately on the signature of the armistice, he argued, left the U.N. Command without "a foot of ground to stand on." He found it "incomprehensible" that a "twelfth hour stand" had been put up over an issue that had already "been built up into enough of a Frankenstein."[27]

Doubts among the allies and within the State Department about the new U.N. Command position were the focus of attention in media reports and public opinion polls in the United States. Eisen-hower's popularity and general public uncertainty as to the most appropriate method for resolving the issues in Korea gave the presi-dent considerable freedom to explore alternative courses of action, and certainly a large percentage of the public—62 percent at the end of March—were ready to contemplate taking "strong steps" even without the support of the allies if necessary. Yet when allied criticisms were voiced in the period May 14–20, these differences with America's partners became, for opinion formers in the U.S. media, the "matter of chief concern in the week's comment." Moreover, Nam Il's eight-point plan of May 7 evoked mixed reactions among observers in the press, radio, and Congress. Some thought the U.N. Command response "reasonable" in the circumstances; others believed its position should be modified. Still others argued that Communist proposals confirmed that Peking and Pyongyang were not truly prepared to concede the question of nonforcible repatriation, whereas some thought their suggestions showed progress was possible and indicated "significant concessions."[28]

The Eisenhower administration could not afford to ignore these doubts and such evidence of disarray in domestic and international opinion. As the acting secretary of state, Walter Bedell Smith, warned the president, the negotiations were at a critical stage, with the U.S. position with its allies "deteriorating daily" and Rhee busy "fomenting public opposition to any armistice along present lines." Despite R.O.K. activity, however, Smith recommended that the administration revert to a position closer to the Indian resolution, thus giving precedence to allied views over those of certain members of Congress and Syngman Rhee. The administration decided it could not risk what threatened to become a major public split with its Western allies over a point that it had recently endorsed at the United Nations.

Nevertheless, despite this decision, U.S. officials also realized that if they were going to reverse their position, urgent discussions with Congress were required to explain this further change in order to maintain support. Only as recently as May 9, the administration had won the agreement of the congressional leaders for the armistice arrangements, on the basis of unanimity voting for the NNRC, Indian troops to take sole custody of the prisoners of war, and an "explanation" period of not more than 60 days. Even so, Knowland had stood out against such arrangements because he believed that an armistice "would have disastrous consequences for us in Asia" and that the failure to unify Korea would "lead to the loss of all Asia to the Communists and the seating of Red China in the UN." Others of his colleagues disagreed, however: though there was "no liking of the situation," there was a recognition that matters had gone so far through the Indian resolution that there was no practical alternative. On May 9 this majority view favoring a continuance of the negotiations on the basis of the new U.S. stand had prevailed. Now, a little over a week later, the administration had to persuade members of Congress that even the position they had accepted only grudgingly could not be adhered to. As Eisenhower told Knowland and others at a meeting at the White House, the terms Congress had agreed to were being rejected elsewhere, and "all over the world" was the idea that the United States had moved away from the Indian resolution, whereas the Communists had moved toward it. Walter Bedell Smith, in a meeting the same day, made a similar appeal for support and with great difficulty managed to secure congressional agreement to a 4–1 voting rule for the NNRC and to the position that all nonrepatriates, including the North Koreans, would be handed over to that commission.[29]

The acting secretary of state had had the unenviable task during Dulles's absence from the country of trying to unite Rhee, Congress, and the Western allies behind the administration's stand. He approached this task by keeping the allies informed of the extent of Rhee's uncooperativeness and of the demands that were emanating from the legislative branch: Smith reminded the British embassy staff in Washington, for example, that Rhee had close connections in the U.S. capital and informed them that the administration was engaged in a "desperate struggle" with the neo-isolationist bloc to reassert its control over foreign policy. He also told the British ambassador that the United States hoped to offer Rhee "the bait of a security guarantee" to get him to support the newly amended U.S. negotiating position.[30]

To secure the Congressional leadership's agreement for the newly modified terms, Smith and the president made clear how critical the allies had become of U.S. policy, and they indicated that rejection of the terms of the modified Indian resolution would be seen to imply a certain bad faith on America's part. But their inducement to congressional leaders to win their support or acquiescence also involved policy concessions concerning China. Smith had discovered in his meetings that concern over the possible future recognition of the P.R.C. underlay most of the criticism of the current negotiations. In consequence, Eisenhower found himself promising that "so long as Red China was constituted on its present basis, under its present leaders, that [he] would *never* be a party to its recognition and its acceptance in the United Nations."[31] Only a promise of this uncompromising kind could maintain unity between the legislative and executive branches.

Despite the energy with which these discussions with the GOP leaders and the allies were pursued, further minor modifications were still to come, however. The 4–1 voting rule for the NNRC, presented anew to key North Atlantic allies, but only at the last moment to Rhee, produced thanks from London and Ottawa that Washington had revised its stand but opposition to that 4–1 voting principle for the NNRC and to the U.S. insistence that, if the U.N. Command's final position was rejected on May 25, the negotiations would be terminated. In his reply to Churchill, Eisenhower expressed disappointment at London's reaction, agreed to one final concession—to revert to simple majority voting for the NNRC—but followed this concession with a threat of congressional and public retribution against the allies if they continued to withhold their support from the United States. The president also made it clear that, despite London's view that differences on what it saw as procedural points were not important, his administration had reached the end of the road where the negotiations were concerned. He confirmed that the U.N. Command would be presenting its final position on May 25 and that Communist failure to accept this last reformulation would mean that the negotiations would be terminated rather than simply recessed. If terminated, Clark would then be authorized to void the agreement on the neutralization of the Munsan-Kaesong-Panmunjom area, to bomb Kaesong, and generally to step up air and naval action. The U.N. commander would also release all nonrepatriate prisoners immediately. Clark later acknowledged that increased naval and air action meant he could launch "conventional attacks on bridges across the Yalu and on bases in Manchuria as soon as the negotiations officially ended."[32]

On May 25 General Harrison presented the U.N. Command's final position. It included acceptance of a five-nation "custodial commission" (the U.S. administration wanted to change the nomenclature for obvious reasons) that would operate on a simple majority voting basis. India was to provide the commission with all necessary armed forces, and all nonrepatriate prisoners were to be handed over to it. The U.N. Command also proposed that, 120 days after the prisoners had been turned over to the commission, any prisoner remaining would be referred to the U.N. General Assembly for final disposal. Nam Il reacted negatively to this final aspect on the grounds that it was equivalent to handing over prisoners "to the control of your side" but otherwise agreed to study the proposals. On June 4 the two sides reconvened, and at this meeting the Communists proposed that after 120 days the prisoners be released to civilian status, a position that Murphy described as far exceeding "our most optimistic expectations." China and North Korea also insisted that there should be ten explaining personnel per 1,000 prisoners, rather than the three Harrison had offered. Two days later, in a final burst of concession/convergence bargaining, the U.S. negotiators offered five personnel for the task and the Communists countered with eight. Finally, on June 8, the two sides accepted seven per 1,000, and the agreement on prisoners of war could at last be drawn up. Rhee immediately disowned the agreement but derived little support for his position outside of his own country. Dulles had another meeting with U.S. senators and found them unhappy with the June 8 agreement but nevertheless willing to go along with the terms worked out for the prisoners of war. Moreover, Knowland offered to "make a statement if we wanted him to," a pledge he fulfilled later that day. Knowland cautioned Rhee not to do anything that would undermine the agreement reached. Casting blame on Truman rather than Eisenhower for the position the United States found itself in, he told his audience: "We must face the facts as they are and not as we would have liked them to be if other decisions had been made long before this Administration came to power." Dulles heartily applauded the speech and thanked the senator for being so statesmanlike, which he appreciated the more because he realized that Knowland had previously been highly critical of various aspects of Korean War policies. By June 17 U.N. Command and Communist negotiators had established a revised demarcation line, and the signature of the final agreement seemed imminent.[33]

Nuclear Threats and the Resolution of the POW Issue

Why the impasse over the POW question was broken at this time has long intrigued analysts of this period of the Cold War. Shortly after the agreement had been reached members of the Eisenhower administration began claiming that "a series of subtle and calculated moves" had been undertaken to convince the Communists that the alternative to an armistice was an enlarged war involving nuclear weapons. This contention was leaked to the press in July 1953, and Dulles and Eisenhower subsequently repeated the notion more publicly. Eisenhower asserted it in his memoirs, for example, and in conversation with his special assistant, Sherman Adams, when the latter asked how an armistice had at last been reached, the president unhesitatingly replied: "Danger of an atomic war. . . . We told them we could not hold it to a limited war any longer if the communists welched on a treaty of truce."[34]

Dulles made a similar claim at the Bermuda conference in December 1953, where he told his British and French counterparts that, had the negotiations not ended satisfactorily, the United States had been "prepared for a much more intensive scale of warfare" utilizing atomic weapons. "It was their knowledge of the U.S. willingness to use force that brought an end to hostilities," he contended. Even more publicly, at the Geneva Conference on Korea in April 1954 Dulles repeated that progress at the talks was due to the Communists' realization that "the battle area would be enlarged so as to endanger the source of aggression in Manchuria."[35]

Certainly the Chinese seemed to realize that the period from mid-May was significant in certain respects. On May 19, for example, the *New China News Agency* reported rumors from Tokyo that the United States was "preparing a new ultimatum." Between the presentation of the U.N. Command's final position on May 25, Bohlen's meeting with V. M. Molotov on May 28, and the basic acceptance of that position on June 4, there had probably been some consultation among Chinese, North Korean, and Soviet leaders. This can be inferred from Molotov's apparent calculation during his meeting with Bohlen as to the number of days left before negotiations were due to be resumed, and his statement on June 3 that although the outcome of the negotiations did not depend on Moscow, he could say "that the path to the successful conclusion of the armistice agreement has been mapped out."[36]

Nevertheless, Eisenhower and Dulles undoubtedly overstated the efficacy of these nuclear threats, as did other members of the administration. As noted earlier, by far the most substantial concessions were made before the U.S. administration had decided to prepare for an expanded, nuclear attack and to communicate a nuclear threat: on March 30 when Chou acknowledged that there was a group of prisoners whose repatriation would prove more difficult to effect, and on May 7 when Nam Il outlined the concrete proposals on which the final armistice agreement was based. Detailed examination of the course of the negotiations in May has also demonstrated that from May 13 the United States was forced into some concessions of its own, ones that the Communists seemed to regard as fundamental, as their press reports indicated.[37]

Moreover, it is seriously to be doubted whether Dulles's rather ambiguous threats made via Nehru, which he believed to have been vital to the success of the plan, ever reached the Chinese government. Subsequently, when rumors abounded about the Indian prime minister's supposed role as conduit for these messages, Nehru recorded a denial of this in his files. And when the U.S. secretary of state was instrumental in giving the matter further publicity through a *Life* magazine article, Nehru took the opportunity to deny strongly that he had ever passed any threatening messages on to the Chinese, going so far as to instruct the Indian ambassador in Washington to inform the State Department that, whatever Dulles believed, Nehru had not felt obliged in his record of their May meetings to make any note of a threat to use nuclear weapons and certainly had not passed anything of that kind on to Peking. Though other Indian officials might have informed Chinese leaders of the American intent, it seems unlikely that Nehru would not have first been consulted, given his known interest in and domination of his country's China policy.[38]

Viewed from the wider perspective of China's strategic doctrine, further questions need to be raised about the likely impact of the Eisenhower-Dulles psychological plan. Mao Tse-tung, throughout his time in power, dominated the expression of strategic thought in the P.R.C., and this made it difficult for others to discuss these areas of policy. It may even have made it problematic for other leaders to raise the consequences of the possible bombing of one or more cities in China, given that the Maoist approach was to analyze nuclear war as one stage of a protracted conflict that China would eventually win, on the basis of its large population and predominantly rural economy. The ideas expressed in Mao's well-known talk with Anna Louise Strong in 1946, when he first declared his belief that nuclear weapons were "paper tigers since the outcome of war is decided by the people, not by one or two new types of weapons," held firm for Mao throughout his lifetime, if not for other Chinese leaders. The P.R.C.'s strategy for deterring a nuclear attack over the Korean War period (and long after) was to deny that such a strike would prove successful against such an undeveloped and vastly populated country. As General Nie Jung-chen, deputy chief of staff of the Chinese People's Liberation Army, said to the Indian ambassador, K. M. Panikkar, in September 1950: "The Americans can bomb us, they can destroy our industries, but they cannot defeat us on land. We have calculated all that. . . . They may even drop atom bombs on us. What then? . . . After all, China lives on the farms." In a similar vein two months later, a current affairs journal told its readers that the bomb could be used only against a "big and concentrated object" or a "huge concentration of troops." Whereas China's population was scattered and its troops hidden in deep, underground fortifications, America's industry was "highly concentrated, hence the atomic bomb is most threatening to the U.S.," it contended.[39] The Chinese "combed Western sources" and made extensive use of U.S. strategic bombing survey reports (produced after Hiroshima and Nagasaki) to show that the United States had greatly exaggerated the destructive capabilities of nuclear weapons and that properly designed underground shelters and tunnels would prove an effective defense against the atomic bomb. Officials also argued that the tunnels that had proved so resilient against conventional bombing would prove their worth in any atomic attack.[40]

Throughout the Korean conflict the Chinese belittled the role of nuclear weapons in battlefield conditions. Propaganda directed at Chinese officers, for example, informed them that such weapons were "for threatening men . . . not for actual combat use." Furthermore, a Chinese journal recorded that they could not be employed without annihilating the users themselves. Much later (and as a consequence of Sino-Soviet polemics), the Chinese revealed more of the assessments they had made at the time of the Korean War, reporting that "U.S. military personnel did not believe that the use of atomic weapons on the Korean battlefield would be effective." A recent study, based in part on interviews in the P.R.C., adds a further dimension to this when it reports the private Chinese view in 1953 that, although caution had to be exercised, "American and world opinion would make it quite improbable that the United States would make good on those threats."[41]

It was not until late in 1954 that Chinese leaders started to reassess their views of nuclear weapons and warfare. Only then did they begin to reconsider the possible role of tactical nuclear weapons and the possibility of surprise or sudden attack in modern war arising out of developments in delivery systems and the greater destructive power of thermonuclear weapons. Most authors attribute this reassessment of strategy primarily to increased Soviet willingness to discuss these developments in the post-Stalin era, and they explain China's decision to follow the lead of Soviet strategists by its need for Moscow's help in providing Peking with the knowledge to develop its own arsenal.[42]

These developments suggest that the Korean War had its effects on China's military and strategic thinking in the longer term. At the time when the nuclear threats were being made, however, Peking's attitude toward nuclear warfare, and particularly its preoccupation with all-out war, together with its limited understanding of the tactical use of such weapons, undermined the credibility of the Eisenhower administration's threats.

This is not to say, however, that nuclear threats played no role whatever in securing final agreement on the outstanding details of the POW issue; it is only to suggest that the centrality subsequently accorded to those threats by Eisenhower and Dulles was misplaced. Certainly, the Chinese did seem to recognize a change of mood with the arrival of the new administration, and they realized that an expanded, nuclear war was possible. A *People's Daily* article on January 23, for example, reported that Eisenhower was contemplating increasing the size of the South Korean army, blockading the China coast, using Chinese Nationalist forces to launch raids on the mainland, bombing northeast China, and using atomic weapons.[43] The Chinese also appeared to understand that the U.N. Command's statement on May 25 at Panmunjom represented a turning point in the talks; this new "take it or leave it" proposal, as one Communist press report put it,[44] together with the Bohlen-Molotov discussion and Clark's letter to the Communist commanders, very likely reinforced the perception that rejection of America's final negotiatory position would mean expanded hostilities, possibly involving the use of nuclear weapons. But, as stated above, the Communist concessions made after May 25 were relatively minor in comparison with those made earlier that year and followed on from a number of U.N. Command concessions. It therefore seems likely that Eisenhower's and Dulles's convictions regarding the effectiveness of their nuclear coercion were exaggerated. Perhaps they claimed this deliberately in order to demonstrate that U.S. power— even if its use was only threatened—could secure Communist acceptance of U.S. objectives, or they may have genuinely believed that these threats had made the crucial difference.

It would have been more plausible for the U.S. administration to argue that it was a combination of military, political, and economic factors that finally tipped the balance and convinced the Chinese to capitulate over their prisoners of war. For domestic economic reasons, all three Communist states had reason to question their continuing involvement in Korea. In the early autumn of 1952, for example, Soviet leaders began to give increased emphasis to internal developments. At the Nineteenth Party Congress in October, the main task for the nation was recognized as being the dampening of the pace of Western military mobilization and the strengthening of the domestic economy in order to concentrate resources on military-related scientific and technological research. In China in December 1952 the government had announced its intention to begin its first five-year plan in early 1953, and from January 1953 it began to devote a great deal of attention in the media to the country's long-term construction needs. North Korean morale toward the close of the war has also been reported as having been near to breaking point. National income had diminished by more than a third, inflation was destroying people's livelihoods and purchasing power, and consequent food hoarding and tax evasion had brought forth harsh confiscatory policies on the part of Kim Il Sung's government. In mid-January 1953 party leaders were reported to have met to discuss "shortcomings" in the field of agricultural organization, admitting that their work had been unsuccessful; and on May 1, North Korean radio exhorted the population to do their utmost to improve the general economic situation and to push ahead with the spring sowing campaign, which, in some areas, had attained less than 30 percent of the target figure.[45] Undoubtedly, the increase in conventional bombing undertaken by the U.N. air force and directed at the dykes and irrigation channels would have further added to the North Korean burden of feeding its population.

Political developments also seem to have been crucial to the Communists' decision to concede on the POW issue. After Stalin's death the emphasis on peaceful coexistence markedly increased. At Stalin's funeral and again on March 15 in a speech to the Supreme Soviet, Georgi Malenkov stated that there was "no disputed or unsettled question that could not be settled peacefully on the basis of mutual agreement between the countries concerned." At the end of the month the U.S. ambassador to the United Nations reported an indirect request for talks between Malenkov and Eisenhower, and significantly, as in October 1950 (see Chapter 2) when the Soviets were also seeking an end to the conflict in Korea, the Norwegian official, Hans Engen, was singled out, first for a response to Chou's March 30 statement, and then for Norwegian views on Soviet-American negotiations. The Soviet official involved in this approach went so far as to specify the kinds of questions that might be raised at a summit with the Americans, including the control of atomic energy and disarmament matters. The linking of the break in the Korean impasse with these broader questions indicated that Moscow was aware that an end to Korean hostilities was a prerequisite for cooperation in other areas.[46]

In April the Soviet press printed in full Eisenhower's "Chance for Peace" address and also offered lengthy editorial comments on it. To the Soviet specialist George Kennan (then at Princeton University on extended leave from the State Department), the editorial revealed "clearly that the present Soviet leaders are definitely interested in pursuing with us the effort to solve some of the present international difficulties" but that progress toward an armistice could not be made while Washington persisted "in acting as though the Chinese were [Moscow's] helpless puppets." An inducement to the Chinese would have to come, Kennan interpreted the Soviets to imply, not only from the U.S.S.R. but also from the United States. Much the same attitude of conciliation was displayed to the new U.S. ambassador when he presented his credentials in Moscow on April 20. Authorized to propose making a settlement in Korea a "litmus test" of American faith in Moscow's friendly gestures, Bohlen reported that the Soviets were "eager to support his statement regarding the importance of an armistice in Korea."[47]

To add to the tangibility of these friendly gestures, Molotov used his influence with Pyongyang at this time to get British and French civilians released from North Korean custody. Eden had initially requested Soviet help with this matter in February, but this appeal did not bear fruit until March and April 1953. Similarly, in April, Moscow agreed to use its good offices to get 13 Americans freed. By early May, Pyongyang had handed over seven American civilians.[48]

Of significance, too, is the timing of Chou's message on the POW question. In February he and Mao were still making speeches calling for an immediate ceasefire in Korea, leaving the POW repatriation issue to be settled subsequently by a specially composed commission. On March 12 the Chinese were continuing to advocate that the commission deal with the repatriation question, and there was still no reference to General Clark's message regarding the exchange of sick and wounded. By the end of the month, however, and immediately on Chou's return from Moscow, this was to change with the acceptance of Clark's proposal and the Chinese premier's new suggestion of handing over the nonrepatriates to a neutral state.[49]

The U.S. consul-general in Hong Kong himself plumped for this political explanation for the March 30 concession (as did the British foreign office): that it had arisen out of the need to consolidate the Communist bloc after Stalin's death. But reports such as these were quickly swept aside, perhaps because they could be seen as implying a kind of credit to the Communists for ending the war and denying the United States a controlling role. An argument based on the efficacy of the nuclear threat was much more valuable to the Eisenhower administration since it could be used to prove that the "New Look" strategy, based on the concept of massive retaliation, was a success,[50] and it served to demonstrate that in the final phase of the war America's military might—even if held in reserve—could ensure the desired outcome at the armistice negotiations.

RHEE'S IMPACT ON THE FINAL AGREEMENT

With the signature of the POW agreement, Clark believed that a full armistice could finally be initialed around June 18. This was not to be, however, because of the actions of America's junior ally in

Asia. In a move that has been described as revenge for the U.N. Command's reversal of its decision to release all North Korean nonrepatriates directly into South Korea, Rhee took the action that Clark and Murphy had been warning of since mid-May: he simply gave orders to R.O.K. troops to release the anti-Communist North Korean prisoners in their custody. Some 25,131 were released on the night of June 17–18, and only 971 were subsequently recaptured. Similar action continued for the next few days until only 8,600 North Korean nonrepatriates were left in U.N. Command compounds. Failure to take steps to prevent Rhee's expected action evoked criticism, not only from the Communists but also from Western allies and from within the U.S. Senate. The U.S. ambassador in London reported his host government's view that U.S. officials had either been "negligent, acquiescent or even directly involved." Senator Robert C. Hendricksen (Republican of New Jersey) obviously felt much the same way and suggested a Senate investigation of the extent of U.S. culpability.[51] (There is no evidence to support these accusations, and Clark was bitter about Rhee's actions; but, as Rhee wrote in a letter to the U.N. commander, he had known of Clark's "personal view regarding this matter" and that the general had been unable to act on it "on account of the international complications.")[52]

As a result of Rhee's release of the prisoners, the armistice negotiations immediately went into recess until the United States could regain control of the South Korean president and ensure his government's adherence to the armistice terms. The administration's earlier offer to sign a mutual defense treaty with South Korea had apparently not been enough of an inducement to gain Rhee's compliance; thus, a variety of new rewards and punishments were now contemplated.

General Clark excoriated Rhee strongly in a letter in which he informed the president that he was "profoundly shocked by this unilateral abrogation of your personal commitment." Washington insisted on publishing this statement despite Walter Robertson's later depiction of it as a public humiliation and Senator Knowland's admonishing of the administration for treating Rhee not as a partner but as a "colonial subject." But Washington realized that Rhee was capable of causing the armistice agreement to unravel—especially when he reiterated his threat to withdraw all R.O.K. army units from the U.N. Command and prosecute the war on his own. The U.S. administration could not allow that unraveling now that it had achieved its basic objectives over the POW question; thus, Eisenhower joined Clark in his criticisms of Rhee, warning him that in the event that the South Koreans continued to defy the U.N. Command, "another arrangement" would be necessary, that "other arrangement" being the withdrawal of U.S. forces from Korea.[53] The executive branch again called on certain senators and congressmen for help with bringing Rhee into line. Senator H. Alexander Smith obliged, stating on the floor of the Senate that it was his judgment that the fighting must cease and that remaining objectives had to be sought through peaceful means.[54]

The administration tried to bring home to Rhee the serious consequences of his obstructive attitude, but there was a certain hollowness to these threats. As the U.S. president acknowledged, America could not forget that Communism was the principal enemy in Korea (even if Rhee seemed a strong candidate at times for that role), and the administration could not walk out on the country and let the Communists simply take it over. Thus, the alternative to threats—which for a brief time included the notion of effecting a military coup against Rhee—was promises. Walter Robertson was sent to Seoul to try to convince Rhee that his future lay with the United States. Rhee's supporters in Congress, and his friend, General Van Fleet, also urged continuing cooperation with the U.S. government and the reestablishment of the close friendship between the two countries.[55]

After a long and difficult time in the South Korean capital, Robertson obtained a lukewarm agreement from Rhee that he would not obstruct the armistice. In exchange, Rhee received "informal assurances" that the Senate would ratify the mutual security treaty; his country also acquired additional economic and military support and a U.S. pledge that, if after 90 days the political conference on Korea was making no progress, the American and R.O.K. government delegations would both withdraw. He also obtained further modifications to the armistice agreement when Washington promised him that all nonrepatriate prisoners of war would go to the DMZ to be interrogated concerning their repatriation wishes rather than remaining in the camps, thus obviating the need for Indian troops and NNRC personnel to be on South Korean territory.[56]

The Chinese and North Korean response to Rhee's release of the prisoners was measured and "comparatively mild" in tone, the Joint Chiefs of Staff were informed. Communist negotiators asked Harrison for guarantees that the U.N. Command could control the South Korean government and army, seeking to know whether the armistice actually included Rhee, and, if not, what assurances they could have that the South Koreans would actually implement the truce arrangements. The Chinese and North Koreans were also concerned about reports that all the released nonrepatriates were being impressed into the South Korean army, reports that Clark substantiated to Washington when he informed the administration that all former prisoners were being inducted into the R.O.K. Army regardless of age.[57]

Despite such provocation, however, which reinforced doubts about Rhee's reliability and constituted a breach of the agreement that on release prisoners would become civilians, despite also a last-minute change regarding the location where prisoners would receive their explanations, the Communists agreed to reconvene plenary sessions on July 10. As Clark had reported, although Communist propaganda emphasized U.S. responsibility for Rhee's actions, there was nothing in it to indicate that the Chinese and North Koreans were not prepared to move toward a final settlement. In some respects, perhaps, Seoul's actions may have spared the North Koreans some embarrassment concerning the repatriation of their prisoners. As the *New China News Agency* recorded on June 19, Rhee's release of prisoners marked the "utter bankruptcy of the hollow pretexts of 'voluntary repatriation' and 'no-forced repatriation' which would not even stand the test of handing over the POWs to neutral custody and disposition." It was "proof of the fear that the POWs would insist on returning home."[58]

Moreover, this enforced delay also allowed the Communist armies time to demonstrate through a ground offensive the futility of Rhee's "March to the North" slogan. In what Premier Chou En-lai told the Indian ambassador was a deliberate act of revenge, the offensive in mid-July directed at R.O.K. forces penetrated their lines along the central front and led to the collapse of the R.O.K. capital division and the near destruction of the Third Division. Before a counterattack could be mounted, R.O.K. troops had been driven back six miles and had suffered the bulk of the U.N. Command's

14,000 casualties. Dulles was concerned about the psychological effects of such a Communist victory from the "standpoint of prestige and morale in that area," but in Collins's view the overall loss of terrain was likely to be insignificant, and any counteroffensive not worth the additional casualties.[59]

By July 20 the offensive was over, yet, in spite of its outcome, Rhee persisted with his spoiling tactics: objecting to Harrison's assurances to the Communists that South Korea would observe the agreement, and stating publicly that the R.O.K. would observe a truce only for 90 days. The political price of these statements was not to be paid to the Communists, however, who still went forward with the armistice, but to the Western allies who became steadily more alarmed at the prospect of signing the Greater Sanction statement. As Lord Salisbury told Washington, a "very widely-held view" in London, and "not merely in Labour circles," was "that the armistice is at present more likely to be broken by Rhee than by the Communists." When the main aim should be to reduce tension, he argued, there seemed no point in releasing an "inflammatory" statement. Dulles, however, made it clear that, in his view, the statement was an integral part of the arrangements that had been made for item 3 of the truce agreement, though the administration did agree that the declaration would not be issued separately but would come in the final U.N. Command report to the United Nations.[60]

At the end, therefore, the U.N. coalition had just about held together, though loose ends still remained untied, involving Syngman Rhee and his probable future actions designed to stymie the political conference, and the Western allies' reluctance to work out the terms of their response to any Communist renewal of aggression in Korea.[61] The administration had also maintained congressional support for its actions as the armistice agreement moved steadily nearer, but this was achieved at the cost of further hardening its policy toward the P.R.C. and toward the terms of any future political conference on Korea. The planning that did take place in Washington designed to force a military conclusion to the conflict probably served to deflect the criticisms of those members of the Joint Chiefs of Staff who had long been arguing for a military solution to be imposed; but advocacy of a course of action involving expanded war was also undercut by the momentum of the negotiations once Chou En-lai had made his statement at the end of March. Though Admiral Fechteler was still wont to suggest that "all bets" should be off if Harrison's position of May 25 were to be rejected by the Communists, he was relatively subdued during these last six months of the war, perhaps as a result of the fast-developing negotiations or perhaps in anticipation of his retirement as naval chief of staff (along with those of the other joint chiefs) in August 1953.[62]

As to the president's role, he had been reluctant to take the lead in all these deliberations, had often appeared to favor aggressive courses of action in NSC discussions, but at times could also soften that belligerence when he brought in the viewpoints of the Western allies or of the American people. Though he wisely encouraged his officials to maintain liaison with members of Congress, he himself remained reluctant to advocate specific courses of action in his own meetings with the legislative branch and primarily used these discussions as fire-fighting exercises.

In a number of respects Eisenhower also remained ambivalent about the signature of the armistice agreement. Though he derived great satisfaction from being the president who had ended the casualties, he and his closest colleagues seemed to regret that they had not been able to inflict a military defeat on the Chinese. As he said to the NSC on December 3, 1953, perhaps in response to that denial of punishment and "with great emphasis," "if the Chinese Communists attacked us again we should certainly respond by hitting them hard and wherever it would hurt most, including Peiping itself."[63]

On July 23 work began on drawing up the final demarcation line, and the date for the signature of the armistice was fixed for July 27. Until the very last minutes of the conflict the U.N. Command continued its bombing: Thunderjet fighter-bombers pummeled the few North Korean airfields and, some 24 minutes before the armistice came into effect, a B-26 dropped its load in a ground-radar-directed close-support mission.[64] At 10:00 P.M. on July 27 this horribly destructive war was finally over. For the first time in its history the United States was not victorious on a foreign battlefield, but it could indeed claim limited territorial satisfaction on the location of the ceasefire line and an ideological victory over the POW question, a policy position that it would claim had wide "free world" support. These were tarnished victories, however, both domestically and in terms of the U.S. global position: tarnished by the costs of reaching agreement over these issues; tarnished by the dubious nature of nonforcible repatriation as it came to be implemented; tarnished by the widely held beliefs outside the United States that negotiating opportunities had been lost, and that the government on whose behalf the war had ostensibly been fought was essentially unworthy.

[8]

Final Acts:
August 1953 to June 1954

A "GREAT PSYCHOLOGICAL VICTORY"?

With the signature of the armistice agreement, the stage was set for the implementation of the POW exchange. In line with the plans that had been developed to exploit this aspect of the armistice, Allen Dulles, the director of the Central Intelligence Agency, described it as "one of the greatest psychological victories so far achieved by the free world against Communism." Between August 5 and September 6, 1953, the U.N. Command in "Operation Big Switch," transferred 75,801 prisoners of war into Chinese and North Korean hands, including about 450 women and 23 children (see Table 1). The Communists for their part handed over 12,773 prisoners to the U.N. Command, including 3,326 Americans. This left about 23,000 nonrepatriates to be moved to the neutral zone to receive explanations concerning their repatriation rights and to make the final choice concerning their future place of abode. On September 23 the U.N. Command turned over 22,604 to the Indian Custodial Forces (CFI) while the Communists placed 359 into Indian care, including 23 Americans and one Briton. These 23,000 were the embodiment of the principle that had delayed the conclusion of the Korean conflict for so many months. It was now the task of the NNRC, led by its Indian chair, General K. S. Thimayya, to ensure that these men could make a choice free from coercion of which regime they wished to live under.[1]

Very few of these 23,000 men changed their minds after interview, ostensibly vindicating the nonforcible repatriation policy. But

Table 1. Final Disposition of Prisoners of War

U.N. Command prisoners turned over in Operation Big Switch		12,773
U.N. Command prisoners turned over to Indian Custodial Forces		359
of whom: Returned to U.N. Command	9	
Returned to D.P.R.K. or P.R.C.	347	
Escaped	1	
Shipped to India	2	
D.P.R.K./P.R.C. prisoners turned over in Big Switch		75,801
D.P.R.K./P.R.C. prisoners turned over to Indian Custodial Forces		22,604
of whom: Returned to D.P.R.K./P.R.C.	629	
Returned to U.N. Command	21,820	
Escaped and missing	13	
Died in Indian custody	38	
Remaining in Indian custody	18	
Shipped to India	86	

Source: Table adapted from RG 319, Records of the Army Staff, box 708, Korean Armistice Negotiations, 1951–58, Feb. 13, 1954, National Archives, Washington, D.C.

as with so many earlier phases of this issue, rules were bent and the spirit of the agreement undermined. Many of those connected with the prisoners in U.N. Command compounds expected the Communist "explainers" to use harsh and intimidatory tactics; they were concerned that such methods, along with some genuine waverers, would obscure the principle that had been fought so long and hard for, as prisoners determined to go home after all. U.N. personnel thus worked to ensure that as many prisoners as possible stuck to the choice they had made during the official poll in April 1952.

PREPARATIONS FOR "EXPLANATIONS"

As the end of the war drew steadily nearer, unrest in the U.N. Command compounds rose to new heights. Philip Manhard sent another of his graphic reports of developments in the camps on June 16, eight days after the POW agreement had been initialed, in which he warned that on Cheju-do, where the Chinese nonrepatriates were being held, "pro-KMT trusties" were "again putting the heat on." There had been an "upsurge in beatings and killings by self-styled anti-Communists of those accused of wavering in their attitude toward Formosa," he informed the U.S. ambassador to Korea. Moreover, these trusties were claiming they were "ready to sacrifice the lives of thousands of fellow POWs in order to preserve their own positions and maintain anti-Communist discipline over the mass of prisoners."[2]

Against this background of uncertainty in the camps, of the POW trusties' perceptions that intimidation was still necessary, and of U.N. Command expectations about Communist methods during the explanatory period, U.S. officers in Korea implemented two courses of action: first, they began schooling the nonrepatriate prisoners in the kinds of questions they would be asked and the pressure that might be put on them when they submitted themselves for explanations; and, second, they arranged for Chiang Kai-shek and Syngman Rhee to broadcast statements to the camps and to send government missions to the compounds—each headed by a high-ranking officer—in order to, as General Clark put it, increase the prospects of an orderly transfer to the DMZ and to strengthen the "will of POWs to resist Communist explainers."[3]

The nonrepatriates—especially the Chinese among them—took part in mock explanations on a daily basis for over two months. A U.S. infantry colonel involved in the process (Kenneth Hansen) later described the series of plays the prisoners were encouraged to put on in every compound, performances in which one figure was made up to appear as the Indian chair of the Repatriation Commission and where others were told to learn certain appropriate lines of "dialogue" such as "hui Taiwan." Chinese and American instructors would also be on hand "every day of the [actual] explanations" since these officers would be serving as "UNC representatives, observers or interpreters." Just before the transfer to the demilitarized zone, Hansen reported that early in September 1953 Korean and Chinese anti-Communists took what he described as an "attitude test." Their answers to questions about, for example, the value of democracy and the role of the United Nations indicated that the orientation program had been "very successful . . . especially among the better educated."[4]

Chiang Kai-shek's broadcast to the Chinese camps on July 30, which the U.N. Command distributed in written form accompanied by his seal and photograph, was designed to indicate to the pris-

oners that a warm welcome awaited them in Taiwan. Chiang urged
the men to "stand firm in your choice of freedom." "Do not suc-
cumb," he advised them, "to Communist enticements or bow to
any form of Communist coercion." Shortly after this gift parcels for
the 14,000 Chinese began to arrive on Cheju-do, flown in by 11
transport planes of the Chinese Nationalist Air Force, together with
letters of welcome from thousands of Chinese now living on the
island of Taiwan.[5] With these additional assurances, the prisoners
could be moved to the DMZ. On U.N. Command insistence, however, they were kept in the same formations in which they had been
held in the camps, which meant that the hold of the compound
leaders over the inmates was maintained. (The Indian chair of the
commission came to see his failure to challenge this procedure as a
serious mistake, since an obvious opportunity had been lost to
remove the powerful trusties.)[6]

On arrival at the DMZ, however, none of the nonrepatriates
would agree to submit themselves to explanations unless it was
accepted that prisoners of war would not be segregated after
screening and that they could attend in groups of 25 or more. The
fear was that the anti-Communist leaders would be divided from
the bulk of prisoners, who might then be subjected to periods of
counterindoctrination and change their allegiances. There was also
the underlying unease that, without the presence of the powerful
leaders, more might, of their own volition, opt for repatriation after
all.

The U.N. Command supported this right of refusal, but the
NNRC did not. In the commission's view, attendance was manda-
tory and prisoners ought to be allowed to attend singly; but enforc-
ing this was a different matter and was likely to result in bloodshed.
The NNRC had little option but to agree that, after explanations,
prisoners would not be separated from those who had not been
interrogated. In mid-October the interviews were at last ready to
begin, only to be further delayed when the U.N. Command allegedly dragged its feet on providing the facilities necessary for
questioning the anti-Communist prisoners. As an exasperated
Nehru was quoted as saying on October 10: "how can we complete
the process [of explanation] when after 41 days the huts are still
incomplete?" This delay led General Thimayya, the Indian chair of

the commission, to warn U.S. officials that if they did not speed up the construction work, the Communists would be allowed to take on the task.[7]

When the prisoners finally began to submit themselves to interrogation, new and rather absurd methods to maintain group solidarity were tried. Each prisoner was issued with either a small Republic of China (R.O.C.) or an R.O.K. flag to hold as he came forward. Other reports indicated that the men arrived wearing headbands with suitable anti-Communist slogans painted on them. A U.S. Air Force captain, operating as an official observer, not to be outdone in the matter of decoration, wore, as appropriate, a hat either with a 3" × 5" Chinese Nationalist or South Korean flag pinned to its side. More seriously for the outcome of this part of the procedure, according to later reports from the British ambassador in Peking, because those that had received explanations were not segregated from the others (until December 20), the same men had been reappearing before the Repatriation Commission, having exchanged identity discs.[8]

Faced with these obstacles, the Indian members of the Repatriation Commission became highly critical of the U.N. Command and thus Indian relations with the U.S., R.O.K. and R.O.C. governments inevitably deteriorated. The Indians objected to the presence of the strong anti-Communist organizations in the camps, which negated the principle of freedom of choice. They abhorred the illegal methods that had been resorted to to facilitate R.O.K. and R.O.C. contact with the nonrepatriates, including the smuggling in of a radio receiving set in a bag of yeast provided from U.N. stores. They also became aware that a general headquarters for POW organization had been established in Seoul under the control of the provost marshal and with direct links with the compounds. The Indian government was also strongly critical of the threats of violence directed against its custodial forces emanating especially from the South Korean but also from the Taiwanese government. Indeed, on October 7 the Indian ambassador in Washington left an *aide-mémoire* with Walter Robertson requesting that the U.S. administration use

[194]

its influence with Rhee to stop his issuing such threatening statements. In an attempt to counter this atmosphere of intimidation
and the effects of the outside interference in the POW camps, the
NNRC issued a leaflet to the inmates, the emphasis of which was on
repatriation, and which expressed sympathy for the pressure that
the prisoners had been experiencing. "No one is entitled to prevent
you from expressing your will," it read. "No one can prevent you
from returning to your homes, nor is any one allowed to compel or
force you to return to your homes. . . . It is our task to prevent
anyone from imposing any pressure on you." This message further
exacerbated relations between the NNRC and U.N. Command.[9]

Thimayya also suggested that he would like to have the period of
explanation extended beyond the 120 days that had been agreed in
order to take account of the disruptions during the early weeks. As
Nehru said to the Indian Parliament, "surely the whole purpose of
this business was to achieve some result, not to follow some paper
time-table." Furthermore, the Indian prime minister also argued
that if the political conference were not held—thereby removing its
role in determining the fate of any remaining POWs—the whole
POW issue might have to be looked at afresh.[10]

Not unexpectedly, in response to these remarks, interpretations,
and the issuance of the leaflet, the U.S. administration renewed its
criticisms of the NNRC, especially of its Indian members, Dulles
stating on October 9 that he was not happy with the commission's
work, and Senator Knowland accusing India of "sabotaging the
peace" as it had the war. These two also assailed Nehru for suggesting that the prisoners were not due for release on January 22,
claiming that he had misinterpreted the POW agreement on this
point.[11]

As befits a nonaligned power, India not only came under criticism
from the United States but also incurred the displeasure of the
P.R.C. The Chinese premier reported to Nedgan Raghavan, the
new Indian ambassador in Peking, that he was annoyed that the
U.N. Command had been allowed to mark time over the provision
of secure facilities for the explanations; he was irritated over the
refusal to segregate those prisoners who had been interrogated; and
he was furious at the eventual Indian decision to release all prisoners as civilians on January 22. But it is unlikely that any extension
of the time period for explanations would have made much differ-

[195]

ence. The Chinese and North Korean personnel designated to inter-view the nonrepatriates found they were having little influence on those that came forward, and as they put more pressure on certain selected individuals who appeared to waver—so much so that on six occasions Thimayya had to intervene to end interviews—more of the precious time period was expended.[12]

By January 22, because of these disruptions and tactics, only 3,224 nonrepatriates had received individual explanations, with 90 Chinese and 47 North Koreans electing to be repatriated as a direct result of these. The remainder who returned asked to be repatriated without having been interviewed, the U.N. Command claiming that these were Communist agents who were getting out while it was still possible to do so. Of the 359 U.S./U.N. nonrepatriates, 255 were interrogated about their repatriation wishes, none was re-patriated as a direct result of interview, but nine asked to return home. Neither the 23 Americans nor the one Briton would submit to explanations, though one asked for release during the 90-day pe-riod and another escaped from the compound. In a letter to those remaining, the U.N. Command reminded them that the time had come to make a "free, intelligent and informed decision," but this communication, along with letters from home, were spurned by the 22. During a U.N. Command broadcast to their compound, they jeered, danced, and sang the Internationale. As in the anti-Commu-nist compounds, the 22 had their appointed leaders who kept con-trol of the waverers and maintained group solidarity through a variety of dubious methods.[13]

The fate of those transferred in "Big Switch" and those who chose not to return home varied considerably, but it cannot be said to have been kind. Not surprisingly, sympathy in the United States quickly waned for the 21 Americans who had chosen to live under Commu-nist regimes. They were all dishonorably discharged from the armed forces, the two who broke away being court-martialed in 1954, one being sentenced to life imprisonment (later commuted to 20 years) and the other to ten years. Of the 21 plus one Briton who stayed behind, it seems that most went to the P.R.C. where they learned the language and studied for higher degrees, and some married. Few settled there for long. In October 1962 the British nonrepatriate, Marine Andrew Condron, returned to the United Kingdom. By 1986 at least 17 of the 20 Americans who had survived had returned to the United States, and another was reported to be in Belgium. Most had applied for exit visas from China in the early to mid-1960s.[14]

Much press attention was focused on the 22—perhaps as much, if not more, than on the large numbers of Chinese who were transported to Taiwan. Possible explanations for their decision to remain behind, amidst the ever-increasing tales of American POW misconduct and collaboration, came to dominate press coverage over earlier themes of Communist atrocities and "brainwashing" techniques. Of the more than 3,000 American prisoners returned home in "Big Switch," many were investigated for having collaborated with their captors or having mistreated fellow prisoners—some 11 percent of U.S. Army men, 26 percent of the Marine Corps, and 39 percent of the Air Force prisoners. (Only 31 U.S. Navy personnel were captured, and no allegations were made against them.) Fourteen U.S. Army officers and men were court-martialed for misconduct and 11 found guilty of offenses ranging from informing on other prisoners to murder. It was a process that occasioned much "national soul searching," and the world probably thought less about Dulles's proclaimed "psychological victory" over the Communists and wondered more about the "curious spectacle of Americans praising the conduct of enemy prisoners on Koje while condemning its own returning prisoners" (especially since such condemnations contradicted psychological warfare operations designed to exploit Communist "brainwashing techniques").[15]

American prisoners, then, were neither received with much sympathy nor covered in glory for battles fought and hardships withstood, though they had behaved little differently from the prisoners held in Japanese camps during World War II where there was a similar loss of morale, with only 12 out of 25,000 to 30,000 managing to escape.[16] But a similar if not a worse fate probably awaited those Chinese and Koreans who returned to Nationalist China and South Korea. Indications of the Koreans' likely future had been provided earlier when the sick and wounded had been returned to the South in April 1953. Then, the South Korean defense minister had confirmed that they would be "re-educated" for six months before being returned to their families. (The U.S. government suggested that the reindoctrination camps ought to be renamed "reception and screening.") In late July reports indicated they were still in isolation, having been allowed no visitors. Those Koreans returning in "Big Switch" underwent a similar period of investigation, and in November the R.O.K. government announced it was considering court-martialing "60 victims of brainwashing" among them.[17]

Those repatriated to Taiwan probably experienced much the same procedure. At the end of a three-month period, the U.S. ambassador in Taipei reported, the ex-prisoner of war would be asked to choose whether to remain in uniform or to become a civilian: "The unanimous forecast is that almost every one of them will choose to remain in the armed forces," Rankin recorded. Colonel Hansen later confirmed a part of this prediction when he visited a Chinese Nationalist Army unit a few months after "freedom day," as he put it, to find it composed entirely of former Communist prisoners of war.[18]

Little is known about the fate of those prisoners who returned to the D.P.R.K., but something was heard of the Chinese who went back to the P.R.C. Though greeted as heroes on their return, the latter were soon treated with suspicion for having allowed themselves to be captured in the first place and then for having been in such close proximity to supposed anti-Communists for such an extended time. Many were demoted to menial posts or sent down to the countryside to be "reformed." A small number who were discovered to have been "turned around" by U.S. and Chinese Nationalist intelligence officers and who received specialized espionage training in Japan were sentenced to life imprisonment.[19]

For most of the prisoners, therefore, it was an unsatisfactory end to a distressing phase of their lives, whether they had been in Communist or in U.N. Command compounds. Yet, despite the unsavory aspects of these last weeks in custody, the United States claimed its psychological victory. Interestingly, however, the Eisenhower administration gave as much emphasis to the view that the establishment of nonforcible repatriation would help to prevent future East-West conflict because of the Soviet bloc's increased fear of defections as it did to the human rights basis of the policy. Nonforcible repatriation had become, in other words, part of America's containment policy. As Gen. John E. Hull, who took over from Mark Clark, publicly stated, the outcome represented a gain in strength for the Western world, for "from this day on, all soldiers of every Communist army may know of a certainty that they may seek and find sanctuary in the Free World." John Foster Dulles also emphasized in public and in private the fear that Soviet leaders must henceforth have that, in the event of a major war, "many of their soldiers and airmen would seize the opportunity to desert or to allow themselves readily to be made prisoners." The Psychological Strategy Board and its successor, the Operations Coordination Board, further exploited this point in broadcasts to "Soviet orbit" countries, as well as the point that the United States and its allies had been willing to sacrifice much blood and treasure in support of this principle. Considerable resources were devoted to the development and implementation of a "National Plan" to exploit all aspects of the POW question—at home, abroad, and within the United Nations.[20]

Three members of the NNRC begged to challenge the assumption underlying this interpretation, however: that the defections that had taken place in Korea were genuine requests for asylum. In the commission's final report, Thimayya agreed with the Czech and Polish representatives that, judging from their experiences in the DMZ, it could not be said that Communist troops had found sanctuary and freedom but only strong anti-Communist POW organizations that "negate[d] all assumptions or assertions about Freedom of Choice." Indeed, it was pointed out, "any prisoner who desired repatriation had to do so clandestinely and in fear of his life." The Swiss and Swedes dissented from this majority argument on the grounds that, although there existed powerful organizations in the camps, there were still many opportunities for the prisoners to ask for repatriation. Such a view overlooked the fact, however, that in this atmosphere of fear and coercion a prisoner was supposed to make his decision in the "fragments of seconds in which he could feel relatively secure."[21]

THE POLITICAL CONFERENCE ON KOREA

If the U.S. administration strove to ensure its psychological victory over the POW issue and used its anti-Communist allies in Asia and their supporters in the U.S. Congress to help in obtaining that outcome, in a sense the quid pro quo for that assistance could be said to have been a political conference on Korea that neither jeopardized President Rhee's position nor extended into other Far Eastern questions affecting Taiwan. Dulles's famous or infamous refusal to grasp the outstretched hand of Chou En-lai at the political conference on Korea needs to be seen in the light of the compromises made with congressional leaders in the period leading up to the signature of the armistice (see p. 174).

A period establishing the parameters of the conference through public statements, and by means of direct talks between Communist and American representatives, preceded its official opening in April 1954. On August 8, 1953, and after discussions in South Korea between the U.S. secretary of state and President Rhee, the two leaders reaffirmed that they would walk out of any political conference after 90 days if there was evidence that the Communists were not negotiating in good faith. The secretary of state accompanied this warning with a pledge that he would not exchange U.N. recognition of the P.R.C. for agreement on Korean unity, thus restricting the scope of the meeting before it had actually been agreed to.[22]

The two major issues of contention between the U.S. and the Communist delegations were the location of the conference and its composition. Rhee had told the Eisenhower administration that he favored holding the meeting in Honolulu or San Francisco. Failing that, a South American country might be appropriate, he stated. A site in Ceylon was definitely not acceptable, he argued, because that country was too susceptible to British and Indian influence. Furthermore, under no circumstances would the South Korean president countenance Indian participation at the conference.[23]

The U.S. position was responsive to a degree to Rhee's preferences. The Eisenhower administration continued to argue for a two-sided conference made up of the belligerents, with the Soviets being arrayed on the Communist side, and with India having little more than observer status. On the question of location, at the first meeting of the preparatory talks in Panmunjom, Arthur Dean, an international lawyer with Dulles's New York firm of Sullivan and Cromwell who had been appointed to lead the U.S./U.N. delegation, proposed Honolulu, Geneva, or San Francisco as possibilities.[24]

The Chinese and North Korean delegates were adamant, however, that the conference should be a "round table" discussion with neutral state participation in order "to facilitate the smooth proceedings of the conference." Such a format and preference for neutral involvement also found favor in Western capitals, such as Canberra, London, and Ottawa, which were obviously sympathetic to the idea of a role for their major Commonwealth ally in Asia. Indeed, the Canadian and Australian governments were openly critical of the U.S. administration for allowing Rhee a veto over New Delhi's participation. London, too, was disappointed at the U.S. attitude toward India. But as Dulles told the British government, "we had no objections to India as long as those who proposed India would assume the responsibility of getting Rhee to sit down." He added, "while we could have a Korean settlement without India, we could not have a settlement without Korea." With both Churchill and Eden ill at this time, Lord Salisbury was prepared to be more circumspect over the matter, reaffirming that although the United Kingdom was committed to proposing Indian involvement, it would not lobby for it. The matter, he contended, simply did not justify a rift with the United States.[25]

The preparatory talks, which began on October 26, were formal, quickly vituperative, and ultimately unproductive, with the matter of composition proving the most difficult problem to resolve. The Chinese delegate, Huang Hua (later a Chinese foreign minister and throughout his career a close associate of Chou En-lai) dominated the proceedings—gone was the facade that North Korea was playing the leading role—and he pushed hard to get agreement on participation by five "neutral" nations—the Soviet Union, India, Indonesia, Pakistan, and Burma. However, decisions would be taken only by unanimous agreement of the signatories of the armistice, he stated. Huang also suggested that the conference be held in New Delhi, starting on December 28. In conversation with Indian officials from the NNRC, the Chinese delegate reported that he could not understand why the United States insisted on Soviet participation on the Chinese and North Korean side, and as a voting member and signatory to any agreement reached, unless it was intended as an insult to the Chinese. After all, he argued, the Chinese were the principal external power involved in North Korea at that time.[26]

In the familiar position of having to juggle Western allied views with those of Rhee and his supporters in the U.S. Congress, the Eisenhower administration maintained its policy of obtaining a two-sided conference, with the Soviets as a voting member on the

Communist side. In order to placate its Western partners, the United States also agreed to invite "some or all governments whose nations are now actually working there or who have current experience in Korea and are currently familiar with its problems," a formula that was obviously intended to encompass Indian participation. In addition, the U.S. administration now suggested that the conference should be convened at Geneva, not less than 28 days nor more than 42 after the termination of the preliminary talks at Panmunjom.[27]

Shortly after this proposal was presented the preliminary discussions were broken off, Dean walking out after Huang had refused to withdraw a charge of "perfidy" against the U.S. government for its "connivance" with Rhee in releasing the nonrepatriate prisoners of war on June 17. Dean cited this accusation in public as the sole reason for terminating the talks, though privately he had earlier advocated recessing the discussions until the nonrepatriate POW problem had been dealt with, since difficulties concerning this were obviously adversely affecting the atmosphere of the talks. What he omitted from his public statement, however—a statement that was notable for directly accusing the U.S.S.R. of "actually instigat[ing] the aggression in Korea in June 1950"—was any indication that the U.S. delegate had replied in kind to Chinese insults. On the day of the perfidy charge, he had labeled the Chinese and North Koreans "Soviet agents," a remark that had "outraged" the Communist delegates. As Prime Minister Nehru stated, having examined the transcripts of the proceedings, the last days of the talks were full of "the most amazing vituperation from both sides."[28]

Before ruffled feathers could be put in order again, however, developments at the Berlin conference of foreign ministers overtook the Panmumjon delegates. On January 27 the Soviet Union had proposed holding a five-power conference, to include the P.R.C., to discuss Far Eastern matters. And in a communiqué from Berlin the four powers—France, the Soviet Union, the United Kingdom, and the United States—agreed that there should be such a meeting in Geneva on April 26 to discuss the problems of Korea and Indochina. Significantly, especially in the context of Sino-Soviet relations, no provision was made for neutral participation (though, in the event, Menon was present in the background).[29]

In light of this decision, the Eisenhower administration switched its attention to preparing a solid allied and domestic front in time for

Geneva. It sought to diminish Chinese prestige (enhanced still further with the invitation to attend a Big Five meeting) and to ensure that any blame for the failure of the conference would lie with the Communists and not with Syngman Rhee or as a result of divisions among America's chief allies. Because "Senatorial misunderstanding" of this invitation to the P.R.C. was high, C. D. Jackson reported, the administration also sought to reassure Chiang Kaishek's supporters in Congress that "neither the invitation to, nor the holding of the . . . conference shall be deemed to imply diplomatic recognition in any case where it has not already been accorded." Senator Knowland nevertheless warned that the administration "would be held accountable if there were any 'slips' that might lead" to P.R.C. recognition: "The American people will not consent to a Far Eastern Munich," he intoned.[30]

Walter Robertson and John Foster Dulles worked hard to get the British in the right frame of mind where China was concerned, especially since the British alongside the Soviets had been appointed the co-chair of the conference. Robertson reminded Eden that the United States did not intend to meet the Chinese as an equal; rather, Washington was "bringing them before the bar of world opinion." The British secretary of state's principal private secretary, Evelyn Shuckburgh, quickly gave an indication of the different perception London held of the Chinese role in Asia. You are not "bringing them," he said, "they are coming." When Dulles, seriously concerned about events in Indochina, tried to obtain British agreement to a preconference statement designed to deter the P.R.C. from open intervention in support of Ho Chi Minh's forces, London argued that such an "anti-Chinese declaration" on the eve of the Geneva meeting "would be regarded by Western opinion as a poor contribution to the success of the Conference."[31]

Difficulties with Western allies were more than matched by those with Rhee. The South Korean president's agreement to participate at Geneva was purchased at the cost of U.S. assistance with the buildup of the R.O.K. military forces; but even so, such assistance did not immediately guarantee Rhee's cooperation with U.S. objectives at the conference. As throughout this period of Korean history, the administration faced the difficult task of maintaining a semblance of unity between Western allies, who wanted a policy that more nearly reflected the realities of power in that part of the world, and Rhee, who wanted, in Walter Bedell Smith's view, "to impose

[the] terms of a conqueror" on the North, including the "uncondi-tional withdrawal Chinese Communist troops, surrender North Korean Army to ROK, leaving ROK in military control of North Korea before elections and unification."[32]

The U.S. administration went to Geneva with three propositions for its allies to consider, the first of which provided for the unifica-tion of Korea through the extension of South Korean authority into the North, elections to be held only in the northern part, and Rhee's government to remain in power. Not unexpectedly, this was not received well in certain quarters. Shuckburgh, reflecting Eden's attitude, described this Rhee-centered plan as "ridiculous," and Eden refused to give his support to it "because he thinks it will seem to the world unreasonable, and he does not agree with putting forward mere bargaining positions publicly." The second proposal, designed to appeal to the Europeans, envisaged the dissolution of the government and constitution of the R.O.K., and the holding of countrywide elections to choose a national assembly that would in turn decide on a new government. The final, compromise proposal called for the retention of the R.O.K. constitution but not of its government, and the holding of free elections under U.N. supervi-sion for members of a national assembly in which representation would be in direct proportion to the indigenous population (thus ensuring a majority for those in the South).[33]

The forging of a consensus between Rhee and the Europeans around this compromise proposal was never accomplished, how-ever. Though the Western allies reacted favorably to this mid-way position (in the British case, in part, because Walter Bedell Smith was around to present it, and they regarded him as a more reason-able man to deal with than Dulles), Rhee remained adamant that he would make no further "concessions." More significant interna-tional events elsewhere soon interrupted the search for an agree-ment, anyway—when the French forces at Dien Bien Phu came under attack and surrendered on May 8. After this catastrophe for the Western powers, as Dulles perceived it, and stymied in his attempts to gain British support for "united action" in Indochina at this time of crisis, the secretary of state quickly came to view staunch anti-Communists like Rhee with greater sympathy. As he told his deputy, Smith, on May 10: "In view of our desire to develop a strong anti-Communist position, with particular relation to Indo-China, and the prospect that we might still intervene there and that this might involve a clash with Communist China, I think it important that we basically follow a line which will keep the confidence of our anti-Communist allies in Asia rather than seem to be working against them with a view to winning favor of Western European countries which are not disposed to be very helpful to us in Asia."[34]

Nevertheless, this growing preference for working more closely with Rhee on the Korean problem because of developments in Indochina did not have as negative an impact on U.S. relations elsewhere as it might have done. Unity was reestablished with the Western allies as the United States forged a common response to a Communist proposal put forward at Geneva. North Korea, with Soviet and Chinese backing, had called for the withdrawal of foreign troops from the peninsula and the establishment of an all-Korea commission, with equal representation for North and South, to arrange for elections throughout the country under NNSC supervision. In the Communists' view, the United Nations could not play a disinterested, neutral role in the electoral process because, as Molotov and Chou explained, they saw that body not as impartial but as a belligerent.[35]

The issue narrowed, then, to one concerning the legitimacy of the United Nations, with the United States struggling to maintain the credibility of that organization's role as peacemaker and a prime maintainer of order in the international system. As a result, the conference became deadlocked over the question of Korea's future, and on June 15 this part of the proceedings was terminated. If the U.S. administration did not gain all of its objectives, at least political disaster had been avoided, and in the final outcome the Western allies had maintained a reasonable semblance of unity.

With regard to the South Korean government, although it did not achieve the unity of the peninsula, it did attain other important objectives. The South was to be materially and militarily strengthened with the provision of a bilateral security treaty with the United States, and with the allocation of vast amounts of American economic and military assistance and the augmentation of its armed forces.[36] Moreover, this backing would also help to secure its political future. In this last phase of the Korean conflict, R.O.K. goals had coincided with larger American objectives at that crucial moment when Washington's leaders were setting out to deal with what they perceived as the next major challenge to international order in Asia.

[9]

Conclusions

At the peace of Westphalia in 1648, the delegates took six months to decide the order in which they would enter and be seated in the conference chamber.[1] In Korea, the United States at least showed a readiness to enter the room in July 1951, but administration officials frequently wished they had not been required to, and often desired to close the door on what was perceived as an unfortunate period in American foreign relations. For the first time in its history (except perhaps for the War of 1812), the nation that had been "dedicated to winning"[2] had been held to a stalemate on the battlefield and forced to negotiate a compromise settlement. Moreover, this had occurred at that moment when its hegemonic position in the international system had been confirmed: when there was a "fit between a con- figuration of material power, the prevalent collective image of world order (including certain norms) and a set of institutions which administer[ed] the order with a certain semblance of universality."[3]

The United States could claim to have obtained certain satisfac- tions at the conference table—some of a material and some of an ideological kind—and these could serve to demonstrate its power and to uphold the notion of the near universality of its interests. U.S. administrations argued, for example, that their enforcement of the principle of no forced repatriation for prisoners of war ex- emplified the respect that Western nations held for individual hu- man rights, demonstrated the extent to which they would sacrifice certain important national goals in pursuit of this principle, showed the illegitimacy of the Communist regimes of North Korea and China given the suspect loyalties of their citizenry, and threatened to weaken all Soviet-bloc nations because of their leaders' fears of troop defections in any future conflict with the West. With Eisenhower and Dulles's later claims that nuclear coercion explained Chinese capitulation on the POW issue, the resolution of this item could be projected as that winning combination of military power in the service of moral rectitude.

The United States also obtained a ceasefire at a defensible military line, more secure than the 38th Parallel (though still requiring the presence of U.S. forces to the present day), and generally above that meridian, thus ensuring greater protection for South Korea. Furthermore, as Nitze had earlier put it, its location demonstrated that Pyongyang and Peking had not achieved "somewhat more than an even military result against 16 nations, including the U.S., U.K., Canada, and France."[4] On the inspection and reinforcement issue, Washington had obtained arrangements it could live with, and the important objective of a pledge (in public at least) of continuing U.N. support for the future of South Korea with the statement that "in the interests of world peace . . . if there is a renewal of the armed attack, challenging again the principles of the United Nations, we should again be united and prompt to resist." This commitment to U.N. principles and South Korean security was also coupled with a threat to expand any future conflict on the peninsula to encompass the territory of the Communist regime in China, a government that the United States had begun to see as the most disruptive of the current international order.

Nevertheless, these were not the kinds of victories that Americans were used to obtaining, and the length of time that it had taken to arrive at these results, together with the costs on the human and material level that had been incurred, caused Washington much international and domestic difficulty. Considerable strain was placed on the notion that a wide measure of agreement existed between the United States and its major allies (though they were no strangers to disagreement where Asian policies were concerned), and that its policies were legitimized by a solid base of domestic support. First, in terms of casualties and physical ruin, the Korean conflict was a terribly destructive war. The U.S. Far Eastern Air Force deputy for intelligence recorded, for example, that in relation to its total resources North Korea suffered greater destruction than the Japanese islands had experienced in World War II.[5] Some

635,000 tons of bombs were dropped (compared with 503,000 in the Pacific theater) and 32,557 tons of napalm.[6] The U.S. embassy in Seoul produced a report illustrating what this meant in material terms: the North's industries had been "flattened," it said; its industrial output was an "insignificant fraction of pre-war production"; and its hydroelectric system was severely damaged. In sum, the "air bombing was so devastating that rebuilding North Korean industry is largely a problem of new construction rather than rehabilitation."[7]

In human terms, the results were even more shocking. Probably some two million to three million civilians were killed in the North and South, and many more were turned into refugees. There were 33,629 U.S. battle deaths, plus 20,617 from other causes, and an estimated 400,000 South Korean military fatalities. Possibly one million to two million Communist troops perished.[8] U.S. statistics showed that 45 percent of its casualties occurred while the negotiations were in progress, and for U.N. Command forces as a whole some 125,000 of them (and perhaps one-quarter of a million on the Communist side) during the 15-month period in which the nonforcible repatriation policy was being debated.[9]

This expenditure of lives, resources, and energy, together with fears that the United States was being drawn too closely into the concerns of Asia to the neglect of Europe, and that its attitude toward the P.R.C. was becoming steadily more counterproductive, led to conflict between the United States and its major Western allies. These allies perceived negotiating opportunities where the United States saw none, and occasions for flexibility when Washington wanted firmness. During the first year of the armistice negotiations the Truman administration had been at its most responsive to these doubts and suggestions, a readiness to listen that the disastrous consequences of Washington's misguided decision to cross the 38th Parallel and march to the Yalu in October 1950 had heightened. Allied opinion thus became an important factor in convincing Truman and Acheson in the early summer of 1951 that the time had come to open negotiations and that there was little to be gained by attempting to push too far into North Korean territory. In the first months of the talks, when Ridgway had urged various breaks in the negotiations, "world opinion," which urged patient discussion, had been a valuable source of support to the administration in its arguments with the U.N. commander for continuing the search for a settlement. After the Communists had retreated from their demand that the ceasefire line should be established at the 38th Parallel, the Truman administration had realized that in order to maintain international approval, and that of some major opinion-formers in the U.S. press, it needed to respond to that concession—hence the rejection of Ridgway's stance on the retention of Kaesong and the agreement to the 30-day time limit at the end of November. In May 1952, the allies—notably, Britain, Canada, and Australia—agitated strongly for some kind of neutral rescreening of the prisoners to confirm their repatriation wishes. This position contributed to the U.S. decision to advance such a proposal at the armistice conference. Such contributions were not fundamental in determining actual policy, but they were important in the area of policy implementation.

Much of this responsiveness is to be explained by the primacy of European security, by the desire to maintain and strengthen the Western allied coalition, by the determination to demonstrate that a universalist institution such as the United Nations continued to support American steps in Korea, and by the realization that the only perceived alternative to ending the armistice talks was expanded hostilities. But as it became apparent to the administration that it could not easily extricate itself from this conflict, and as it became obvious that it could not consider the interests of the Western constituency alone, other influences of a less "globalist" kind received attention. Courses that were acceptable to North Atlantic allies were not acceptable to the South Korean government, whose value as a partner had increased because of the country's symbolic role as the battleground between East and West, and, more prosaically, because its armed forces held two-thirds of the front line. Understanding that his power had significantly increased as a result of his country's status in the war, Rhee frequently took actions designed to disrupt the negotiations: his partisan forces violated the neutrality of the conference site; he influenced Ridgway to attempt to retain Kaesong behind U.N. Command lines; the R.O.K. president persuaded Clark to recommend that all North Korean non-repatriates be released immediately on the signature of an armistice agreement; and, when thwarted in this, he released a large part of this group from custody on the eve of a final settlement, thus prolonging the conflict for another month.

On the domestic political level, the declining popularity of the

Truman administration, the charges that had been made against it concerning corruption within and pusillanimity in dealing with Communists, coupled with the mass public's sympathy for General MacArthur's allegation that Truman was waging war "with no hope for victory," sharpened comment on this indecisive conflict and reinforced the sense of malaise and enervation that surrounded the Democrats. The inability to end the war could, then, become the focus for a number of deeper strains within the American body-politic: between internationalism and unilateralism; between a "Europe first" and an "Asia first" outlook; between an intellectual pro-European such as Dean Acheson and a pro-Asian anti-Communist such as Douglas MacArthur.

To simplify the argument: in relation to progress at the armistice negotiations, the former position in each of these sets of dichotomous relationships implied greater flexibility at the talks and the latter, greater inflexibility. The idea of a negotiating continuum between the two extremes of flexibility and inflexibility aids an understanding of the kinds of coalitions that could form at or near one of these polar opposites. Though the composition of groupings tended to vary over time, arrayed toward the inflexible end of the continuum, there would be the military commanders in Korea (including the U.N. commanders, generals Ridgway and Clark), certain members of the Pentagon in Washington, the South Korean government, the "Asia-firsters" among the GOP, and, after the first few months of the negotiations, the mass public. Vital to the maintenance of this coalition was the belief that the United States could afford to invest more air and naval resources in an expanded effort and that such additional military pressure would not lead to the overt entry of Soviet forces into the fighting in support of its Asian Communist allies.[10] Conversely, toward the flexible end of the continuum there were the Western allies, certain members of the State Department, and editorial opinion, especially the views of editors expressed in the more widely respected East Coast newspapers. This group argued in essence that constraints on U.S. military resources and an expanded war that would divert much-needed equipment from NATO forces and risk global conflict required the United States to continue with the talks. Where Truman and Acheson chose to settle along this continuum was, of course, vital to the nature of the policies arrived at.

In the last months of the Truman administration, as the negotiations entered their second year, there was a definite hardening in the administration's attitude toward the truce talks. The president's personal preference for "tough" action partly explains this tendency, as does the emergence of an issue (nonforcible repatriation) that was perceived as having widespread benefits, thus facilitating the development of a consensus between Truman and Acheson and between the departments of Defense and State. Admiral Fechteler's beliefs were also crucial, since, with the support of successive U.N. commanders in Korea, he had maintained a consistent argument that a more aggressive stance at Panmunjom and intensified air action would more quickly secure the desired outcome at the talks. He and others in the Pentagon would also claim that the advantages deriving from the military pressure were already apparent in the second half of 1952; hardly surprising, in their view, since, as Lovett contended, Communist judgment was "influenced solely by force."

The attractiveness of the naval chief's solution was many-faceted, while the fact that it was election year also increased its appeal. Fechteler's approach projected an image to the domestic audience of principled behavior coupled with aggressiveness, both important when the Democrats were being accused of "appeasement." His solution also appealed to the deeper beliefs within a society that had never attached much importance to the art of negotiation because it had rarely needed to. It also had the attraction of being simple and straightforward, less devious in a sense, because all it required was for the U.N. Command team in Korea to state its position and keep up the military pressure until the other side agreed to it. Fechteler's solution avoided, then, the ambiguities of bargaining, and the ever-present fear that America's negotiators were being led into traps.

Also at the root of this, however, was a less clearly articulated perception, which expressed itself in concrete bureaucratic form in a division between State and Defense, until it was resolved in the Pentagon's favor in the late summer of 1952. Members of the State Department believed that the United States could best secure its dominant role in world politics and, in this instance, in the Korean operation through obtaining the consent of its allies to its policy positions. As Nitze said, he wanted to show America's partners that the administration had "exhausted every possible scheme for securing an armistice," believing that, once it had obtained their legitimizing support, the room for policy maneuver would expand. The view that came to prevail in the Defense Department, on the other hand, articulated most strongly by the U.S. Navy and Air Force chiefs of staff, or their deputies, was that less attention should be given to allied opinion and greater efforts should be made to demonstrate firmness and resolve in order to impress the Communists. Once impressed, the Chinese and North Koreans would concede the remaining issues in dispute at the conference, which in turn would lead the Western allies to rally and once more to associate themselves with a victorious America. The Defense Department had explained the unilateralist elements within this argument as early as November 1951, when it reminded State that "among the Western nations the United States is now the dominant power in the Western Pacific. Consequently, in any conflict of interest arising between the United States and other Western Powers which may affect the position of the United States in the Far East, the United States should in its own interest insist that the United States security considerations in that area be overriding."[11] By 1952, irritated even more at allied criticisms of the U.S. military conduct of the war—including the bombing of the hydroelectric installations and the use of napalm—Pentagon members argued that less time should be devoted to the consideration of allied reactions and of possible areas for compromise, and more attention focused on the impact that the bombing program was having on the Communist position. As State officials discerned the Defense Department's position, military punishment of the enemy had begun to take precedence over allied unity, and over the signing of an armistice agreement that allowed for the redeployment of U.S. forces.

In a number of respects Eisenhower had much more leeway than Truman when it came to devising a strategy for ending the war. This, after all, had been "Truman's war" as it could be said to be Truman's peace negotiations, and the Republican president could always state that, in bringing the war to a close, he was making the best of an unsatisfactory situation. Eisenhower also enjoyed far better relations with Congress than Truman had maintained, though this support was obtained at a price where China policy was concerned. Moreover, he had achieved a solid victory at the polls and obviously held the confidence of the general public, which served to reduce the domestic sniping at his policy.

In other areas, however, there were certain similarities between the two administrations, especially in the belief that the Communists were responsible for the delay in reaching agreement and that "deeds" not "words" were the only things that would influence the Chinese and North Koreans. Eisenhower was determined to (and was expected to) bring matters to a head, and thus he took the significant decision to present the U.N. Command's final stand at the armistice talks on May 25, on the understanding that if these terms were rejected, the negotiations would be broken off and military operations would be stepped up. The Eisenhower administration also made the contingent decision on May 20 to extend hostilities into China, utilizing nuclear weapons, if it became clear that the Communists were not going to come to terms. Importantly, although Washington understood that its Western partners approved of none of these actions at a time when final agreement at the talks was so close, and though it was accepted that an extension of hostilities—especially if it involved nuclear weapons—"would severely strain and possibly break the Western alliance,"[12] the president claimed that he believed that if an expanded war proved successful, any damage done to allied relationships would soon be repaired. The under secretary of state, Walter Bedell Smith, put it more plainly when he stated that if such military action produced the desired results, "many of our friends who had fallen away at the outset would climb back on the victorious bandwagon."[13]

Many would subsequently argue that Eisenhower's success in ending the Korean conflict proved that if tougher military steps had been taken earlier, the armistice agreement would have been signed that much sooner. In 1952 the U.N. commander, the Joint Chiefs of Staff, and the secretary of defense all stated that the enhanced pressure from the air was already forcing Communist concessions at the truce talks, though no detailed evidence to support these arguments was provided. Neither were any studies undertaken of the difficulties of conducting coercive diplomacy through bombing, which became evident whenever it was attempted. Technical and planning problems often interfered with the timing of operations; and the punishment inflicted bore differentially on China and North Korea, with the former—the major force behind the negotiations—suffering far less than its ally. Moreover, it was never considered that the effects of the air attacks might be making the Communists more intransigent: that the Chinese and North Koreans were in earnest when they repeated the refrain that neither Peking nor Pyongyang would give in to such cruel and obvious tactics. Indeed, in June 1952, what might have been a promising opening was closed off, by Chou En-lai and the Soviet official, Zinchenko, after the hydroelectric installations along the Yalu were put out of action (echoes of which were to be found in Vietnam in 1965 when the negotiating operation "Marigold" was scuppered as U.S. jet bombers attacked the Hanoi area).[14] Finally, those who linked increased air pressure and nuclear threats with Communist concessions in the last months of the talks gave scant attention to the contribution made to this decision by the fundamental increase in political vulnerability that had occurred in the Communist bloc with the death of Stalin.

If such analyses of these arguments had been undertaken, other more compelling reasons, primarily of a political nature, would have emerged to explain the slow pace of these armistice talks, including those noted earlier such as the difficulties of determining policy positions that would satisfy both the South Koreans and the Western partners; the adversarial nature of American domestic politics, further heightened in 1952; and the general dislike of the negotiating process. Furthermore, factors directly connected with the conduct of the talks also added to the difficulties of reaching agreement. Neither those giving advice to the U.N. Command mediators nor the negotiating team itself gave detailed consideration to possible Communist reactions to certain of its policy positions or analyzed what Communist objectives might be at various stages of the talks. Intelligence reports that were produced tended to concentrate on the general question of whether the Communists wanted an armistice at that stage or not, and they did not consider which points might be of particular importance to them or why certain positions were valued. There were individuals who demonstrated greater sensitivity, of course: General Bradley for one realized that it would take time for the Communists to give up their attachment to a ceasefire line at the 38th Parallel; and Charles Bohlen argued that reciprocity was important to the Chinese and North Koreans and that mutual concessions would bring results. But these remarks were exceptional and had little impact on the day-to-day tone of negotiations, which was influenced by the U.S. negotiators' belief that the talks were "doomed to failure" anyway, and by

Ridgway's "personal sense of outrage" and his "stubbornness . . . motivated in considerable part by personal factors."[15] The U.N. Command negotiators looked upon the Communists as being "utterly inflexible"; hence, when the Chinese and North Koreans issued hints that they might be about to modify their stand on particular issues—such as the ceasefire line or the resumption of the talks after the August suspension—these signals tended to be overlooked.[16]

This tendency to ignore Communist hints arose out of a lack of familiarity with the art of negotiation, the mediators' insecurities about their skills for the task, and a deep distrust of their opponents—which the latter's behavior at Kaesong on the eve of the talks had exacerbated. But the lack of firm instructions from Washington also compounded the problem. At times, the U.S. negotiators seemed to spend as much energy trying to work out and influence the administration's position as they gave to the Communist statements. This came about because U.S. policy positions, notably on the inspection and POW items, were formulated during the course of the negotiations, rather than prior to them.

With regard to the inspection issue, the previously firm commitment to unlimited observation throughout the whole of Korea was quickly undermined when Ridgway acknowledged that it would only lead to many instances of unresolved friction between the U.N. and Communist supervisory teams; when Rusk admitted that even if unlimited inspection were won, the Americans would only want to inspect at key locations; and when another State official pointed out that the U.N. Command would be unlikely to take action on a buildup of supplies or troops, unless such increases were followed by an overt act of aggression. These points led to the development of the Greater Sanction proposal, which, because it required allied agreement, took some time to become operational. The POW policy similarly took until late February to be worked out, though discussions began on this item at Panmunjom in December 1951. Moreover, in this case not only had the policy not been thought through in Washington when it was first introduced into the talks, but also little consideration was being given to probable Chinese Communist reaction to nonforcible repatriation, though it was realized that a large number of their prisoners might refuse to return home. Neither was any analysis offered of the manner in which conditions in the camps might affect attitudes toward repatriation.

That an advanced state with an efficient bureaucracy had not given more consideration to the administration of POW camps for those who were bound to be captured in the Korean conflict was surprising, but perhaps understandable as a result of the speed with which U.N. Command fortunes improved after September 1950. Nevertheless, administration officials did point to some of the possibly adverse results of MacArthur's decision to recruit officials from Taiwan as guards, as interpreters in the compounds, and as instructors in the civil information and education program. Yet, when the official polling of prisoners drew near, the factionalism and violence that had arisen among prisoners from countries that had so recently been divided and been engaged in civil war, factionalism that the recruits from Taiwan, the POW-trusties, and the R.O.K. guards all encouraged, it seemed to take the administration by surprise and to render it supine. Reports on the eve of the screening indicated that it would be virtually impossible to determine which prisoners genuinely feared returning home, and it also became known in February that possibly thousands of Chinese would refuse to go back to the P.R.C. Both of these points had been established before the POW policy was fully determined—although the president was probably only aware of the latter—but the implications of neither one of them were fully explored. Any such exploration would have revealed that the humanitarian dimension of the policy was much more ambiguous than allowed for and the consequences for ending the conflict, given the large number of nonrepatriate Chinese, possibly enormous. But the administration, reluctant to delay or to consider such measures that might remove or reduce the powerful influence of the POW trusties, became locked into this policy from that time on. Truman's commitment to nonforcible repatriation was perceived as being so firm that those who raised the possibility of exploring such questions did so with little vigor and virtually no support. It was a prime example of the manner in which the authority of the presidential office can foreclose a detailed discussion of the implications of certain policies.

Thus, the lengthy nature of these armistice negotiations can largely be explained by a U.S. unwillingness or inability to consider Communist objectives and probable reactions to U.N. Command

[216]

policy positions, and to a lack of clarity in and detailed examination of the objectives the administration sought at talks where it was not a victor and could not impose terms. On the other hand, once the U.S. position was determined, the distrust of the Communists was so great as to require the development of all facets of a particular policy in considerable detail.

The sources of these difficulties also explain why various tentative opportunities to end the conflict were left unexplored. Leaving aside the striking nature of the Soviet offer made in October 1950, when U.S./U.N. forces were poised to cross the 38th Parallel, and the "second alternative" that Chou put forward in June 1952, to be quickly withdrawn after the bombing of the power installations, there were other occasions when it seemed that the Communists might be ready to end the war. The Hallinan proposal, taken up in the Soviet press, which suggested an immediate ceasefire, with the question of the prisoners left for civilian representatives to resolve, mirrored some of the suggestions that had arisen in the State Department and among the Western allies. But as a possible opening it was left unexplored. In early November, before the U.N. debate, Soviet and Chinese officials suggested that if the United States did not make too much of its victory over the POW issue, and provided that the nonforcible repatriation principle could be obscured, the Chinese might accept that they would not get all their prisoners back. These suggestions, which, if developed successfully, would have served to deny the administration a clear-cut victory over POW repatriation, also coincided with the hardening of the administration's stance regarding the negotiations at Panmunjom and thus would not be examined either.

Little direct evidence is available about Chinese or North Korean objectives at the talks, of course, but certain inferences can still be drawn. It is better understood now that China's original decision to enter the fighting had been difficult for the new regime to take,[17] but what is less well known is that there was a continuing controversy about the country's involvement. Mao's speech at the war's end indicated some of these difficulties. Though in September 1953 the party leader noted that Chinese troops had gained military experience and had "taken on the measure of the U.S. armed forces," important because it showed that "U.S. imperialism is not terrifying, nothing to make a fuss about," he also confirmed that the "agricultural tax" to support the war effort had been "a shade on the heavy side," that "some people raised an outcry" as a result and "wanted us to give up the war."[18] The protracted nature of the conflict had had, then, some bonuses in terms of experience, but, more significantly, it had divided the leadership and had imposed severe burdens on the economy.

But in the United States at the time and subsequently many chose to believe that Peking was deliberately engaging Washington in a war of attrition, and that any hint of flexibility on China's part was disingenuous, being primarily designed to impress the nonaligned or divide the United States from its allies. Moreover, official studies of the war often alleged that the U.N. Command team had "compromised on point after point in the discussions," and psychological warfare plans were specifically designed to promote the view that any progress was solely "due to the sincere efforts of the UN delegation."[19] Other U.S. officials, who had come to realize otherwise and that the Chinese and North Koreans had indeed come to the DMZ to negotiate an armistice, were rarely heard, however, at least in the public arena. In March 1952 a State Department Office of Intelligence and Research report had noted the Communist concessions on the agenda, the 38th Parallel, and change of site from Kaesong to Panmunjom.[20] In February 1953 John Allison of the Bureau of Far Eastern Affairs wrote that although the Communists had "indicated a tough bargaining attitude," this "could not be interpreted as an unwillingness to enter into an armistice." Rather, they had accepted the "basic substantive positions of the UNC," such as no withdrawal of foreign troops, a ceasefire at the line of contact between opposing forces, behind-the-lines inspection, and the rotation of forces and equipment.[21] If he had written this memorandum two months later, he could also have added that the Communists had accepted the U.N. Command position on nonforcible repatriation for Chinese prisoners, as they had done for the Koreans in March 1952.

Even on this most difficult of issues regarding the prisoners of war, Peking had shown a consistency of approach from June 1952 to March 1953 that indicated that the P.R.C. might have accepted nonforcible repatriation provided the principle itself was masked and the prisoners were taken out of the hands of those who had allowed them to be influenced or intimidated. In June 1952, for

[218]

example, Chou, in private conversations with Panikkar, was supposed to have suggested that the prisoners be taken to a neutral area, there to be interviewed by representatives from four neutral states—an argument that quite closely resembled the arrangements finally arrived at in June 1953. In November 1952 the Indians believed the Chinese had been interested in Menon's proposed U.N. resolution when it remained rather "vague" about no forced repatriation and when it put the emphasis on placing the prisoners in the hands of a neutral commission for final disposition. In March 1953, in the first indication that acknowledged that there was a repatriation problem, the Chinese premier spoke of sending those who did not wish immediately to be exchanged "to a neutral state so as to ensure a just solution to the question of their repatriation." The similarities between these three proposals suggests that there probably was, as Nitze put it in May 1952, "an area of possible negotiation in connection with the manner and timing of the rescreening of the POWs."[22]

Chinese stubbornness on the propaganda elements of the POW issue paralleled some of Washington's reasoning for its determination to retain clarity. For the new government in China, the specter of thousands of its soldiers' embracing what it saw as the illegal alternative regime on Taiwan struck at the heart of its contention that it had come to power with the support of a loyal Red Army and backed by the gratitude of a united populace. For the United States, the allure of many Chinese voting with their feet for Chiang rather than Mao validated a policy toward Nationalist China that was unpopular internationally, at the same time as it demonstrated to Truman's domestic critics that his administration was taking action that gave succor to the Generalissimo. On a more general level, America's staunch adherence to a difficult policy could indicate to members of the international community just how steadfast the United States could be in support of a high moral principle. Not for them the past expediency of the British, or the callousness and cynicism of the Soviet Union. Moreover, nonforcible repatriation could be projected as a valuable adjunct to the policy of containment, helping to prevent future Soviet aggression because members of its armed forces, if sent abroad to fight, would probably take the first opportunity they could to opt for the freedoms offered in the West. Finally, an obvious victory on nonforcible repatriation—

provided it could remain unsullied—could provide a justification for all that the war had entailed in terms of lives lost and treasure spent.

These arguments, however, if they had been held up for close inspection, would have been difficult to sustain. Though Chiang's and Rhee's supporters in the United States were no doubt gratified by the outcome of nonforcible repatriation, too much had filtered through to Western governments and to the Asian nonaligned about the intimidation employed against the Chinese prisoners, in particular, to demonstrate convincingly to non-Communist governments that the regime in China was either unpopular or regarded as illegitimate. The reports of A. Sabin Chase and Philip Manhard, who had been sent by the State Department to investigate the reasons behind the poll results, also confirmed that the figures did not indicate a significant lack of support for the Chinese Communists, but instead were a reflection of the terror tactics that had been deployed to ensure defections. These same intimidatory means, and the riots and deaths in the camps, also tended to flaw the moral victory that would be claimed (a victory that was further undermined later on with the revelations about the behavior of U.S. prisoners and the willingness of the 22 to reject the West). As regards future surrenders by enemy forces, it was obvious from POW statistics that most enemy troops had given themselves up as the result of the failure of particular military campaigns. Few Chinese surrendered, for example, after the disastrous fifth offensive in April and May 1951, and the troops gave up then only because they were out of supplies, exhausted, and starving.

The benefits of this policy, therefore, would have been seen to have been questionable if they had been explicitly considered alongside the costs required to enforce it: in terms of casualties, the prolongation of the period of captivity for U.N. Command prisoners, relations with allies, and, for Truman, the standing of the Democratic party with the electorate. Though it is the case that, once the administration became publicly committed to this policy, the possibility of retreat was virtually nonexistent, the awareness of the doubtful basis of the position and of the price it was exacting should have encouraged a greater willingness to explore some of the areas of compromise that had been suggested. Personal fears of appearing weak, political accusations of appeasement, and an as-

[220]

sumption that the Communists would find a way of subverting the policy of nonforcible repatriation if its final stages were taken out of U.S. hands, have all been shown to have contributed to the decision to reject compromise. But important, too, were the attractions and opportunities offered by such a telling policy: that despite the lack of a battlefield victory, here was an issue of fundamental principle that if starkly projected could demonstrate the essential moral difference between East and West, and which if resolved in the West's favor could make plain "in a way which leaves no shadow of doubt in anyone's mind that our will has been imposed on the enemy."[23]

The impact of the war on future U.S. policy toward Asia in general and China in particular was profound. The concept that force would not be used to return prisoners home lived on in Vietnam, though it never led to the wholesale defections among Communist troops that had been predicted for it. During this later war the United States decided to turn over all those captured to the Saigon regime. The result was rather as it had been in Korea: those persuaded to remain with Saigon were alleged to be in far better physical shape than those who chose to be repatriated; and the South Vietnamese authorities organized nonrepatriate participation in numerous anti-Communist demonstrations.[24] The U.S. military responded to the alleged failure of its forces to maintain morale during their period of captivity in Korea by teaching the next generation that, if taken prisoner, they had a duty to conduct themselves as though they were still joined in battle. It became a legal obligation for U.S. armed forces to "resist and harass their captors," a law that represented a fundamental rejection of the Geneva Convention.[25]

The belief generated during the Korean conflict in the value of saturation bombing as a way of forcing enemy concessions was also transferred to the Vietnam theater, Gen. Maxwell Taylor stating that a graduated bombing program against Hanoi would yield results as it had in that earlier Asian war.[26] Yet, although the punishment inflicted on North Vietnam was colossal, it was no more responsible for the ending of that conflict than it had been in Korea. As Ho Chi Minh was to tell Lyndon Johnson, much as Chou En-lai and Kim Il Sung told Harry Truman: "The Vietnamese people will never submit to force; they will never accept talks under the threat of bombs."[27]

After the Korean conflict had ended and, possibly because Eisenhower and Dulles believed that nuclear coercion had been so successful in forcing final concessions out of Peking, the administration continued to threaten the P.R.C. with atomic warfare: during the Indochina crisis in 1954, for example, and in the two Taiwan Straits crises of 1955 and 1958. These threats were designed to show the efficacy of the massive retaliation doctrine and to demonstrate that, despite China's alliance with the U.S.S.R., Peking's military options were limited. One effect, however, was to accelerate China's development of its own nuclear arsenal, an outcome that seriously alarmed future U.S. administrations, given their perceptions of the P.R.C. as an irrational and violent revolutionary power.

In the 1950s domestic political constraints and a determination not to add to the international prestige of the P.R.C. made the Eisenhower administration unwilling to negotiate seriously with Peking, whether about tensions in the Taiwan Strait, or about U.N. recognition, or on trading links. Though intermittent diplomatic contact was maintained from 1954 onward, the debates remained sterile, and the only agreement reached concerned the return of a number of Americans who had been imprisoned in China.[28]

Some within the executive branch came to recognize the drawbacks of such a stultifying policy and argued that the U.S. refusal to break out of the diplomatic straitjacket it had imposed on itself jeopardized its relations with Japan, India, and the Western powers;[29] but a fundamental redirection of policy could not be countenanced. New directions, it was stated during the second term of Eisenhower's presidency, would have the unwelcome effect of adding to Peking's prestige and disposing others in Asia to seek to regularize relations with Mao's regime. Moreover, accommodation with the P.R.C. would not encourage it to adopt those forms of international behavior that the United States thought appropriate.[30] Not until U.S. leaders discerned, in the late 1960s, the emergence of a new international power configuration could a significant departure in China policy be contemplated.

Notes

ABBREVIATIONS USED IN NOTES

DDEL	Dwight D. Eisenhower Library
DDRS	Declassified Documents Reference System
HSTL	Harry S. Truman Library
JCS	U.S. Joint Chiefs of Staff
NA	National Archives
NSC	U.S. National Security Council
PPS	Policy Planning Staff
PRO	Public Record Office
PSF	President's Secretary File
RG	Record Group
SCMP	*Survey of the China Mainland Press*
SGML	Seeley G. Mudd Library

CHAPTER 1

1. C. Thorne, *The Issue of War: States, Societies, and the Far Eastern Conflict of 1941–1945* (London: Hamish Hamilton, 1985), pp. 211–12; Robert Dallek, "The Post-War World," in Sanford J. Ungar, ed., *Estrangement: America and the World* (New York: Oxford University Press, 1985), p. 30; E. A. Brett, *The World Economy since the War* (London: Macmillan, 1985), p. 63.

2. Thorne, *Issue of War*, pp. 212–13; Michael L. Dockrill, "The Foreign Office, Anglo-American Relations and the Korean War, June 1950–June 1951," *International Affairs* (London) 62 (1986): 475.

3. Robert W. Cox, "Social Forces, States and World Orders: Beyond International Relations Theory," *Millennium: Journal of International Studies* 10 (Summer 1981): 137. See also Stephen Gill, "American Hegemony: Its Limits and Prospects in the Reagan Era," in ibid. 15 (Winter 1986); Robert Keohane, *After Hegemony: Cooperation and Discord in the World Political Economy* (Princeton, N.J.: Princeton University Press, 1984), esp. chap. 8.

4. Burton I. Kaufman, *The Korean War: Challenges in Crisis, Credibility, and Command* (Philadelphia: Temple University Press, 1986), p. 356.

5. See the arguments in John L. Gaddis, "Reconsiderations—Was the Truman Doctrine a Real Turning Point?" *Foreign Affairs* 52 (Jan. 1974), but note, too, Melvyn P. Leffler, "The American Conception of National Security and the Beginnings of the Cold War, 1945–1948," in *American Historical Review* 89 (April 1984).

6. E.g., see Truman Papers, National Security Council Minutes, June 29, 1950, HSTL; ibid., PSF, Aug. 6–8, 1950, HSTL; DEFE 4, Chiefs of Staff 50, Minutes, 101st meeting, July 3, 1950, PRO.

7. See Harold Nicolson, *Diplomacy* (London: Thornton Butterworth, 1939), p. 144.

8. For a useful summary of the points of friction in Anglo-American relations during the truce negotiations, see Michael Dockrill, "The Foreign Office, Anglo-American Relations and the Korean Truce Negotiations, July 1951–July 1953," in James Cotton and Ian Neary, eds., *The Korean War in History* (Manchester: Manchester University Press, 1989), pp. 100–119.

9. For further details see Denis Stairs, *The Diplomacy of Constraint: Canada, the Korean War and the United States* (Toronto: University of Toronto Press, 1974), and Robert O'Neill, *Australia in the Korean War, 1950–53*, Vol. 1: *Strategy and Diplomacy* (Canberra: Australian War Memorial and Australian Govt. Publishing Services, 1981).

10. *Foreign Relations of the United States 1951*, vol. 7: *Korea* (Washington, D.C.: Government Printing Office, 1983), pp. 27–28, Jan. 5 (hereafter cited as *Foreign Relations*); PREM 11, Nov. 11, 1952, no. 111, PRO; *Foreign Relations*, 1952–54, 15:1302, July 2, 1953.

11. E.g., see David Caute, *The Great Fear: The Anti-Communist Purge under Truman and Eisenhower* (New York: Simon & Schuster, 1978); Thomas C. Reeves, *The Life and Times of Joe McCarthy: A Biography* (New York: Stein & Day, 1982).

12. Richard H. Ullman, "Paths to Reconciliation: The United States in the International System of the Late 1980s," in Ungar, *Estrangement*, p. 281.

13. Ronald J. Caridi, *The Korean War and American Politics: The Republican Party as a Case Study* (Philadelphia: University of Pennsylvania Press, 1968). Robert A. Divine, *Foreign Policy and U.S. Presidential Elections, 1952–60* (New York: New Viewpoints, 1974).

14. Rosemary Foot, *The Wrong War: American Policy and the Dimensions of the Korean Conflict, 1950–1953* (Ithaca, N.Y.: Cornell University Press), 1985, chap. 7; Richard K. Betts, *Nuclear Blackmail and Nuclear Balance* (Washington, D.C.: Brookings Institution, 1987), pp. 37–42.

15. John E. Mueller, *War, Presidents and Public Opinion* (New York: John Wiley, 1973), pp. 51, 229–30; RG 59, Office of Public Opinion Studies, box 12, NA.

16. Michael Hunt, *Ideology and US Foreign Policy* (New Haven: Yale University Press, 1987), p. 180.

17. Kaufman, *Korean War*, p. 282.

18. Dean Acheson, *Present at the Creation: My Years in the State Department* (New York: Norton, 1969), p. 533.

19. The U.N. Command negotiating team was led in the first year by Adm. Charles Turner Joy, who was assisted by Rear Adm. Arleigh Burke, Maj. Gen. Henry Hodes (Army), and Maj. Gen. Lawrence Craigie (Air Force). The first South Korean officer attached to the team was Maj. Gen. Paik Sun Yup. Though well liked by the American officers, he was never treated as a full member and never spoke at the negotiating table.

20. RG 218, JCS Records, CCS 383.21 Korea (3-19-45), sec. 51, July 2, 1951, NA; The

History of the Joint Chiefs of Staff, by James F. Schnabel and Robert J. Watson: The Joint Chiefs of Staff and National Policy, vol. 3, The Korean War, p. 568 (cited hereafter as History of the JCS).

21. John W. Dower, *War Without Mercy: Race and Power in the Pacific War* (New York: Pantheon, 1986), passim.

22. *Foreign Relations*, 1951, 7:785–89, Aug. 7; ibid., 1952–54, 15: 513, Sept. 15, 1952; William H. Vatcher, Jr., *Panmunjom: The Story of the Korean Military Armistice Negotiations* (New York: Praeger, 1958), p. 204; Herbert Goldhamer, "The Korean Armistice Conference," a declassified RAND study, Dec. 1951, pp. 237–38.

23. Goldhamer, "Korean Armistice," p. 46. As a possible defense against this feared charge of incompetence, Admiral Joy, who led the U.N. Command negotiating team for the first year, described the negotiations as "doomed from the start." Ibid.

24. Robert F. Randle, *The Origins of Peace: A Study of Peacemaking and the Structure of Peace Settlements* (New York: Free Press, 1973), p. 449.

25. U. Alexis Johnson, *The Right Hand of Power* (Englewood Cliffs, N.J.: Prentice Hall, 1984), pp. 127–28.

26. Callum A. MacDonald, *Korea: The War before Vietnam* (London: Macmillan, 1986), p. 117; RG 59, 695A.0024, May 20, 1952, NA; Wilfred Burchett, *At the Barricades* (London: Quartet Books, 1980), p. 161; Wu Hsiu-chuan (Wu Xiuquan), *Eight Years in the Ministry of Foreign Affairs* (Peking: New World Press, 1985), chap. 3, esp. p. 85; for details of the organization established for the U.N. Command negotiators, see History of the JCS, 3:589–92.

27. RG 218, JCS Records, CCS 383.21 Korea (3-19-45), sec. 53, July 13, 1951, NA; RG 319, Korea 091 Army Ops., box 38A, July 5, 1951, NA; NSC 118/2, Dec. 20, 1951, NA.

28. For a useful discussion of these conflicting pressures see RG 84, 350 Korea, "Estimate of World-Wide Reactions to, and Consequences of, a Korean Armistice," an intelligence estimate prepared by Office of Intelligence Research (I.E. no. 24), box 1340, July 16, 1951, Moscow Files, Washington National Records Center.

29. D. Druckman discusses an idea similar to this in terms of dual responsiveness "where a negotiator monitors for movement on the opposing side and for evidence of preferences on one's own side": "Boundary Role Conflict: Negotiation as Dual Responsiveness," in I. W. Zartman, ed., *The Negotiation Process: Theories and Applications* (Beverly Hills, Calif.: Sage, 1978). Leon Sigal in *Fighting to a Finish: The Politics of War Termination in the United States and Japan, 1945* (Ithaca, N.Y.: Cornell University Press, 1988), p. 285, also notes that war termination requires agreement within governments, among allies, as well as between opponents.

30. Truman Papers, PSF, Longhand Notes Files, Jan. 27, May 18, 1952, box 333, HSTL.

31. Deborah Welch Larson, *Origins of Containment: A Psychological Explanation* (Princeton, N.J.: Princeton University Press, 1985), pp. 144–47; William A. Williams, *Empire as a Way of Life* (New York: Oxford University Press, 1980), p. 182.

32. Gaddis Smith, *Dean Acheson* (New York: Cooper Square, 1972), p. 161; MacDonald, *Korea*, p. 24; Larson, *Origins of Containment*, p. 306.

33. Ole Holsti, "The 'Operational Code' Approach to the Study of Political Leaders: John Foster Dulles' Philosophical and Instrumental Beliefs," *Canadian Journal of Political Science* 3 (March 1970). See also Richard J. Barnet, *Roots of War: The Men and Institutions behind U.S. Foreign Policy* (Harmondsworth: Penguin, 1971), p. 56; and Richard D. Challener, "The National Security Policy from Truman to Eisenhower," in

Norman A. Graebner, ed., *The National Security: Its Theory and Practice, 1945–1960* (New York: Oxford University Press, 1986), pp. 56–57. Both authors refer to Dulles's reluctance to negotiate.

34. For example, see Ungar, *Estrangement*, p. xi; Barnet, *Roots of War*, p. 25.

35. Colin S. Gray, "National Style in Strategy: The American Example," *International Security* 6 (Fall 1981): 24.

36. For a fuller discussion of these arguments, see (e.g.) Donald J. Devine, *The Political Culture of the United States* (Boston: Little Brown, 1972); Hunt, *Ideology and U.S. Foreign Policy*; Christopher Thorne, *American Political Culture and the Asian Frontier, 1943–1973* (London: The British Academy Sarah Tryphena Phillips Lecture, 1988).

37. Alexander George, David K. Hall, and William E. Simons, *The Limits of Coercive Diplomacy* (Boston: Little Brown, 1971), p. 1.

38. Kaufman, *Korean War*, p. 261; *Congressional Record*, 82d Cong., 2d sess., 98, May 15, 1952, p. A3007.

39. Lucian Pye, *Chinese Commercial Negotiating Style* (Cambridge, Mass.: Oelgeschlager, Gunn & Hain, 1982), p. 74. Perhaps, though, this approach to negotiation owes more to Asian cultural characteristics since there are similarities here with Japanese bargaining techniques. The Japanese, too, have tended to portray their objectives as "just, proper, or fair" in the belief that the other side would submit in recognition of the rectitude of Tokyo's position. See Michael Blaker, *Japanese International Negotiating Style* (New York: Columbia University Press, 1977), chap. 1, passim.

40. For a useful discussion of the pragmatic elements in Chinese Communist party foreign policy, see James Reardon-Anderson, *Yenan and the Great Powers* (New York: Columbia University Press, 1980).

41. These attributes, discovered in relation to the Korean armistice negotiations, are also seen to be more generally descriptive of U.S. and Chinese bargaining methods. See, for example, Fred Iklé, *How Nations Negotiate* (New York: Harper & Row, 1964); Pye, *Chinese Commercial Negotiating Style*; Kenneth Young, *Negotiating with the Chinese Communists: The United States Experience, 1953–1967* (New York: McGraw-Hill, 1968); Kinhide Mushakoji, "The Strategies of Negotiation: An American-Japanese Comparison," in J. A. LaPonce and Paul Smoker, eds., *Experimentation and Simulation in Political Science* (Toronto: University of Toronto Press, 1972); Alfred Donovan Wilhelm, Jr., "Sino-American Negotiations: The Chinese Approach," Ph.D. diss., University of Kansas, 1986.

42. Walter C. Hermes, *Truce Tent and Fighting Front* (Washington, D.C.: Government Printing Office, 1966), p. 26; Burchett, *At the Barricades*, p. 161; *Foreign Relations, 1951*, 7:629, July 6.

43. Arthur Lall, *How Communist China Negotiates* (New York: Columbia University Press, 1968), p. 6; Wu Hsiu-chuan, *Eight Years in the Ministry*, p. 74.

CHAPTER 2

1. *Foreign Relations 1950*, 7:312–13, July 6, 1950; 7:329–31, July 7; Michael L. Dockrill, "The Foreign Office, Anglo-American Relations and the Korean War, June 1950–June 1951," *International Affairs* (London) 62 (1986): 461.

2. *Foreign Relations, 1950*, 7:340, July 10; William Whitney Stueck, Jr., *The Road to Confrontation: American Policy toward China and Korea, 1947–1950* (Chapel Hill: University of North Carolina Press, 1981), pp. 199–200.

3. *Foreign Relations*, 1950, 7:372–73, July 13; 7:401, July 16.

4. RG 59, PPS Records, box 23, July 7, 1950, NA.

5. *Foreign Relations*, 1950, 7:348, July 10.

6. Burton I. Kaufman, *The Korean War: Challenges in Crisis, Credibility and Command* (Philadelphia: Temple University Press, 1986), p. 56.

7. George F. Kennan, *Memoirs, 1925–1950*, vol. 1 (Boston: Little, Brown, 1967), pp. 691–92.

8. *Foreign Relations*, 1950, 7:556, Aug. 11; 7:586–87, Aug. 15.

9. Ibid., 1950, 7:556, Aug. 11.

10. For a longer discussion of the bureaucratic debate on crossing the parallel, see Rosemary Foot, *The Wrong War: American Policy and the Dimensions of the Korean Conflict, 1950–1953* (Ithaca, N.Y.: Cornell University Press, 1985), pp. 70–74.

11. James T. Patterson, *Mr Republican: A Biography of Robert A. Taft* (Boston: Houghton Mifflin, 1972), p. 455.

12. Matthew J. Connelly Papers, Sept. 29, 1950, HSTL. (In this case, as with a number of other similar materials, the quotation attributed to Acheson relies on the accuracy of the note taker, in this instance, on Connelly.)

13. *Foreign Relations*, 1950, 7:831, Sept. 30; 7:883–84, Oct. 5; 7:838, Oct. 2; 7:878, Oct. 5; Gavan McCormack, *Cold War, Hot War: An Australian Perspective on the Korean War* (Sydney: Hale & Iremonger, 1983), p. 111.

14. Stueck, *Road to Confrontation*, p. 208; Foot, *Wrong War*, p. 79. For a discussion of the debate in Peking over intervention, see the memoirs of generals Peng Te-huai [Peng Dehuai], *Memoirs of a Chinese Marshal: The Autobiographical Notes of Peng Dehuai* (Peking: Foreign Languages Press, 1984), and Nie Jung-chen [Nie Rongzhen], *Huiyi Lu (Memoirs)* (Peking: PLA Publishers, 1984), chap. 23.

15. Foot, *Wrong War*, pp. 78–85.

16. *Foreign Relations*, 1950, 7:1108–9, Nov. 9; RG 319, Records of the Army Staff, G3 091 Korea TS, Nov. 20, box 36A, NA.

17. Harry S. Truman, *Memoirs*, vol. 2: *Years of Trial and Hope, 1946–1952* (Garden City, N.Y.: Doubleday, 1956), p. 432; *Foreign Relations*, 1950, 7:1182, Nov. 17; 7:1196, Nov. 20; 7:1206–1207, Nov. 21.

18. *Foreign Relations*, 1950, 7:1229, Nov. 24; Peter Farrar, "Britain's Proposal for a Buffer Zone South of the Yalu in November 1950: Was It a Neglected Opportunity to End the Fighting in Korea?" *Journal of Contemporary History* 18 (1983): esp. 344–45. Farrar has concluded that the British plan for a zone was initiated about six weeks too late for it to have had any chance of succeeding. See "A Pause for Peace Negotiations: The British Buffer Zone Plan of November 1950," in James Cotton and Ian Neary, eds., *The Korean War in History* (Manchester: Manchester University Press, 1989), esp. p. 77. Dockrill, "The Foreign Office," pp. 463–64.

19. *Foreign Relations*, 1950, 7:1197, Nov. 20.

20. Ibid., 1950, 7:1365, Dec. 4. For discussion of the Truman-Attlee summit, see Roger Dingman, "Truman, Attlee and the Korean War Crisis," in *The East Asian Crisis, 1945–1951*, *International Studies* (International Centre for Economics and Related Disciplines, London School of Economics), 1982/1; Dockrill, "The Foreign Office," p. 465; Rosemary Foot, "Anglo-American Relations in the Korean Crisis: The British Effort to Avert an Expanded War, December 1950–January 1951," *Diplomatic History* 10, no. 1 (1986). Excerpts from Truman's diary are in Robert Ferrell, ed., *Off the Record: The Private Papers of Harry S. Truman* (New York: Harper & Row, 1980), see p. 203.

21. *Foreign Relations*, 1950, 7:1524–25, Dec. 12.

22. For further details on the Chinese visit to the United Nations, see the memoirs of General Wu Hsiu-chuan (Wu Xiuquan), *Eight Years in the Ministry of Foreign Affairs* (Peking: New World Press, 1985), esp. chap. 2. *Foreign Relations*, 1951, 7:64, Jan. 11.

23. *Foreign Relations*, 1951, 7:91–92, Jan. 17; 7:117, Jan. 22; 7:130, Jan. 25. The text of Chou's reply is in RG 59, Records of the Director of the Office of North East Asian Affairs, U. Alexis Johnson, box 4, Jan. 22, 1951, NA.

24. Acheson Papers, Dec. 1, 1950, HSTL; Selected Records of the Department of State and Department of Defense, box 9, Dec. 3, 1950, HSTL.

25. *Foreign Relations*, 1950, 7:1383, Dec. 5; 7:1348, Dec. 4; James F. Schnabel, *Policy and Direction: The First Year* (Washington, D.C.: Government Printing Office, 1972), pp. 290–91.

26. NSC 95, Dec. 12, 1950, NA.

27. Dean Acheson, *Present at the Creation: My Years in the State Department* (New York: Norton, 1969), p. 513; Kaufman, *Korean War*, p. 132; *Foreign Relations*, 1950, 7:1541, Dec. 13.

28. *Foreign Relations*, 1951, 7, part 2: 1476–1716, passim, esp. Jan. 1951, pp. 1479–80; 7:1561, Feb. 5.

29. Ibid., 1951, 7:98, Jan. 18.

30. Ibid., 1951, 7:153, Feb. 2. As we now know, Chinese losses were considerable in that campaign. U.N. air superiority, supply problems, and the cold weather took their toll. Some 45,000 men, for example, are believed to have frozen to death in the unsuccessful attempt to block an American retreat from the east coast. See Jurgen Domes, *Peng Te-huai: The Man and the Image* (Stanford, Calif.: Stanford University Press, 1985), p. 62.

31. *Foreign Relations*, 1951, 7:177, Feb. 13; 7:233, March 15; 7:247, March 19.

32. Ibid., 1951, 7:254, March 21; *New York Times*, March 25, 1951. The Athenians stated to the Melians: "You, by giving in, would save yourself from disaster . . . your actual resources are too scanty to give you a chance of survival against the forces that are opposed to you at this moment." Thucydides, *History of the Peloponnesian War* (London: Penguin Books, 1972), Book V, pp. 402 and 406. MacArthur's statement is also in RG 59, PPS Records, 1947–53, box 20, March 25, 1951, NA.

33. John Lewis Gaddis, *The Long Peace: Inquiries into the History of the Cold War* (New York, Oxford University Press, 1987), p. 171. *Foreign Relations*, 1951, 7:448, May 23; *Department of State Bulletin*, May 28, 1951, pp. 843–48; Callum A. MacDonald, *Korea: The War before Vietnam* (London: Macmillan, 1986), p. 103. *Foreign Relations*, 1951, 7:1661–1662, May 9.

34. *Foreign Relations*, 1951, 7:243, March 17; 7:304–305, April 5; Michael Hunt, *Ideology and US Foreign Policy* (New Haven: Yale University Press, 1987), pp. 163–64.

35. Kaufman, *Korean War*, p. 185; Peng Te-huai, *Memoirs of a Chinese Marshal*, p. 480; Nie Jung-chen, *Huiyi Lu (Memoirs)*, pp. 741–42; *Foreign Relations*, 1951, 7:484, May 31; 7:507–511, June 5.

36. *Foreign Relations*, 1951, 7:560, June 27.

37. FO 371/92785, June 28, 1951, PRO.

38. *BBC Monitoring Reports, Summary of World Broadcasts*, Part 5: Far East, nos. 115 and 116, June 23–29, 1951, and June 30–July 6, 1951; Robert Simmons, *The Strained Alliance: Peking, Pyongyang, Moscow and the Politics of the Korean Civil War* (New York: Free Press, 1975), p. 199.

39. William H. Vatcher, Jr., *Panmunjom: The Story of the Korean Military Armistice Negotiations* (New York: Praeger, 1958), p. 24; *Foreign Relations*, 1951, 7:606, June 30.

40. Kaufman, *Korean War*, p. 202.

41. RG 59, PPS Records, Marshall to Nitze, Feb. 12, 1951, NA.

42. Kaufman, *Korean War*, pp. 185–86; MacDonald, *Korea*, pp. 114–15.

43. *Foreign Relations*, 1951, 7:598–600, June 30.

44. Gerald Segal, *Defending China* (London: Macmillan, 1986), p. 97.

45. Nikita Khrushchev, *Khrushchev Remembers* (Boston: Little, Brown, 1970), pp. 367–69. But see, too, in connection with this, the review of *Khrushchev Remembers* by John Merrill, *Journal of Korean Studies* 3 (1981).

1. *Foreign Relations*, 1951, 7:587, June 29; 7:609, July 2.

2. RG 218, JCS Records, CCS 383.21 Korea (3-19-45), sec. 51, July 2, NA.

3. *Foreign Relations*, 1951, 7:617, July 3.

4. *BBC Monitoring Reports, Summary of World Broadcasts*, Part 5: Far East, no. 116, July 2, 1951.

5. I. William Zartman and Maureen R. Berman, *The Practical Negotiator* (New Haven: Yale University Press, 1982).

6. *Foreign Relations*, 1951, 7:683, July 15.

7. *World Broadcasts*, no. 116, July 10, 1951.

8. *Foreign Relations*, 1951, 7:652–53, July 10.

9. RG 59, Records of the Bureau of Far Eastern Affairs, "Black Book on Ceasefire," lot 55D 128, box 1, July 10, 1951, NA. (Hereafter, RG 59, "Black Book on Ceasefire.")

10. *World Broadcasts*, no. 122, Aug. 11, 1951; Alfred Donovan Wilhelm, Jr., "Sino-American Negotiations: The Chinese Approach," Ph.D. diss., University of Kansas, 1986, p. 145.

11. U.S. Congress, Senate, *Military Situation in the Far East*, Hearings before the Committee on Armed Services and the Committee on Foreign Relations, 82d Cong., 1st sess. (Washington, D.C.: Government Printing Office, 1951; rpt. Arno Press, 1979), 3:1782–83, 1:454; Bevin Alexander, *Korea: The First War We Lost* (New York: Hippocrene Books, 1986), p. 426.

12. *Military Situation*, 3:2126.

13. *Foreign Relations*, 1951, 7:652, July 10. After an initial confusion regarding the definition of "foreign troops," General Nam returned to this point and said "by foreign troops we mean those troops not Korean, not in Korean armies."

14. RG 59, PPS Records 1947–53, Nitze, "Considerations with respect to the location of the Demilitarized Zone," Aug. 2, 1951, box 20, Korea, NA; ibid., Davies, "Kansas Line versus 38 Parallel," Aug. 3 1951, NA.

15. *World Broadcasts*, no. 120, July 29, 1951.

16. *Foreign Relations*, 1951, 7:735–37, July 26; 7:739–45, July 27, esp. p. 743.

17. Herbert Goldhamer, "The Korean Armistice Conference," RAND study, Dec. 1951, p. 114, p. 125; *Foreign Relations*, 1951, 7:748–49, 753, July 28.

18. *Foreign Relations*, 1951, 7:777, Aug. 3; 7:807, Aug. 11.

19. RG 59, Korean Situation File—H. Freeman Matthews, lots 53D 413, 55D 107, Aug. 17, 1951, NA; *Foreign Relations*, 1951, 7:830, Aug. 17; 7:845, Aug. 20. Note, however, the cautious way in which Admiral Joy responded to these developments. Unlike Ridgway in his message to the joint chiefs, Joy expressed doubts that this represented a serious proposal. Allen E. Goodman, ed., *Negotiating While Fighting:*

The Diary of Admiral C. Turner Joy at the Korean Armistice Conference (Stanford, Calif.: Hoover Institution Press, 1978), Aug. 20, 1951, p. 32.

20. RG 59, "Black Book on Ceasefire," July 24, 1951, NA.

21. *Foreign Relations*, 1951, 7:850, Aug. 23.

22. Goodman, ed., *Joy Diary*, p. 34; RG 59, Korean Situation File, Aug. 23, 1951, NA.

23. DDRS, no. 2467 (1987), Daily Korean Bulletin, Aug. 20, 1951 (President's Secretary's Files, Harry S. Truman Library).

24. FO 371/92792, Aug. 28, 1951, PRO.

25. RG 59, Korean Situation File—H. Freeman Matthews, Aug. 28, 1951, NA.

26. *World Broadcasts*, nos. 124 and 125, Sept. 1, 1951.

27. RG 59, "Black Book on Ceasefire," Aug. 23 and 24, 1951, NA.

28. *Foreign Relations*, 1951, 7:923–24, Sept. 20; FO 371/92793, Sept. 12, 1951, PRO.

29. FO 371/92795, Sept. 29, 1951, PRO.

30. Rosemary Foot, *The Wrong War: American Policy and the Dimensions of the Korean Conflict, 1950–1953* (Ithaca, N.Y.: Cornell University Press, 1985), p. 151.

31. RG 330, Secretary of Defense, "Memo for the Secretary," box 233, Oct. 10, 1951, NA. Bohlen also gave an oral briefing to the 104th meeting of the NSC. See the minutes of this in Truman Papers, PSF, Oct. 11, 1951, HSTL.

32. Goodman, ed., *Joy Diary*, Sept. 30, 1951, pp. 51–52. On the other hand, Goldhamer, in "The Korean Armistice Conference," claims that the visit put pressure on the delegation to "get results" (pp. 168–69).

33. *Foreign Relations*, 1951, 7:846, Aug. 21.

34. Ibid., 7:1065, Oct. 26; 7:1072, Oct. 28; 7:1076, Oct. 31; FO 371/92796, Nov. 6, 1951, PRO.

35. Goldhamer, "Korean Armistice Conference," p. 200.

36. *Foreign Relations*, 1951, 7:1117, Nov. 11.

37. Ibid., 7:1147, Nov. 17.

38. Goldhamer, "Korean Armistice Conference," pp. 122–24, 140–41.

39. Ibid., p. 249.

40. Matthew J. Connelly Papers, July 6 and 13, 1951, HSTL.

41. *Foreign Relations*, 1951, 7:682, July 15; 7:711–13, July 20; 7:714–18, July 23 and 21.

42. RG 59, "Black Book on Ceasefire," Aug. 6, 1951, NA; *Foreign Relations*, 1951, 7:787–88, Aug. 7.

43. *Foreign Relations*, 7:790, Aug. 7, n. 2.

44. Ibid., 7:882, Sept. 5; 7:923, Sept. 20; 7:928, Sept. 21; 7:931, Sept. 22. Ridgway was sufficiently upset by this admonishment that he sent an "eyes only" telegram to Collins expressing his "inner feelings" about the teleconference: "You know beyond any shadow of doubt the completeness of my efforts to comply with instructions," he told the army chief of staff, but in his view those instructions had "the clear pattern of a consistent search for measures whereby, in one form or another, we accede to Communists' demands." J. Lawton Collins Papers, box 17, Sept. 26, 1951, DDEL.

45. *Foreign Relations*, 1951, 7:956, Sept. 26.

46. Ibid., 1951, 7:810–12, Aug. 11.

47. Ibid., 1951, 7:934, Sept. 24; 7:960, Sept. 26. Additional comments on Ridgway's inability to compromise or be flexible are contained in Clay Blair, *The Forgotten War: America in Korea, 1950–1953* (New York: Times Books, 1987), p. 938.

48. *Foreign Relations*, 1951, 7:957, Sept. 26; RG 330, "Memorandum for the Secretary," Oct. 4, 1951, box 233, NA.

49. *Foreign Relations*, 1951, 7:1074, Oct. 30.

50. Sir William Strang, permanent under secretary at the British foreign office, had also suggested the device of a time limit "within which remaining items on armistice talks agenda must be settled." Sir Esler Dening, the British political representative in Tokyo, believed that the proposal to leave the demarcation line to the end of the talks was a new demand by the U.N. Command and one that had not been thought through. FO 371/92796 and 92797, Nov. 9, 1951, PRO.

51. *Foreign Relations*, 1951, 7:1123, Nov. 12.

52. Ibid., 7:1126, Nov. 13; 7:1129–30, Nov. 13.

53. Ibid., 7:1131, Nov. 14; 7:1147, Nov. 17.

54. Quoted in Walter C. Hermes, *Truce Tent and Fighting Front* (Washington, D.C.: Government Printing Office, 1966), p. 506.

55. *Foreign Relations*, 1951, 7:606–607, June 30.

56. Ibid., 7:707, July 20.

57. RG 59, PPS Records, J. P. Davies, "Kansas Line versus 38 Parallel," Aug. 3, 1951, box 20, NA.

58. *Foreign Relations*, 1951, 7:774–76, Aug. 3.

59. Ibid., 7:928, n. 1, Sept. 20; Goodman, ed., *Joy Diary*, p. 68.

60. *Congressional Record*, 1951, 82d Cong., 1st sess., 97, pp. A4357, A 4361, A 4369; RG 59, 795.00 Korea, box 4274, July 10, 1951, NA; R. Caridi, *The Korean War and American Politics: The Republican Party as a Case Study* (Philadelphia: University of Pennsylvania Press, 1968), p. 191.

61. *Congressional Record*, 82d Cong., 1st sess., 97, 1951, p. 12300, Sept. 28; pp. 12537–40, Oct. 3.

62. Hermes, *Truce Tent*, p. 33; *Foreign Relations*, 1951, 7:718–19, July 21; 7:730–31, July 25; History of the JCS, 3:625.

63. Callum MacDonald, *Korea: The War before Vietnam* (London: Macmillan, 1986), p. 119, pp. 124–25; Hermes, *Truce Tent*, p. 507; J. Lawton Collins, *War in Peacetime: The History and Lessons of Korea* (Boston: Houghton Mifflin, 1969), p. 323.

64. Hermes, *Truce Tent*, p. 507; William H. Vatcher, Jr., *Panmunjom: The Story of the Korean Military Armistice Negotiations* (New York: Praeger, 1958), p. 73; Matthew B. Ridgway, *The Korean War* (Garden City, N.Y.: Doubleday, 1967), p. 190; DDRS (1977), no. 3B, "Intelligence Report: Asian Communist Employment of Negotiations as a Political Tactic," Nov. 1966, p. 25. But note Gen. J. Lawton Collins's negative remarks about the Van Fleet operation in *War in Peacetime*, p. 323.

65. Alexander L. George, David K. Hall, and William E. Simons, eds., *The Limits of Coercive Diplomacy: Laos, Cuba, Vietnam* (Boston: Little Brown, 1971), chap. 1; Wallace J. Thies, *When Governments Collide: Coercion and Diplomacy in the Vietnam Conflict, 1964–68* (Berkeley: University of California Press, 1980).

66. Bevin Alexander, *Korea: The First War We Lost*, pp. 440–47; Blair, *The Forgotten War*, pp. 947–50.

67. NSC 48/5, May 17, 1951, NA.

68. See, for example, FO 371/92793, Sept. 7, 1951, and 92795, Nov. 9, 1951, PRO.

69. Shiv Dayal, *India's Role in the Korean Question* (Delhi: Chand, 1959), p. 143; Burton I. Kaufman, *The Korean War: Challenges in Crisis, Credibility, and Command* (Philadelphia: Temple University Press, 1986), p. 212.

70. *Foreign Relations*, 1951, 7:716, July 21; 7:993, Oct. 4.

71. Ibid., 7:768, Aug. 1; RG 59, 795.00 Korea, box 4275, Sept. 26, NA; Kaufman, *Korean War*, p. 209.

72. *Foreign Relations*, 1951, 7:1105, Nov. 9; 7:1120–22, Nov. 12.

73. RG 59, PPS Records, "Meeting of the US–UK Foreign Ministers, Washington D.C.," box 20, Sept. 10, 1951, NA; Foot, *Wrong War*, p. 169.

74. James Aronson, *The Press and the Cold War* (Indianapolis, Ind.: Bobbs-Merrill, 1970), pp. 114–15; *Time Magazine*, July 23 and Aug. 20, 1951; Goodman, ed., *Joy Diary*, Oct. 31, 1951, p. 68; Kaufman, *Korean War*, p. 211; Gavan McCormack, *Cold War, Hot War: An Australian Perspective on the Korean War* (Sydney: Hale & Iremonger, 1983), p. 143; *Foreign Relations*, 1951, 7:1093, Nov. 6.

75. *Foreign Relations*, 1951, 7:714–15, July 23.

76. Ibid., 7:917–19, Sept. 17.

77. Ibid., 7:939–44, Sept. 25; 7:955–62, esp. p. 957, Sept. 26; Bohlen papers, Memorandum (undated), box 5, NA.

78. Robert Jervis, *Perception and Misperception in International Politics* (Princeton, N.J.: Princeton University Press, 1976), p. 82.

79. *Foreign Relations*, 1951, 7:955–62, Sept. 26.

80. Goldhamer, "The Korean Armistice Conference," p. 263.

81. Goodman, ed., *Joy Diary*, Aug. 17, 1951, p. 29; *Foreign Relations*, 1951, 7:673–74, July 13; 7:1013–14, Oct. 10.

82. *Foreign Relations*, 1951, 7:847, Aug. 22; 7:1099, Nov. 8.

83. Mao Tse-tung, "Great Victories in Three Mass Movements," *Selected Works* (Peking: Foreign Languages Press, 1977), 5:60–61.

84. FO 371/92797, Nov. 19, 1951, and 92798, Nov. 27, 1951, PRO.

85. Alexander George, *The Chinese Communist Army in Action: The Korean War and Its Aftermath* (New York: Columbia University Press, 1967); John Gittings, *The Role of the Chinese Army* (London: Oxford University Press, 1967), pp. 119–24.

86. *World Broadcasts*, no. 120, July 29, 1951; *Foreign Relations*, 1951, 7:1158, Nov. 21.

CHAPTER 4

1. *Foreign Relations*, 1951, 7:1243, Dec. 5; 7:1380, Dec. 19; 7:1435, Dec. 24 and nn; RG 59, "Black Book on Ceasefire," box 3, Jan. 21 1952, NA.

2. *Christian Science Monitor*, Feb. 6, 1952; *New York Times*, Feb. 8; *New York Herald Tribune*, Feb. 10; J. Lawton Collins, *War in Peacetime: The History and Lessons of Korea* (Boston: Houghton Mifflin, 1969), pp. 338–39; History of the JCS, 3:719; V. K. Wellington Koo Papers and Diaries, box 147, Butler Library, Columbia University, New York.

3. Nam Il's reaction to inspection is noted in *Foreign Relations*, 1951, 7:697, July 18; 7:617, July 3; Burton I. Kaufman, *The Korean War: Challenges in Crisis, Credibility, and Command* (Philadelphia: Temple University Press, 1986), p. 233.

4. *Foreign Relations*, 1950, 7:1519, Dec. 11; 1951, 7:599, June 30, 1951.

5. Ibid., 1951, 7:998, Oct. 4.

6. FO 371/92795, Oct. 9, 1951, PRO.

7. *Foreign Relations*, 1951, 7:999, n., Oct. 23; 7:1081–85, Nov. 2; RG 59, 795.00 Korea, box 4276, Nov. 2, 1951.

8. RG 59, 795.00 Korea, box 4276, Nov. 16, 1951.

9. *Foreign Relations*, 1951, 7:1176, Nov. 24.

10. RG 59, State-JCS Meeting, 795.00 Korea, box 4276, Nov. 26, 1951.

11. *Foreign Relations*, 1951, 7:1186, Nov. 26.

12. Ibid., 7:1156–58, Nov. 21; 7:1189–93, Nov. 28; FO 371/99598, Dec. 11, 1951, PRO.

13. FO 371/92759, C.O.S. Committee, Minutes, Nov. 30, 1951, PRO; *Foreign Relations*, 1951, 7:1221–23, Dec. 3; 7:1331–32, Dec. 14.

14. FO 371/99564, Dec. 17, 1951, PRO; Acheson Papers, Memorandum of Conversation, Jan. 7, 1952, HSTL; Truman Papers, PSF, Truman-Churchill Talks, Jan. 9, 1952, HSTL.

15. *Foreign Relations*, 1951, 7:1254–57, Dec. 6; 7:1410–12, Dec. 21; 7:1415–17, Dec. 12; 7:1458–60, Dec. 28; 1952–54, 15:4, Jan. 3, 1952.

16. Truman Papers, PSF, General, Dec. 10, 1951, HSTL; *Foreign Relations*, 1951, 7:1281, n. 2, Dec. 8.

17. *Foreign Relations*, 1952–54, 15:11, Jan. 7, 1952; 15:17, Jan. 12, 1952; 1951, 7:1372, Dec. 18; 7:1377–81, Dec. 19.

18. Ibid., 7:1187–88, Nov. 27; 7:1194–95, Nov. 28; 7:1202, Nov. 29.

19. *World Broadcasts*, no. 138, Dec. 1, 1951.

20. Walter C. Hermes, *Truce Tent and Fighting Front* (Washington, D.C.: Government Printing Office, 1966), p. 125; *Foreign Relations*, 1951, 7:1229–30, Dec. 3.

21. Hermes, *Truce Tent*, p. 126.

22. *Foreign Relations*, 1951, 7:1279, Dec. 8; 7:1320, Dec. 12; 7:1333, Dec. 14.

23. Ibid., 7:1381–82, Dec. 19; 7:1420–21, Dec. 22; Allen E. Goodman, ed., *Negotiating While Fighting: The Diary of Admiral C. Turner Joy at the Korean Armistice Conference* (Stanford, Calif.: Hoover Institution Press, 1978), p. 139, Dec. 19; RG 59, 795.00 Korea, box 4276, Jan. 2, 1952.

24. William H. Vatcher, Jr., *Panmunjom: The Story of the Korean Military Armistice Negotiations* (New York: Praeger, 1958), p. 103; RG 59, 795.00 Korea, box 4277, Feb. 1, 19, and 26, 1952. History of the JCS, 3:721ff.; *New York Times*, Dec. 24, 1951; *New York Herald Tribune*, Jan. 25, 1952; *New York Times*, Jan. 30 and 31; *Daily Worker*, Feb. 1, 1952; *New York Times*, Feb. 2, 1952; *Christian Science Monitor*, Feb. 4, 1952; *New York Times*, Feb. 12, 23, and 24, 1952.

25. *New York Times*, Feb. 16, 1952; RG 59, 795.00 Korea, box 4276, Feb. 16; *World Broadcasts*, no. 149, Feb. 16, 1952; *New York Times*, Feb. 25, 1952; RG 59, 795.00 Korea, box 4277, Feb. 26; RG 59, "Black Book on Ceasefire," box 4, Feb. 22, March 5; box 5, April 4, NA. *Foreign Relations*, 1952–54, 15:111, n. 5, March 20, 1952; 15:83, March 12.

26. *Foreign Relations*, 1951, 7:600, June 30; RG 59, 795.00 Korea, box 4274, July 3, 1951, NA; *Foreign Relations*, 1951, 7:622, July 4.

27. RG 319, Army Ops, General Decimal Files, G3 383.6 TS, box 174, July 5, July 31, and Aug. 27, 1951, NA.

28. *Foreign Relations*, 7:857–59, Aug. 27; RG 59, 693.00 China, box 3003, Aug. 27, NA; Mark R. Elliott, *Pawns of Yalta: Soviet Refugees and America's Role in Their Repatriation* (Urbana: University of Illinois Press, 1982), p. 107 and chap. 5, passim. Truman may have been more influenced than Acheson appeared to be by the experiences of 1945 and 1946. Then, he had presided over an administration that had gradually shifted away from the earlier U.S. policy of forced repatriation of Soviet refugees, a shift that had come about as a result of the appalling consequences of trying to enforce the repatriation agreements signed at Yalta in February 1945. Ibid. The drawing up of the Geneva Convention in 1949 is discussed in J. A. C. Gutteridge, "The Repatriation of Prisoners of War," *International and Comparative Law Quarterly* 2 (1953). See also Allan Rosas, *The Legal Status of Prisoners of War: A Study in International Humanitarian Law Application in Armed Conflicts* (Helsinki: Suomalainen Tiedeakatemic, 1976), p. 482.

29. Robert H. Ferrell, ed., *Off the Record: The Private Papers of Harry S. Truman* (New York: Harper & Row, 1980), pp. 250–51.

30. RG 59, PPS Records, James Webb, "Meeting with the President, Monday, October 29, 1951, Korean Negotiations," NA; Deborah Welch Larson, *Origins of Containment: A Psychological Explanation* (Princeton, N.J.: Princeton University Press, 1985), pp. 146–47. Consider, too, the remark in Henry Wallace's diary: "Everything [Truman] said was decisive. It almost seemed as though he was eager to decide in advance of thinking." Quoted in Leon Sigal, *Fighting to a Finish: The Politics of War Termination in the United States and Japan, 1945* (Ithaca, N.Y.: Cornell University Press, 1988), p. 211.

31. *Foreign Relations*, 1951, 7:1244, n. 4, Dec. 5; 7:1277, Dec. 7.

32. Barton J. Bernstein, "The Struggle over the Korean Armistice: Prisoners of Repatriation?" in Bruce Cumings, ed., *Child of Conflict: The Korean-American Relationship, 1943–1953* (Seattle: University of Washington Press, 1983), pp. 278–79; DDRS (1986), no. 2343, Psychological Strategy Board, Dec. 28, 1951.

33. *Foreign Relations*, 1952–54, 15:40–43, Feb. 8, 1952.

34. RG 59, "Black Book on Ceasefire," box 3, Jan. 4 and Feb. 4, NA; *Foreign Relations*, 1952–54, 15:38, Feb. 2, 1952.

35. Bernstein, "The Struggle over the Korean Armistice," p. 280; *Foreign Relations*, 1952–54, 15:43–45, Feb. 8, 1952; Larson, *Origins*, p. 308.

36. RG 59, 795.00 Korea, box 4277, Feb. 27, 1952, NA. A useful discussion of the germ warfare campaign is contained in Callum MacDonald, *Korea: The War before Vietnam* (London: Macmillan, 1986), pp. 161–62.

37. FO 371/99631, Jan. 29, 1952, Feb. 13, March 25, PRO.

38. FO 371/99568, Feb. 1952, PRO. Nikolai Tolstoy, *Victims of Yalta* (London: Hodder and Stoughton, 1977), passim.

39. RG 59, 795.00 Korea, box 4277, Feb. 6, 1952, NA; Robert O'Neill, *Australia in the Korean War, 1950–1953*, vol. 1: *Strategy and Diplomacy* (Canberra: Australian War Memorial and Australian Government Publishing Service, 1981), p. 270; *Foreign Relations*, 1952–54, 15:68–69; Feb. 27, 1952; RG 59, 795.00 Korea, box 4278, Feb. 29 and March 12, 1952, NA.

40. *New York Times*, Nov. 24, 1951; RG 59, Office of Public Opinion Studies, box 39, March 3, 1952, NA; Bernstein, "The Struggle over the Korean Armistice," p. 283; *New York Times*, March 21, 1952.

41. RG 319, G3 383.6 TS, box 126, Feb. 19, 1952, NA; *Foreign Relations*, 1952–54, 15:58–59, Feb. 25, 1952; Goodman, ed., *Joy Diary*, p. 252, Feb. 14, 1952. The New Zealand government was told on Feb. 18 that the administration had reason to believe that only 10 percent of the Chinese would forcibly resist repatriation. RG 59, "Black Book on Ceasefire," box 4, Feb. 18, 1952, NA.

42. *Foreign Relations*, 1952–54, 15:92, March 17, 1952; 15:97, March 19.

43. *Foreign Relations*, 1952–54, 15:98–9, March 19. The points made in these reports concerning the fear in the camps and the brutal way in which the trustees ran them are explored in the following chapter.

44. The account of the State Department meeting with the joint chiefs at which U. Alexis Johnson performed such a crucial role is in *Foreign Relations*, 1952–54, 15:112–14, March 21, 1952; Goodman, ed., *Joy Diary*, April 1, 1952, p. 343.

45. *Foreign Relations*, 1951, 7:1306, Dec. 11; David P. Forsythe, *Humanitarian Politics: The International Committee of the Red Cross* (Baltimore: Johns Hopkins University Press, 1977), pp. 8–9 and 147.

46. *Foreign Relations*, 7:1311, Dec. 12; Goodman, ed., *Joy Diary*, Dec. 12, pp. 119–20; *Foreign Relations*, 1951, 7:1344, Dec. 15; 7:1374, Dec. 18; RG 59, 795.00 Korea, box 4276, Dec. 18.

47. *Foreign Relations*, 1951, 7:1422, Dec. 23. According to British records, the United States calculated the number of men missing in action in an expansive way. It added together those (1) missing believed killed, (2) missing believed taken prisoner, and (3) missing, whereas the United Kingdom used only (2) for its estimates. See FO 371/105583, April 9, 1953, PRO.

48. Goodman, ed., *Joy Diary*, Jan. 2, 1952, p. 178; *Foreign Relations*, 1952–54, 15:6, Jan. 3, 1952.

49. *World Broadcasts*, no. 143, Jan. 5, 1952; no. 145, Jan. 20–23 1952; no. 152, March 13, 1952; RG 59, 795.00 Korea, box 4277, Jan. 22, 1952, NA; Goodman, ed., *Joy Diary*, Jan. 24, 1952, p. 214.

50. RG 59, 795.00 Korea, box 4277, Jan. 18, 1952; box 4278, March 7, 1952; box 4277, Feb. 21, 1952; all at NA. *Foreign Relations*, 1952–54, 15:127, April 1, 1952. The Communists also referred to a dispatch from Koje-do dated March 14 from the Central News Agency of Taiwan that reported the tattooing and signing of petitions in blood. Quoted in Goodman, ed., *Joy Diary*, March 15, 1952, pp. 307–8.

51. *New York Times*, Jan. 28, 1952; Goodman, ed., *Joy Diary*, March 19, p. 314, and March 21, p. 319; *Foreign Relations* 1952–54, 15:108–9, March 20, 1952; RG 59, "Black Book on Ceasefire," box 4, March 21–24, NA.

52. Goodman, ed., *Joy Diary*, March 21, p. 319, April 1, p. 343; *Foreign Relations*, 1952–54, 15:136, editorial note; RG 59, "Black Book on Ceasefire," box 4, April 1–3, NA.

53. *Foreign Relations*, 1952–54, 15:151, April 14, 1952; Goodman, ed., *Joy Diary*, April 12, p. 354; Connelly Papers, April 25, 1952, HSTL; Bernstein, "The Struggle over the Korean Armistice," p. 284.

54. *Congressional Record*, 82d Cong., 2d sess., 98, April 24, 1952, pp. 4355–56; p. A2677, May 1; *Foreign Relations*, 1952–54, 15:172–73, April 26, 1952.

55. *Foreign Relations*, 1952–54, 15:171, April 26; FO 371/99632, April 23, 28, and 15, 1952; PREM 11, no. 116, April 15, 1952; *Times*, May 8, 1952.

56. I. William Zartman and Maureen R. Berman, *The Practical Negotiator* (New Haven: Yale University Press, 1982), p. 179.

57. *Foreign Relations*, 1952–54, 15:102–4 and 107, March 19, 1952; RG 59, 795.00 Korea, box 4278, March 13, 1952, NA; RG 330, CD 383.6, box 363, Feb. 11, 1952, NA. As on previous occasions, Ridgway was supported by Admiral Fechteler. *Foreign Relations*, 1952–54, 15:84, March 12, 1952.

58. *Foreign Relations*, 1952–54, 15:173–76, and 179–80, April 26; *Times*, May 2, 1952; RG 59, statement by the President, Press Release, May 7, 1952, NA.

59. Herbert Goldhamer, "The Korean Armistice Conference," RAND study, Dec. 1951, p. 271.

60. Admiral C. Turner Joy, *How Communists Negotiate* (New York: Macmillan, 1955), p. 129; Goldhamer, "The Korean Armistice Conference," p. 7. Burke is quoted in History of the JCS, 3:621; *New York Herald Tribune*, Dec. 2, 1951; Presidential News Conference in Key West, Florida, *Foreign Relations*, 1951, 7:1199–1200, editorial note, Nov. 29.

61. Hermes, *Truce Tent*, p. 507; History of the JCS, 3:610 and 622–25; Kaufman, *Korean War*, p. 220.

62. Peng Te-huai [Peng Dehuai], *Memoirs of a Chinese Marshal: The Autobiographical Notes of Peng Dehuai* (Peking: Foreign Languages Press, 1984), p. 482; Truman Papers, PSF, Memorandum for the President, Summary of discussion at 101st meeting of NSC, Aug. 30, 1951, HSTL; RG 330, Defense Records, box 233, Memorandum for the Secretary, Oct. 4, 1951, NA.

63. Hermes, *Truce Tent*, p. 192; Robert Jackson, *Air War over Korea* (London: Ian Allan, 1973), p. 102; Kaufman, *Korean War*, p. 222.

64. Zartman and Berman, *Practical Negotiator*, chap. 5.

65. Goodman, ed., *Joy Diary*, April 21, 1952, p. 375.

66. That the U.N. Command felt uneasy about having given out this figure of 116,000 to the Communists is indicated by the statement on April 25 of the general headquarters of the U.N. Command's public information office. According to this statement, "The UN Command, reluctant to guess at a figure and unwilling to arrive at one arbitrarily, reiterated to the Communists that only an actual screening of POWs and civilian internees could disclose the numbers to be ultimately turned over to Communist control." Mark W. Clark Papers, DDEL.

CHAPTER 5

1. RG 59, statement by the president, May 7, 1952, NA; David Carlton, *Anthony Eden: A Biography* (London: Allen & Unwin, 1986), p. 319.

2. RG 59, PPS Records, box 20, C. B. Marshall to Paul Nitze, Jan. 28, 1952, NA; RG 59 695A.0024, Dec. 1, 1952, NA; Allen E. Goodman, ed., *Negotiating While Fighting: The Diary of Admiral C. Turner Joy at the Korean Armistice Conference* (Stanford, Calif.: Hoover Institution Press, 1978), May 20, p. 429.

3. Samuel M. Meyers and Albert B. Biderman, eds., *Mass Behavior in Battle and Captivity: The Communist Soldier in the Korean War* (Chicago: University of Chicago Press, 1968), chap. 5. This authoritative study, which this chapter will draw on extensively, came out of a request from Army Command in the Far East, which wanted research to be undertaken on the motivations of the prisoners of war. Burton I. Kaufman, *The Korean War: Challenges in Crisis, Credibility, and Command* (Philadelphia: Temple University Press, 1986), p. 266; Callum A. MacDonald, *Korea: The War before Vietnam* (London: Macmillan, 1986), pp. 135–36; RG 59, 695A.0024, July 2, 1952, NA.

4. FO 371/99638, PRO; RG 59, 695A.0024, May 3, 1952, NA; MacDonald, *Korea*, p. 135; RG 319, Records of the Army Staff, G3 091 Korea, box 39, May 4, 1953, NA; RG 59, 695A.0024, July 2, 1952, NA.

5. Meyers and Biderman, *Mass Behavior*, pp. 256, 309.

6. Max Hastings, *The Korean War* (London: Michael Joseph, 1987), pp. 329–30; FO 371/99638, March 24, 1952, PRO; 99640, Sept. 15, 1952, PRO.

7. "The Handling of Prisoners of War during the Korean Conflict," prepared by the Military History Office, Office of the Assistant Chief of Staff, G3, HQ US Army, June 1960, box 626, p. 5, NA (hereafter cited as Center for Military History MS); Truman Papers, Naval Aide File, Selected Records Relating to the Korean War, box 11, File 42, May 12, 1952, HSTL; RG 319, Records of the Army Staff, G3 091 Korea, box 39, May 4, 1953, NA; James Cameron, *Point of Departure* (Stocksfield, Northumberland: Oriel Press, 1967), pp. 131–32; RG 59 695A.0024, July 2, 1952, NA.

8. RG 59, 695A.0024, July 2, 1952, NA; Alexander George, *The Chinese Communist Army in Action: The Korean War and Its Aftermath* (New York: Columbia University Press, 1967), pp. 9 and 83–85; Meyers and Biderman, *Mass Behavior*, pp. 77, 244–56; *Foreign Relations*, 1952–54, 15:98–99, March 14, 1952.

9. Meyers and Biderman, *Mass Behavior*, pp. 254, 311, 329.

10. MacDonald, *Korea*, p. 137; John J. Muccio Oral History, pp. 100–101, HSTL.

11. Meyers and Biderman, *Mass Behavior*, p. 262; RG 59, 695A.0024, Oct. 20, 1952, NA; RG 59, 693.95A0024, box 3005, July 7, 1952, NA.

12. Meyers and Biderman, *Mass Behavior*, pp. 211, 300–301, 287; General Mark Clark, *From the Danube to the Yalu* (New York: Harper & Row, 1954), pp. 58–70.

13. NSC 81/1, Sept. 9, 1950, in *Foreign Relations*, 1950, 7:718; Meyers and Biderman, *Mass Behavior*, pp. 219, 258–59; RG 59, 693.0024, China, box 3003, Aug. 19, 1951, NA; MacDonald, *Korea*, pp. 137–38; RG 59, Records of the Office of Chinese Affairs, box 22, March 19, 1951, NA.

14. Meyers and Biderman, *Mass Behavior*, p. 258; Kenneth K. Hansen, *Heroes Behind Barbed Wire* (Princeton, N.J.: Van Nostrand, 1957), p. 70; Center for Military History MS, "Handling of the POWs," pp. 102–7.

15. The ICRC recommendation is in RG 319, G3 383.6, box 309, May 12, 1952, NA. For the short period that Gen. Haydon Boatner was in charge of the camps, he stopped the program entirely, because he claimed that his Chinese interpreter from Taiwan was misrepresenting his statements and using his own highly inflammatory words. Haydon L. Boatner Papers, boxes 7 and 8, Hoover Institution, Stanford, Calif.

16. C. D. Jackson Records, box 4, "Psychological Operations Plan Incident to Korean Cease-fire Negotiations," Oct. 25, 1951, DDEL.

17. RG 319, G3 383.6, box 309, "Interim Report on Progress of Educational Program for POWs," Jan. 28, 1952, p. 23, NA; *Foreign Relations*, 1952–54, 15:98–99, March 14, 1952.

18. Goodman, ed., *Joy Diary*, April 12, 1952, p. 355.

19. RG 319, G3 383.6 TS, box 126, April 12, 1952, NA; *Foreign Relations*, 1952–54, 15:360, June 28, 1952; RG 59, 695A.0024, July 5, 1952, NA.

20. RG 319, Army Ops, Bulky Decimal Files, 383.6, box 408, Jan. 28, 1953, NA.

21. Ibid., box 309, "POW Activities in FECOM," NA; Meyers and Biderman, *Mass Behavior*, p. 296.

22. The ICRC report is in RG 59, 695A.0024, May 3, 1952, NA. See also ibid., 795.00 Korea, box 4277, Feb. 21, 1952, NA.

23. In February it had been left to General Van Fleet's discretion as to whether to give any "off the record" briefing to the press, though if he did, he was told to ensure the press realized that any "publicizing of this disturbance at this time might easily provide Communists with material for their propaganda machine." RG 59, "Black Book on Ceasefire," box 4, Feb. 20, 1952, NA.

24. Walter C. Hermes, *Truce Tent and Fighting Front* (Washington, D.C.: Government Printing Office, 1966), p. 252.

25. *New York Times*, March 15, 1952; Truman Papers, Naval Aide File (ICRC Report), Selected Records Relating to the Korean War, box 11, file 42, May 12, 1952, HSTL; Meyers and Biderman, *Mass Behavior*, p. 299. These authors add: "The fact that the Communists resisted frequently and deliberately should not obscure the fact that the anti-Communists were almost equally capable of creating serious trouble when and if they considered it necessary." They "repeatedly held noisy patriotic mass demonstrations with U.N. permission or in defiance of U.N. orders throughout the last year of the conflict." See p. 320 and note.

26. RG 59, 695A.0024, Oct. 20, 1952, NA.

27. Center for Military History MS, "Handling of Prisoners of War during the Korean Conflict," pp. 43–44, NA; ICRC report in RG 319, 091. Korea, box 39, May 4, 1953, NA.

28. U.K. Ministry of Defence, *Treatment of British Prisoners of War in Korea* (London: Her Majesty's Stationery Office, 1955); Capt. Anthony Farrar-Hockley, *The Edge of the Sword* (London: Frederick Muller, 1954); Francis Jones, *No Rice For Rebels: A Story of the Korean War* (London: Bodley, 1956), pp. 158ff. See also C. D. Jackson Records, box 5, Prisoner Exchange File, May 12, 1953, DDEL.

29. MacDonald, *Korea*, pp. 146–47; Edgar S. Schein, "The Chinese Indoctrination Program for Prisoners of War: A Study of Attempted 'Brainwashing,'" *Psychiatry* (1956): 149–72; Farrar-Hockley, *Edge of the Sword*, p. 95; William Lindsay White, *The Captives of Korea: An Unofficial White Paper on the Treatment of War Prisoners* (New York: Scribners, 1957), pp. 84, 88; Hastings, *Korean War*, p. 336.

30. MacDonald, *Korea*, p. 147; Schein, "Chinese Indoctrination," pp. 154–67; Virginia Pasley, *22 Stayed* (London: Allen, 1955), p. 24. Mail was also used as a weapon in order to make the prisoners feel even more alone and reliant on their guards. Many of the few letters allowed through contained only bad news. MacDonald, *Korea*, p. 151.

31. Defence Ministry, *Treatment of British Prisoners of War*.

32. H. H. Wubben, "American Prisoners of War in Korea: A Second Look at the 'Something New in History' Theme," *American Quarterly* 22 (Spring 1970): 7; State Department report of Defense views is dated Feb. 18, 1953 and quoted in MacDonald, *Korea*, p. 152.

33. Meyers and Biderman, *Mass Behavior*, p. 334; RG 59, Stelle to Nitze, PPS Records, box 20, "The POW Issue in the Armistice Negotiations," Jan. 24, 1952, NA; RG 59, 695A.0024, Feb. 2, 1952, NA; RG 59, 693.0024 China, box 3003, Aug. 19, 1951, NA.

34. *Foreign Relations*, 1952–54, 15:98–99, March 19, 1952; 15:141–42, April 7, 1952; U. Alexis Johnson, *The Right Hand of Power* (Englewood Cliffs, N.J.: Prentice Hall, 1984), p. 148; RG 319, 091 Korea TS, box 18, March 19, 1952, NA; *Foreign Relations*, 1952–54, 15:105, March 20, 1952.

35. Goodman, ed., *Joy Diary*, p. 355.

36. RG 59, 695A.0024, May 20, 1952, NA.

37. C. D. Jackson Records, box 1, "National Operations Plan to Exploit Communist Bacteriological Warfare Hoax, Mistreatment of POWs, and other Atrocities . . . ," Oct. 13, 1953; box 4, Dept. of State InfoGuide Bulletin 411, July 24, 1953; White House Office, National Security Council Staff, OCB Central Files, box 117, Oct. 30, 1953; White House Office, Office of the Special Assistant for National Security, Status of Projects Subseries, "Status of U.S. National Security Program on June 30 1953"—all at DDEL.

38. MacDonald, *Korea*, p. 145; RG 59, 695A.0024, July 2, 1952, NA.

39. Hansen, *Heroes behind Barbed Wire*, p. 1; RG 59, Dulles speech before the American Legion, Saint Louis, Sept. 2, 1953, Dept. of State Press Release no. 469, Sept. 1, 1953, NA; RG 59, 695A.0024, Dec. 1, 1952, NA.

40. Boatner is quoted in Barton J. Bernstein, "The Struggle over the Korean Armistice: Prisoners of Repatriation?" in Bruce Cumings, ed., *Child of Conflict: The Korean-American Relationship, 1943–1953* (Seattle: University of Washington Press, 1983), p. 286.

CHAPTER 6

1. Dean Acheson Papers, memorandum of conversation, box 67, April 3, 1952, HSTL; RG 84, 350 USSR, Intelligence Report, no. 5751.2, "The USSR in 1951," March 14, 1952, Foreign Service Posts, Moscow, Washington National Records Center.

2. *Time* magazine, June 2, 1952, p. 23.

3. *New York Times*, June 10, 1952; Burton I. Kaufman, *The Korean War: Challenges in Crisis, Credibility, and Command* (Philadelphia: Temple University Press, 1986), p. 268; *Foreign Relations* 1952–54, 15:371–72, July 2, 1952; 15:402, July 11; 15:413, July 13.

4. *Foreign Relations*, 1952–54, 15:188–89, May 2, 1952; RG 59, 795.00 Korea, box 4279, May 13, 1952, NA; *Foreign Relations*, 1952–54, 15:198, May 14, 1952; RG 59, PPS Records, box 20, "Future Courses of Action on the POW issue," June 11, 1952, NA; RG 59, PPS Records, box 20, "Discussion of NSC 118/2 by Policy Planning Staff," May 28, 1952, NA; RG 59, 795.00 Korea, box 4281, June 12, 1952, NA.

5. *Foreign Relations*, 1952–54, 15:198, May 14, 1952; 15:262–63, May 28.

6. This suggestion was never carried out in part because of the marked lack of enthusiasm for the task expressed by those governments approached. RG 59, PPS Records, box 20, "Memorandum of Conversation with the President," June 12, 1952, NA; and Connelly Papers, June 13, 1952, HSTL.

7. FO 371/99574, May 22, 1952, PRO.

8. *Foreign Relations*, 1952–54, 15:366, June 30, 1952; RG 59, 795.00 Korea, box 4281, June 30, NA; FO 371/99575, June 6 and 11, 1952, PRO.

9. FO 371/99581, July 18; 99583, Aug. 25, 1952, PRO. In support of Panikkar, however, note how close Chou's second alternative was to the final agreement. (See Chapter 7.)

10. *Foreign Relations*, 1952–54, 15:341, June 18, 1952; FO 371/99575, June 17, 1952, PRO.

11. *Foreign Relations*, 1952–54, 15:345, June 19, 1952.

12. RG 59, Records of the Assistant Secretary of State, Far Eastern Affairs, lot 55D282, box 1, July 1 and May 21, 1952, NA.

13. FO 371/99573, May 21; 99632, May 23, 1952, PRO.

14. *The Scotsman*, May 10, 1952; RG 59, "Black Book on Ceasefire," May 27, 1952, NA; Kaufman, *The Korean War*, p. 277.

15. *Times*, May 31, 1952; *Foreign Relations*, 1952–54, 15:352, June 24, 1952.

16. *Foreign Relations*, 1952–54, 15:352–54, June 24, 1952; Kaufman, *The Korean War*, pp. 276–78.

17. *Foreign Relations*, 1952–54, 15:195, May 14, 1952.

18. Ibid., 1952–54, 15:256–62, May 28, 1952.

19. Ibid., 1952–54, 15:209, May 19, 1952; 15:213, May 21, 1952.

20. Robert F. Futrell, *The United States Air Force in Korea, 1950–53* (New York: Duell, Sloan and Pearce, 1961), p. 444; RG 218, JCS Records, Recently Declassified JCS Documents, Korea, April 3, 1952, NA.

21. Futrell, *U.S. Air Force*, pp. 449–51.

22. FO 371/99598, June 24, 1952, PRO; *Time* magazine, June 30, 1952, p. 24.

23. *World Broadcasts*, no. 167, June 27, 1952; *Foreign Relations*, 1952–54, 15:384, July 9, 1952; Futrell, *US Air Force*, p. 481; Truman Papers, PSF, National Security Council, Psychological Strategy Board Report on period July 1 1952–September 30 1952, Oct. 30, 1952, HSTL; History of the JCS, 3:876.

24. FO 371/99581, July 16, 1952, PRO.

25. *Foreign Relations*, 1952–54, 15:638, Nov. 16, 1952.

26. Ronald J. Caridi, *The Korean War and American Politics: The Republican Party as a Case Study* (Philadelphia: University of Pennsylvania Press, 1968), p. 211; RG 59, Office of Public Opinion Studies, 1943–56, box 12, Monthly Survey, July 1952, NA.

27. *Congressional Record*, 82d Cong., 2d sess., 98, p. 2042, March 10, 1952; Kaufman, *The Korean War*, pp. 261, 290; Robert Divine, *Foreign Policy and U.S. Presidential Elections, 1952–60* (New York: New Viewpoints, 1974), p. 34; Rosemary Foot, *The*

Wrong War: American Policy and the Dimensions of the Korean Conflict, 1950–1953 (Ithaca, N.Y.: Cornell University Press, 1985), pp. 191–93; Gary W. Reichard, *Politics as Usual: The Age of Truman and Eisenhower* (Arlington Heights, Ill.: Harlan Davidson, 1988), p. 81. Eisenhower's speech in San Francisco is in the C. D. Jackson Records, box 2, Oct. 8, 1952, DDEL.

28. Matthew Mantell, "Opposition to the Korean War: A Study in American Dissent" (Ph.D. diss., New York University, 1973), pp. 217–18.

29. *Congressional Record*, 82d Cong., 2d sess., 98, p. 5145, May 14, 1952; p. 6933, June 10, 1952; RG 330, CD 383.6, box 363, June 24, 1952, NA; *Congressional Record*, 82d Cong., 2d sess., 98, p. A3111, May 20, 1952.

30. *Congressional Record*, 82d Cong., 2d sess., 98, pp. A3507–8, May 22, 1952; RG 59, 695B.1124, July 20, 1952, NA; RG 59, "Black Book on Ceasefire," box 8, Aug. 22, 1952, NA; *Foreign Relations*, 1952–54, 15:715, Dec. 22, 1952.

31. RG 59, 795.00 Korea, box 4283, Sept. 15, 1952, NA; RG 59, Office of Public Opinion Studies, box 39, Aug. 13 and Sept. 15, 1952, NA.

32. Mantell, "Opposition to the Korean War," pp. 269, 190; and, e.g., see *Congressional Record*, 82d Cong., 2d sess., 98, p. 4355, April 24, 1952, and ibid., p. A2323, April 9, 1952; RG 59, 695.0029, May 19, 1952, NA; RG 59, "Black Book on Ceasefire," box 6, June 4, 1952, NA.

33. RG 59, 695B.1124, July 20, 1952, NA.

34. Truman Papers, PSF, NIE 55/1, July 30, 1952, HSTL.

35. RG 59, 795.00 Korea, box 4283, Aug. 28, 1952, NA; *Foreign Relations*, 1952–54, 15:463–64, Aug. 27, 1952.

36. RG 59, "Black Book on Ceasefire," box 8, Aug. 19, 1952, NA.

37. *Foreign Relations*, 1952–54, 15:467–70, Sept. 1, 1952; 15:417, July 21, 1952; RG 319, G3091 Korea TS, box 20, Sept. 8, 1952, NA; *Foreign Relations*, 1952–54, 15:466, Sept. 1, 1952.

38. *Foreign Relations*, 1952–54, 15:469, Sept. 1, 1952; 15:466, Sept. 1, 1952.

39. Ibid., 15:492–99, Sept. 8, 1952.

40. Ibid., 15:493, Sept. 8, 1952; 15:475, Sept. 2, 1952.

41. Ibid., 15:506–507, Sept. 11, 1952.

42. Ibid., 15:512–14, Sept. 15, 1952.

43. Truman Papers, PSF, NSC Minutes, Oct. 11, 1951, HSTL; *Foreign Relations*, 1952–54, 15:514–21, Sept. 16, 1952; 15:481, Sept. 2, 1952.

44. Futrell, *US Air Force*, p. 488; DDRS (1981), 543C, Aug. 27, 1952.

45. Futrell, *U.S. Air Force*, pp. 488–92, 496; FO 371/99602, Sept. 30, 1952, PRO.

46. Acheson Papers, memorandum of conversation, Sept. 17, 1952, HSTL.

47. RG 319, 092 Korea TS, box 10, Sept. 17, 1952, NA.

48. Acheson Papers, box 67a, undated but marked as about Sept. 16, 1952, HSTL.

49. Truman Papers, PSF, Sept. 24, 1952, HSTL.

50. *Foreign Relations*, 1952–54, 15:544, Sept. 26, 1952; 15:545–48, Sept. 29; *Department of State Bulletin*, Oct. 20, 1952, p. 600.

51. Deborah Welch Larson, *Origins of Containment* (Princeton, N.J.: Princeton University Press, 1985), p. 131.

52. *Foreign Relations*, 1952–54, 15:520, Sept. 16, 1952.

53. Ibid., 1952–54, 15:527–28, Sept. 23, 1952; 15:548–50, Sept. 29, 1952.

54. Acheson Papers, memorandum of conversation, box 67, Sept. 17, 1952, HSTL.

55. FO 371/99583, Aug. 29, 1952; *Foreign Relations*, 1952–54, 15:453–56, Aug. 14, 1952; RG 59, 695.00, box 3024, Aug. 27, 1952, NA.

56. Acheson Papers, memorandum of conversation, box 67, Sept. 17, 1952, HSTL.

57. Truman Papers, Naval Aide File, Nov. 6, 1952, HSTL.

58. Roger Bullen, "Great Britain, the United States and the Indian Armistice Resolution on the Korean War: November 1952," in *Aspects of Anglo-Korean Relations, International Studies* (International Centre for Economics and Related Disciplines, London School of Economics and Political Science), 1984/1, p. 30.

59. *Foreign Relations*, 1952–54, 15:567, Oct. 29, 1952; 15:590, Nov. 8, 1952.

60. The development of this debate is covered in some detail in ibid., 15:558ff.

61. PREM 11, no. 111, Nov. 11, 1952, PRO; Barton J. Bernstein, "The Struggle over the Korean Armistice: Prisoners of Repatriation?" in Bruce Cumings, ed., *Child of Conflict: The Korean-American Relationship, 1943–1953* (Seattle: University of Washington Press, 1983), p. 303; *Foreign Relations*, 1952–54, 15:637, Nov. 16, 1952; Callum A. MacDonald, *Korea: The War before Vietnam* (London: Macmillan, 1986), p. 171.

62. *Foreign Relations*, 1952–54, 15:674–75, Nov. 24, 1952; MacDonald, *Korea*, pp. 171–72; Foot, *Wrong War*, p. 185.

63. Futrell, *U.S. Air Force*, p. 565; RG 59, PPS Records, box 20, "Transcript of a Statement by . . . Acheson . . . in Committee One," Nov. 24, 1952, NA.

64. RG 59, 795.00 Korea, Nov. 6, 1952, NA; S. Gopal, *Jawaharlal Nehru: A Biography*, vol. 2: *1947–56* (London: Jonathan Cape, 1979), p. 145.

65. Dean Acheson, *Present at the Creation: My Years in the State Department* (New York: Norton, 1969), pp. 700–705; White House Office: Office of the Special Assistant for National Security, Status of Projects Subseries, box 3, NSC 142, The Psychological Program, Jan. 21, 1953, DDEL. *Foreign Relations*, 1952–54, 15:659, Nov. 19, 1952.

66. RG 59, PPS Records, box 20, Stelle to Nitze, "Our Korea Policy," Nov. 13, 1952, NA.

CHAPTER 7

1. Dwight D. Eisenhower, *The White House Years: Mandate for Change, 1953–56* (Garden City, N.Y.: Doubleday, 1963), 1:96–97; Rosemary Foot, *The Wrong War: American Policy and the Dimensions of the Korean Conflict, 1950–1953* (Ithaca, N.Y.: Cornell University Press, 1985), p. 205; John Foster Dulles Papers, Subject Series, box 8, SS Helena notes, Dec. 11, 1952, DDEL.

2. FO 371/104578, Jan. 6, 1953, PRO; U. Alexis Johnson, *The Right Hand of Power* (Englewood Cliffs, N.J.: Prentice Hall, 1984), p. 162; Edward C. Keefer, "President Dwight D. Eisenhower and the End of the Korean War," *Diplomatic History* 10 (Summer 1986): 268.

3. Dwight D. Eisenhower, Papers as President of the United States (Ann Whitman File), Cabinet Series, box 2, March 27, 1953, DDEL; C. D. Jackson Records, box 4, Memorandum on Recent Polls on Korea, June 2, 1953, DDEL. Although 69 percent of respondents stated in April they would approve of an armistice being signed, 54 percent in April and 74 percent in May did not think it likely to happen in the next month or so. Ibid. *Foreign Relations*, 1952–54, 15:826–27, March 31, 1953.

4. Eisenhower, Papers as President (Whitman File), Cabinet Series, box 2, Jan. 23, 1953, DDEL. Robert Bowie also reported that Dulles made considerable efforts to prevent sniping from Congress by keeping its members in close touch with developments and soliciting their opinions. Robert R. Bowie, Oral History, p. 21, DDEL.

5. *Congressional Record*, 83d Cong., 1st sess., 99, 1953, p. 4275, April 6; p. 4860, May 13; pp. 4872–73, May 13; *Christian Science Monitor*, June 1, 1953; Foot, *The Wrong War*, p. 221.

6. John Foster Dulles Papers, Subject Series, box 8, Nov. 26, 1952, DDEL.

7. Mark W. Clark, Oral History Project, Butler Library, Columbia University, New York, p. 9; Eisenhower, *White House Years*, 1:180; RG 10, Douglas A. MacArthur, "Memorandum on Ending the Korean War," Dec. 14, 1952, MacArthur Memorial Library, Norfolk, Va.

8. *Foreign Relations*, 1952–54, 15:827, March 31, 1953; 15:977, May 6, 1953.

9. Ibid., 15:815, March 21, 1953; 15:826, March 31, 1953; Jackson Records, box 5, P. file, March 30, 1953, DDEL; Dulles Papers, Telephone Calls Series, box 1, April 7, 1953, DDEL; Eisenhower, Papers as President, NSC meeting, April 8, 1953 (Whitman File), box 4, DDEL.

10. *Foreign Relations*, 1952–54, 15:817–18, March 27, 1953; 15:1014, May 13, 1953. Roger Dingman has written a valuable study of Truman and Eisenhower administration policy toward nuclear weapons. See his "Atomic Diplomacy during the Korean War," *International Security* 13 (Winter 1988/9).

11. Foot, *The Wrong War*, pp. 206–7; *Foreign Relations*, 1952–54, 15:1014, May 13, 1953.

12. *Foreign Relations*, 1952–54, 15:1066–68, May 20, 1953; Richard K. Betts, *Nuclear Blackmail and Nuclear Balance* (Washington, D.C.: Brookings Institution, 1987), p. 42.

13. *Foreign Relations*, 1952–54, 15:1068, May 21, 1953; Roger Dingman, "Atomic Diplomacy," p. 86; FO 371/105496, May 25, 1953. The high commissioner added, "I gathered impression, however, that Indians had not, repeat not, passed this onto Chinese."

14. *Foreign Relations*, 1952–54, 15:1103, May 26, 1953; Walter C. Hermes, *Truce Tent and Fighting Front* (Washington, D.C.: Government Printing Office, 1966), p. 430.

15. Barry M. Blechman and Robert Powell, "What in the Name of God is Strategic Superiority?" *Political Science Quarterly* 97 (Winter 1982–83): 591; Robert F. Futrell, *The United States Air Force in Korea, 1950–53* (New York: Duell, Sloan and Pearce, 1961), p. 570, pp. 626–27; David Rees, *Korea: The Limited War* (New York: St. Martin's Press, 1964), pp. 381–82. Hermes, *Truce Tent*, p. 461; Robert Jackson, *Air War over Korea* (London: Ian Allan, 1973), pp. 156–57; John Gittings, "Talks, Bombs and Germs: Another Look at the Korean War," *Journal of Contemporary Asia* 5, no. 2 (1975): 215.

16. RG 319, Army Ops General Decimal File, 1953 383.6, box 205, Feb. 16, 1953, NA; RG 59, Bureau of Far Eastern Affairs, Lot 55D388, box 3, Feb. 4, 1953, NA; Mark Clark Papers, Dec. 22, 1952, DDEL; *Foreign Relations*, 1952–54, 15:785–86, Feb. 18, 1953; 15:788–89, Feb. 19; 15:818–19, March 28.

17. Eisenhower, Papers as President (Whitman File), Dulles-Herter Series, box 1, April 2, 1953, DDEL; *Foreign Relations*, 1952–54, 15:857, April 4, 1953; RG 59, 795.00 Korea, box 4285, April 21, 1953, NA.

18. *Foreign Relations*, 1952–54, 15:865–77, April 3, 1953. Special Estimate no. 37, March 9, 1953, even recorded that "large-scale and sustained air and naval bombardment of key Chinese Communist transportation lines in conjunction with a naval blockade could sharply reduce Chinese Communist military capabilities, but would probably not in itself induce the Communists to accept a Korean settlement on UN terms." Freedom of Information Act request.

19. RG 319, Army Ops, General Decimal File 1953, 383.6, box 205, March 30, NA; History of the JCS, 3:965; *New York Times*, March 31, 1953; *Foreign Relations*, 1952–54, 15:831, April 1, 1953; 15:903–4, April 11; FO 371/105485, April 9, 1953, PRO; *Department of State Bulletin*, April 20, 1953, pp. 575–76.

20. *Department of State Bulletin*, April 27, 1953; RG 59, PPS Records, box 19, March 31, 1953, NA; *Foreign Relations*, 1952–54, 15:974, May 5, 1953.

21. *Foreign Relations*, 1952–54, 15:979–81, May 7, 1953.

22. Ibid., 15:982, May 7, 1953; Hermes, *Truce Tent*, pp. 425–26.

23. *Foreign Relations*, 1952–54, 15:1020, May 14, 1953; *Survey of the China Mainland Press (SCMP)* (Hong Kong: U.S. Consulate General, 1953), nos. 572 and 575, May 16 and 20 (hereafter cited as *SCMP*); RG 59, 695A.0024, box 3024, May 16, 1953, NA.

24. RG 59, Bureau of Far Eastern Affairs, Lot 55D388, box 1, April 24, 1953, NA; *Foreign Relations*, 1952–54, 15:953, April 29, 1953; RG 59, PPS Records, box 19, June 23, 1953, NA.

25. *Foreign Relations*, 1952–54, 15:832, April 1, 1953; *Congressional Record*, 83d Cong., 1st sess., 99, May 13, 1953, p. 4860.

26. RG 59, 795.00 Korea, May 18, 1953, NA; *Foreign Relations*, 1952–54, 15:1019, May 12, 1953; Denis Stairs, *The Diplomacy of Constraint: Canada, the Korean War and the United States* (Toronto: University of Toronto Press, 1974), pp. 276–77; RG 59, 695.0029, May 2, 1953; Burton I. Kaufman, *The Korean War: Challenges in Crisis, Credibility, and Command* (Philadelphia: Temple University Press, 1986), pp. 315–16; Callum A. MacDonald, *Korea: The War before Vietnam* (London: Macmillan, 1986), p. 187; RG 59, 695.0029, May 6, 1953, NA.

27. RG 59, 795.00 Korea, May 18, 1953, NA; White House Office, Office of the Special Assistant for National Security, Status of Projects Subseries, NSC 161, vol. 11 (3), the Psychological Program—no. 8, July 30, 1953, DDEL; *Foreign Relations*, 1952–54, 15:1057, May 19, 1953.

28. RG 59, Office of Public Opinion Studies, box 39, Jan. 29 and March 23, 1953, NA; RG 59, 795.00 Korea, box 4286, May 20, 1953, NA.

29. Dulles Papers, Subject Series, box 9, May 9, 1953, DDEL; RG 59, 611.95A241, May 11, 1953, NA; *Foreign Relations*, 1952–54, 15:1046–47, May 18, 1953; 15:1051, May 18, 1953; White House Office, Office of the Staff Secretary Records, Legislative Meetings Series, box 1, May 19, 1953, DDEL; RG 59, 695.0029, May 22, 1953, NA.

30. FO 371/105497 and 105495, May 18, 1953, PRO.

31. Eisenhower, Papers as President (Whitman File), Cabinet Series, box 2, May 29, 1953, DDEL; Eisenhower, Papers as President, Diary Series, box 3, June 2, 1953, DDEL. Dulles had a similar experience to Walter Bedell Smith when he spoke to Sen. H. Alexander Smith, ostensibly about Korea, but found him expressing his "great concern over Red China." Dulles Papers, Telephone Calls Series, box 1, May 30, 1953, DDEL.

32. RG 59, 695.0029, May 22, 1953, NA; Barry M. Blechman and Robert Powell, "Strategic Superiority?" p. 595, n. 17.

33. *Foreign Relations*, 1952–54, 15:1097, May 25, 1953; 15:1138, June 4, 1953; William H. Vatcher, Jr., *Panmunjom: The Story of the Korean Military Armistice Negotiations* (New York: Praeger, 1958), p. 193; Eisenhower, Papers as President, Name Series, June 8, 1953, DDEL; Dulles Papers, Subject Series, box 9, June 8, 1953, DDEL; Knowland Papers, Letter from Dulles to Knowland, June 8, 1953, The Bancroft Library, University of California, Berkeley.

34. *New York Herald Tribune*, July 22, 1953; Eisenhower, *The White House Years*, 1:179–80; Sherman Adams, *Firsthand Report: The Inside Story of the Eisenhower Administration* (London: Hutchinson, 1962), p. 102.

35. *Foreign Relations*, 1952–54, 5:1811–13, Dec. 7, 1953; Lawrence Freedman, *The Evolution of Nuclear Strategy* (London: Macmillan, 1983), p. 85.

36. *World Broadcasts*, no. 253, May 19, 1953; *Foreign Relations*, 1952–54, 15:1111, May 28, 1953; RG 59, 795.00 Korea, box 4268, June 3, 1953, NA.

37. *World Broadcasts*, no. 254, May 21, 1953; *SCMP*, nos. 572–75, May 16–21, 1953.

38. Sarvepalli Gopal, *Jawaharlal Nehru: A Biography*, vol. 2: *1947–1956* (London: Jonathan Cape, 1979), p. 148; Escott Reid, *Envoy to Nehru* (Oxford: Oxford University Press, 1981), p. 45. The magazine article inspired by the secretary of state was entitled "How Dulles Averted War," Jan. 16, 1956.

39. Mao Tse-tung, *Selected Works* (Peking: Foreign Languages Press, 1969), 4:100; William R. Harris, "Chinese Nuclear Doctrine: The Decade Prior to Weapons Development (1945–1955)," *China Quarterly* 21 (Jan.–March 1965): 90–91; *Current Background* (Hong Kong: U.S. Consulate General), no. 32, Nov. 29, 1950.

40. Mark A. Ryan, "Chinese Attitudes toward Nuclear Weapons: China and the United States during the Korean War" (Ph.D. diss., Georgetown University, 1986), esp. pp. 122–57.

41. H. Goldhamer, "Communist Reaction in Korea to American Possession of the A-Bomb and Its Significance for U.S. Political and Psychological Warfare," U.S. Air Force, Project RAND, Research Memorandum 903 (Santa Monica, Calif.: Rand Corporation, Aug. 1, 1952), pp. 38–39; Harris, "Chinese Nuclear Doctrine," p. 91; Raymond L. Garthoff, ed., *Sino-Soviet Military Relations* (New York: Praeger, 1966), p. 231; John Wilson Lewis and Xue Litai, *China Builds the Bomb* (Stanford: Stanford University Press, 1988), p. 15.

42. Harris, "Chinese Nuclear Doctrine," pp. 93 and 95; Charles Horner, "The Production of Nuclear Weapons," in William W. Whitson, ed., *The Military and Political Power in China in the 1970s* (New York: Praeger, 1972); Alice Langley Hsieh, *Communist China's Strategy in the Nuclear Era* (Englewood Cliffs, N.J.: Prentice Hall, 1962), pp. 20–26.

43. *World Broadcasts*, no. 221, Jan. 23, 1953.

44. Ibid., no. 253, May 19, 1953.

45. Garthoff, *Sino-Soviet Military Relations*, p. 85. For a discussion of the impact of the war on China's domestic policies, see Lawrence C. Weiss, "Storm Around the Cradle: The Korean War and the Early Years of the People's Republic of China, 1949–1953" (Ph.D. diss., Columbia University, 1981). For some indication of the probable tension caused by the military expenditure on the war effort, see Mao, "Our Great Victory in the War to Resist U.S. Aggression and Aid Korea and our Future Tasks," in *Selected Works*, 5:119. Robert A. Scalapino and Chong-sik Lee, *Communism in Korea*, part 1 (Berkeley: University of California Press, 1972), esp. pp. 413–22; *World Broadcasts*, no. 217, Jan. 20, 1953, and no. 247, May 1, 1953.

46. Dulles Files, Telephone Conversation Memoranda, box 1, March 31, 1953, SGML; RG 59, 695A.0024 North Korea, box 3027, March 30, 1953, NA; Robert Simmons, *The Strained Alliance: Peking, Pyongyang, Moscow and the Politics of the Korean Civil War* (New York: Free Press, 1975), p. 233.

47. RG 59, PPS Records, box 19, April 25, 1953, NA; RG 84, Foreign Service Posts, Moscow, box 1392, April 20, 1953, Washington National Records Center, Suitland, Md.

48. *New York Times*, March 21, 1953; *Observer*, March 29; *Christian Science Monitor*, April 10; *New York Times*, April 11; *Times*, May 4; FO 371/105588, April 10, 1953, PRO.

49. *World Broadcasts*, nos. 223–24, Feb. 10 and 12, 1953; *SCMP*, no. 530, March 12.

50. *Foreign Relations*, 1952–54, 15:828, March 31, 1953; RG 59, 695A.0024, March 31, 1953, NA; FO 371/105485, April 9, 1953, PRO. For discussion of the "New Look," see Samuel F. Wells, Jr., "The Origins of Massive Retaliation," *Political Science Quarterly* 96 (Spring 1981).

51. MacDonald, *Korea*, p. 192; Kaufman, *The Korean War*, p. 328; *New York Times*, June 19, 1953.

52. Clark Papers, June 18, 1953, DDEL. See also Rhee's public statement on June

18: "Most of the United Nations authorities with whom I have spoken about our desire to release these prisoners are with us in sympathy and in principle." In a letter Clark wrote on July 8 to Roy W. Howard of Scripps-Howard newspapers but which he did not send, he alleged that Rhee was as "unscrupulous a dictator as ever lived. Anyone who raises his voice against him is beaten up by thugs." All at DDEL.

53. *American Foreign Policy, 1950–55* (Washington, D.C.: Department of State, June 20, 1953), pp. 2659–60; Walter S. Robertson, Oral History Project, Butler Library, Columbia University, p. 59; RG 59, Bureau of Far Eastern Affairs, box 1, June 30, 1953, NA; *Foreign Relations, 1952–54*, 15:1200, June 20, 1953. Robert D. Murphy obviously felt as angry as General Clark. In a confidential, unofficial letter that, in the end, was not sent, dated July 6, he alleged that Rhee bore the responsibility for thousands of extra casualties because without the South Korean president's interference Murphy believed that an armistice would have been signed in time to avoid them. Murphy Papers, Hoover Institution, Stanford University, Calif.

54. Dulles Papers, Subject Series, box 9, June 25, 1953, DDEL.

55. Arthur Minnich, cabinet notes, June 19, 1953, DDEL; RG 59, 795.00 Korea, July 1, 1953, NA.

56. Keefer, "President Eisenhower and the End of the Korean War," p. 287; *Foreign Relations, 1952–54*, 15:1270, June 25, 1953; 15:1270, June 27, 1953.

57. RG 218, CCS 383.21 Korea (3-19-45), box 44, June 30, 1953, NA; *Foreign Relations, 1952–54*, 15:1224, June 20, 1953; 15:135, June 22, 1953; RG 218, CCS 383.21 Korea (3-19-45), box 44, July 2, 1953, NA. In early July a *New York Times* reporter stated that some 1,400 anti-Communist prisoners of war released by Rhee's troops had been taken through the city in broad daylight waving flags en route to the South Korean army replacement center. July 3, 1953.

58. RG 218, JCS Records, 383.21 Korea (3-19-45), box 44, June 30, 1953, NA; *SCMP*, no. 594, June 19, 1953.

59. *World Broadcasts*, no. 271, July 28, 1953; Kaufman, *The Korean War*, p. 335; Humphrey Trevelyan, *Living with the Communists* (Boston: Gambit, 1971), p. 69; Dulles Papers, 1952–59, Telephone Call Series, box 1, July 15, 1953, DDEL.

60. *Foreign Relations, 1952–54*, 15:1404, July 21, 1953; RG 59, Bureau of Far Eastern Affairs, box 1, lot 55D388, July 23, 1953, NA.

61. See, e.g., the British position as outlined in DEFE 6, C.O.S. Cmt., Joint Planning Staff Memoranda, 104, Aug. 11, 1953, PRO.

62. This assessment of Fechteler is based on a reading of the *Foreign Relations* volume for 1953.

63. Eisenhower, Papers as President (Whitman File), NSC Series, box 5, Dec. 3, 1953, DDEL.

64. Futrell, *U.S. Air Force in Korea*, p. 641.

CHAPTER 8

1. *Foreign Relations, 1952–54*, 15:1730, Jan. 23, 1954; RG 319, PW Statistics, Office, Deputy Chief of Staff Military Operations, box 708, Korean Armistice Negotiations, 1951–58 (hereafter RG 319, PW Stats.), Feb. 13, 1954, NA.

2. RG 59, 695A.0024, June 16, 1953, NA. Manhard also warned in this report that the Indians would soon discover when they took over the camps that the U.N. Command did not have and had never had "anything resembling adequate POW records." In light of this, "suspicion will flourish," he argued, "that we had little basis on which to judge the political attitude of the prisoners, [and] almost no knowledge of the most elementary information" about them. Ibid.

3. William Lindsay White, *The Captives of Korea: An Unofficial White Paper on the Treatment of War Prisoners* (New York: Scribners, 1957), p. 250; Kenneth K. Hansen, *Heroes behind Barbed Wire* (Princeton, N.J.: Van Nostrand, 1957), p. 127; RG 218, CCS 383.21 Korea (3-19-45), box 45, July 22, 1953, NA. The joint chiefs' reply is in ibid. also dated July 22.

4. Hansen, *Heroes behind Barbed Wire*, pp. 145–46, pp. 134, 108.

5. *Free China Information*, Aug. 18, 1953; *South China Morning Post*, Aug. 28 and 24, 1953.

6. Shiv Dayal, *India's Role in the Korean Question* (Delhi: Chand, 1959), p. 197.

7. Callum A. MacDonald, *Korea: The War before Vietnam* (London: Macmillan, 1986), p. 251; *Times*, Oct. 26 and 31, 1953; RG 59, Bureau of Far Eastern Affairs, box 1, Lot 55D388, Oct. 10, 1953, NA; *New York Times*, Oct. 9, 1953.

8. Hansen, *Heroes behind Barbed Wire*, pp. 179, 248; FO 371/105597, Dec. 23, 1953, PRO.

9. Dayal, *India's Role*, pp. 207, 201; White, *Captives of Korea*, p. 298; FO 371/110625, Jan. 24, 1954, PRO; *Hindu*, Oct. 4, 1953; *Foreign Relations*, 1952–54, 15:1525, Oct. 7, 1953.

10. Dayal, *India's Role*, pp. 236–37, 239; *New York Times*, Nov. 16, 1953.

11. Dayal, *India's Role*, pp. 203–4; *Hindu*, Oct. 9, 1953; *New York Times*, Nov. 17, 1953; *Times*, Nov. 18, 1953. Knowland rang Dulles about Nehru's statement, and the secretary promised to comment on that statement at his next press conference. Dulles Papers, telephone conversations series, box 2, Nov. 16, 1953, DDEL.

12. *Foreign Relations*, 1952–54, 15:1688, n. 8, Dec. 29, 1953; 15:1725, Jan. 15, 1954; Dayal, *India's Role*, p. 219.

13. RG 319, PW Stats., Feb. 13, 1954, NA; Hansen, *Heroes behind Barbed Wire*, pp. 160–61; Virginia Pasley, *22 Stayed* (London: Allen, 1955), p. 17; *New York Times*, Dec. 19, 1953, Dec. 22 and 23, 1953; RG 319, 383.6 Korea, box 206, Dec. 19, 1953, NA; FO 371/105597, Dec. 24, 1953, PRO.

14. Pasley, *22 Stayed*, p. 160; *New York Times*, Nov. 3, 1986. See also *Time* magazine for an account of the return of number twelve. Aug. 27, 1965.

15. Albert Biderman, *March to Calumny: The Story of American POW's in the Korean War* (London: Macmillan, 1963), p. 190; David Rees, *Korea: The Limited War* (New York: St. Martin's Press, 1964), p. 346; MacDonald, *Korea*, pp. 253, 256. Aspects of a "National Operations Plan to Exploit Communist Bacteriological Warfare Hoax, Mistreatment of Prisoners of War, and other Atrocities Perpetrated by Communist Forces during the Korean War" are described in C. D. Jackson Records, box 1, Oct. 13, 1953, DDEL.

16. Harold H. Wubben, "American Prisoners of War in Korea: A Second Look at the 'Something New in History' Theme," *American Quarterly* 22 (Spring 1970): 8–9.

17. *New York Herald Tribune*, April 21, 1953, and July 22, 1953; *Christian Science Monitor*, Nov. 6, 1953; FO 371/110621, Jan. 19, 1954, PRO.

18. RG 59, 695A.0024, box 3029, Feb. 2, 1954, NA; Hansen, *Heroes behind Barbed Wire*, p. 129.

19. Jean Pasqualini (Bao Ruo-wang), *Prisoner of Mao* (New York: Coward, McCann & Geoghegan, 1973), pp. 160–61; Jon Halliday and Bruce Cumings, *Korea: The Unknown War* (London: Viking, 1988), pp. 208–9.

20. Hansen, *Heroes behind Barbed Wire*, pp. 304–5; RG 59, Department of State Press Release, no. 469, Sept. 1, 1953, NA. Further details of these psychological warfare plans are contained at the close of Chapter 5. See also C. D. Jackson Records, "National Operations Plan . . . ," box 1, Oct. 13, 1953, DDEL.

21. Dayal, *India's Role*, pp. 248, 210. White, *Captives of Korea*, pp. 325–26. W. G.

Graham of the British Legation in Seoul also remarked, "Only a man of strong character, whose mind was fully made up, would be able to avail himself of such a fleeting opportunity" to choose repatriation. FO 371/110623, Jan. 25, 1954, PRO.

22. *New York Times*, Aug. 8, 1953, and July 29. See also RG 59, Department of State Press Release, no. 403, July 28, 1953, NA.

23. *Foreign Relations*, 1952–54, 15:1468, Aug. 8, 1953.

24. RG 59, Bureau of Far Eastern Affairs, lot 55D388, box 1, Oct. 26, 1953, NA. For details of the workings of Sullivan and Cromwell, see Nancy Lisgor and Frank Lipsius, *A Law unto Itself: The Untold Story of the Law Firm Sullivan and Cromwell* (New York: William Morrow, 1988).

25. RG 59, Bureau of Far Eastern Affairs, lot 55D388, box 1, Oct. 10, 1953, and Aug. 24, 1953, NA; *Daily Telegraph*, Aug. 14, 1953; *Foreign Relations*, 1952–54, 15:1498–99, Aug. 18, 1953; Dulles Papers, telephone calls series, Subseries—White House, box 10, Aug. 27, 1953, DDEL.

26. *Foreign Relations*, 1952–54, 15:1742, Nov. 30, 1953, n. 5; 15:1699, Jan. 7, 1954.

27. *Department of State Bulletin*, Dec. 21, 1953, pp. 877–78. Dean's proposal was made on December 8.

28. *Foreign Relations*, 1952–54, 15:1656–57, Dec. 12; 15:1629, Dec. 1, 1953; 15:1673, Dec. 21, 1953; 15:1692, Jan. 5, 1954, n. 3; 15:1710, Jan. 8, 1954; RG 59, Department of State Press Release, no. 667, Dec. 21, 1953, NA.

29. Dayal, *India's Role*, p. 277; *Foreign Relations*, 1952–54, 15:1750, editorial note.

30. Townsend Hoopes, *The Devil and John Foster Dulles* (Boston: Little Brown, 1973), p. 206, C. D. Jackson Records, box 3, May 3, 1953, DDEL; Henry W. Brands, Jr., "The Dwight D. Eisenhower Administration, Syngman Rhee and the 'Other' Geneva Conference of 1954," *Pacific Historical Review*, Feb. 1987, p. 67. This next section will draw extensively on this helpful article.

31. Evelyn Shuckburgh, *Descent to Suez: Diaries, 1951–56* (London: Weidenfeld and Nicolson, 1986), pp. 164, 161. See for further discussion on the "united action" debate and Anglo-American relations during the Indochina crisis: James Cable, *The Geneva Conference of 1954 on IndoChina* (London: Macmillan, 1986).

32. Brands, "The 'Other' Geneva Conference," p. 70; *Foreign Relations*, 1952–54, 16:249, May 11, 1954.

33. Brands, "The 'Other' Geneva Conference," p. 73; Shuckburgh, *Descent to Suez*, pp. 182, 185; U.S. Department of State, *American Foreign Policy, 1950–55*, vol. 2, parts X–XX, "Geneva Conference."

34. Shuckburgh, *Descent to Suez*, p. 190; Brands, "The 'Other' Geneva Conference," p. 78. See also Henry W. Brands, Jr., *Cold Warriors: Eisenhower's Generation and American Foreign Policy* (New York: Columbia University Press, 1988), p. 74 and pp. 82–84 for discussion of the productive relationship between Walter Bedell Smith and the British at Geneva and earlier in Smith's career. *Foreign Relations*, 1952–54, 16:243, May 10, 1954.

35. Dayal, *India's Role*, p. 277; *American Foreign Policy*, "Geneva Conference."

36. Brands, "The 'Other' Geneva Conference," pp. 80–81.

CHAPTER 9

1. Herbert C. Kelman, ed., *International Behavior: A Social-Psychological Analysis* (New York: Holt, Rinehart and Winston, 1965), p. 472.

2. Richard J. Barnet, *Roots of War: The Men and Institutions behind U.S. Foreign Policy* (Harmondsworth: Penguin, 1971), p. 338.

3. Robert W. Cox, "Social Forces, States and World Orders: Beyond International Relations Theory," in *Millennium: Journal of International Studies* 10 (Summer 1981): 139.

4. RG 59, PPS Records, 1947–53, box 20, Aug. 2, 1951, NA.

5. Robert F. Futrell, *The United States Air Force in Korea, 1950–53* (New York: Duell, Sloan and Pearce, 1961), p. 648.

6. Guenter Lewy, *America in Vietnam* (New York: Oxford University Press, 1978), pp. 143, 385.

7. RG 59, Bureau of Far Eastern Affairs, 1953, box 1, lot 55D388, Oct. 21, 1953, NA.

8. Lewy, *America in Vietnam*, p. 450. Jon Halliday and Bruce Cumings in *Korea: The Unknown War* (London: Viking, 1988), pp. 200–201, put the fatalities, especially for Communist troops, much higher.

9. Walter C. Hermes, *Truce Tent and Fighting Front* (Washington, D.C.: Government Printing Office, 1966), p. 500.

10. The details of this debate form a large part of the analysis in my book *The Wrong War: American Policy and the Dimensions of the Korean Conflict, 1950–1953* (Ithaca, N.Y.: Cornell University Press, 1985).

11. *Foreign Relations*, China, 1951, 7:2050, Nov. 21.

12. NSC 147, April 2, 1953, NA.

13. Dwight D. Eisenhower, *White House Years: Mandate for Change, 1953–56* (Garden City, N.Y.: Doubleday, 1963), 1:180; *Foreign Relations*, 1952–54, 15:1015, May 13, 1953.

14. David Kraslow and Stuart H. Loory, *The Secret Search for Peace in Vietnam* (New York: Vintage Books, 1968), p. 39.

15. Herbert Goldhamer, "The Korean Armistice Conference," RAND, Dec. 1951, pp. 143, 146.

16. Ibid., pp. 262–63.

17. Allen S. Whiting, *China Crosses the Yalu: The Decision to Enter the Korean War* (Stanford, Calif.: Stanford University Press, 1960). See also the memoirs of General Peng Te-huai and General Nie Jung-chen, which both discuss the debates in September and October 1950.

18. Mao Tse-tung, "Our Great Victory in the War to Resist U.S. Aggression and Aid Korea and Our Future Tasks," in *Selected Works* (Peking: Foreign Languages Press, 1977), 5:115–20.

19. Futrell, *U.S. Air Force in Korea*, p. 448. See also Adm. C. Turner Joy's *How Communists Negotiate* (New York: Macmillan, 1955). C. D. Jackson Papers, President's Committee on International Information Activities (Jackson Committee), box 12, DDEL.

20. RG 84, Foreign Service Posts, Moscow, Intelligence Report, no. 5751.2, March 14, 1952, box 169, Washington National Records Center.

21. RG 59, Records of the Bureau of Far Eastern Affairs, box 1, lot 55D388, Feb. 10, 1953, NA.

22. *Foreign Relations*, 1952–54, 15:262–63, May 28, 1952.

23. RG 59, PPS Records, box 20, "Our Korea Policy," Nov. 13, 1952, NA.

24. Allan Rosas, *The Legal Status of Prisoners of War: A Study in International Humanitarian Law Applicable in Armed Conflicts* (Helsinki: Suomalainen Tiedeakatemic, 1976), p. 174.

25. David P. Forsythe, *Humanitarian Politics: The International Committee of the Red Cross* (Baltimore: Johns Hopkins University Press, 1977), p. 186.

26. Wallace Thies, *When Governments Collide: Coercion and Diplomacy in the Vietnam Conflict, 1964–68* (Berkeley, Calif.: University of California Press, 1980), p. 219.

27. Kraslow and Loory, *The Secret Search*, p. 215.

28. For further details on this see Kenneth Young, *Negotiating with the Chinese Communists: The United States Experience, 1953–1967* (New York: McGraw-Hill, 1968); and my chapter "The Search for a Modus-Vivendi: Anglo-American Relations and China Policy in the Eisenhower Era," in Warren I. Cohen and Akira Iriye, eds., *The Great Powers in East Asia* (New York: Columbia University Press, 1990).

29. *Foreign Relations*, 1955–57, China, 3:545–49, June 19, 1957.

30. Ibid., 3:558–66, June 28, 1957. Similar sentiments were expressed at the close of Eisenhower's term of office. See DDRS, no. 1286 (1983), Nov. 10, 1960, "US Policy in the Far East," reaffirming policy conclusions in NSC 5913/1, Sept. 25, 1959.

Bibliography

PRIMARY SOURCES

Manuscript Collections

Acheson, Dean. Papers. Harry S. Truman Library, Independence, Missouri.

Almond, Edward M. Papers. U.S. Army Military History Institute, Carlisle Barracks, Pennsylvania.

Alsop, Joseph, and Stewart Alsop. Papers. Library of Congress, Washington, D.C.

Ayers, Eben A. Papers. Harry S. Truman Library, Independence, Missouri.

Bevin, Ernest. Private Collections, Ministers and Officials. F.O. 800, Public Record Office, London.

Boatner, Haydon L. Papers. Hoover Institution on War, Revolution and Peace, Stanford, California.

Bohlen, Charles. Papers. National Archives, Washington, D.C.

Bradley, Omar. Files. Military Branch, National Archives, Washington, D.C.

Byers, Clovis E. Papers. Hoover Institution on War, Revolution and Peace, Stanford, California.

Clark, Mark. Papers. Dwight D. Eisenhower Library, Abilene, Kansas.

Collins, J. Lawton. Papers. Dwight D. Eisenhower Library, Abilene, Kansas.

Connelly, Matthew J. Papers. Harry S. Truman Library, Independence, Missouri.

Deuel, Wallace. Writings and Journals. Library of Congress, Washington, D.C.

Drumwright, Everett F. Papers. Hoover Institution on War, Revolution and Peace, Stanford, California.

Dulles, John Foster. Papers. Dwight D. Eisenhower Library, Abilene, Kansas.

Dulles, John Foster. Files. Seeley G. Mudd Library, Princeton University, Princeton, New Jersey.

Eisenhower, Dwight D. Papers as President of the United States 1953–1961. Dwight D. Eisenhower Library, Abilene, Kansas.

Eisenhower, Dwight D. Records. White House Central Files. Dwight D. Eisenhower Library, Abilene, Kansas.

Elsey, George M. Papers. Harry S. Truman Library, Independence, Missouri.

Feis, Herbert. Papers. Library of Congress, Washington, D.C.

Jackson, C. D. Records. Papers. Dwight D. Eisenhower Library, Abilene, Kansas.

Jessup, Philip C. Papers. Library of Congress, Washington, D.C.

Judd, Walter H. Papers. Hoover Institution on War, Revolution and Peace, Stanford, California.

Kennan, George. Papers. Seeley G. Mudd Library, Princeton University, Princeton, New Jersey.

Knowland, William F. Papers. The Bancroft Library, University of California, Berkeley, California.

Koo, Wellington, V. K. Papers, Diaries. Butler Library, Columbia University, New York, New York.

Krock, Arthur. Papers. Seeley G. Mudd Library, Princeton University, Princeton, New Jersey.

Lloyd, David D. Files. Harry S. Truman Library, Independence, Missouri.

MacArthur, Douglas A. MacArthur Memorial Library, Norfolk, Virginia.

Minnich, Arthur. Cabinet Notes. Dwight D. Eisenhower Library, Abilene, Kansas.

Murphy, Robert D. Papers. Hoover Institution on War, Revolution and Peace, Stanford, California.

Pulitzer, J., Jr. Papers. Library of Congress, Washington, D.C.

Reid, Helen Rogers. Papers. Library of Congress, Washington, D.C.

Ridgway, Matthew B. Papers. U.S. Army Military History Institute, Carlisle Barracks, Pennsylvania.

Smith, H. Alexander. Papers. Seeley G. Mudd Library, Princeton University, Princeton, New Jersey.

Taft, Robert A. Papers. Library of Congress, Washington, D.C.

Truman, Harry S. Papers. President's Secretary File. Naval Aide File. NSC File. Harry S. Truman Library, Independence, Missouri.

Vatcher, William H. Papers. Hoover Institution on War, Revolution and Peace, Stanford, California.

Willoughby, Charles A. Papers. U.S. Army Military History Institute, Carlisle Barracks, Pennsylvania.

Public Records: Unpublished

Legislative Branch, National Archives, Washington, D.C.
RG 46, MacArthur Hearings
National Security Council Documents

Diplomatic Branch, National Archives, Washington, D.C.
RG 59, General Records of the Department of State, 1950–54. Decimal File:
    611.93 China.
    611.95 Korea.
    611.95A North Korea.
    611.95B South Korea.
    693.00 China.
    694.A Formosa.
    695.00 Korea.
    695.A North Korea.
    695.B South Korea.
    793.00 China.
    793.A Manchuria.
    795.00 Korea.
    795.A North Korea.

795.B South Korea.
Lot Files:
  Office of the Executive Secretariat. Summaries of the Secretary's Daily Meetings, 1949–1952.
  Under Secretary's Meetings. Summaries.
  Under Secretary's Meetings. Minutes. Memoranda.
  Office of North East Asian Affairs.
  Records of the Office of Chinese Affairs.
  Records of the Bureau of Far Eastern Affairs—"Black Book on Ceasefire."
  Records of the Bureau of Far Eastern Affairs—1953.
  Korean Situation File—H. Freeman Matthews.
  Records of the Assistant Secretary of State for Far Eastern Affairs—John Moore Allison.
  Records of the Director of the Office of North East Asian Affairs—U. Alexis Johnson.
  Records of the Office of Public Opinion Studies.
  Records of the Policy Planning Staff, 1947–1953.
  Office of Intelligence Research Reports.

Washington National Records Center, Suitland.
RG 84, Foreign Service Posts of the Department of State; Korea—Seoul, Moscow, Tokyo.

Military Branch, National Archives, Washington, D.C.
RG 218, Records of the U.S. Joint Chiefs of Staff.
RG 319, Records of the Army Staff.
RG 330, Records of the Office of the Secretary of Defense.
RG 338, Far East Command.
The History of the Joint Chiefs of Staff
  The Joint Chiefs of Staff and National Policy, vol. 3: The Korean War, Parts I and II, by James F. Schnabel and Robert J. Watson, Historical Division, Joint Secretariat, Joint Chiefs of Staff, April 1978, March 1979.
  The Joint Chiefs of Staff and National Policy, vol. 4: 1950–1952, by Walter S. Poole, Historical Division, Joint Secretariat, Joint Chiefs of Staff, December 1979.

Public Record Office, London, 1950–1954
FO 371 Foreign Office Files. Far Eastern—China, Korea; American—United States.
PREM 11, 8. Prime Minister's Office.
DEFE 4. Chiefs of Staff Committee, Minutes of Meetings.
DEFE 5. Chiefs of Staff Committee, Memoranda.
DEFE 6. Chiefs of Staff Committee, Joint Planning Staff Reports.
CAB 128. Cabinet Minutes.
CAB 129. Cabinet Memoranda.
CAB 131. Cabinet Defence Committee.
CAB 134. Far Eastern Official Committee.

Declassified Documents Reference System
Research Publications. Retrospective Collection. Collections, 1975–1988. Woodbridge, Conn.

Public Records: Published

Congressional Record, 1950–1953. Washington, D.C.: Government Printing Office.

United Kingdom. *Parliamentary Debates.* Hansard, 1950–1953.

United Kingdom. Ministry of Defence. *Treatment of British Prisoners of War in Korea.* London: Her Majesty's Stationery Office, 1955.

U.S. Congress. Senate. Committees on Armed Services and Foreign Relations. *Military Situation in the Far East.* Hearings, 82nd Cong., 1st sess., 1951. Washington, D.C.: Government Printing Office, 1951.

U.S. Congress. Senate. Committee on Foreign Relations. *The United States and the Korean Problem, Documents, 1943–1953.* 83rd Cong., 1st sess., 1953. Washington, D.C.: Government Printing Office, 1953.

U.S. Congress. Senate. Sub-Committee on National Security and International Operations. *Peking's Approach to Negotiation.* Washington, D.C.: Government Printing Office, 1969.

U.S. Department of State. *American Foreign Policy, 1950–1955.* Basic Documents. Washington, D.C.: Government Printing Office, 1957.

U.S. Department of State. *Department of State Bulletin.* Washington, D.C.: Government Printing Office, 1950–1954.

U.S. Department of State. *Foreign Relations of the United States.* Washington, D.C.: Government Printing Office.

1950, vol. 1: *National Security Affairs.* 1977.

1950, vol. 3: *Western Europe.* 1976.

1950, vol. 6: *East Asia and the Pacific.* 1976.

1950, vol. 7: *Korea.* 1976.

1951, vol. 1: *National Security.* 1979.

1951, vol. 2: *The United Nations; The Western Hemisphere.* 1979.

1951, vol. 6: *Asia and the Pacific* (two parts). 1977.

1951, vol. 7: *China and Korea* (two parts). 1983.

1952–1954, vol. 3: *United Nations Affairs.* 1979.

1952–1954, vol. 5: *Western European Security* (two parts). 1979.

1952–1954, vol. 13: *Indochina* (two parts). 1982.

1952–1954, vol. 14: *China and Japan* (two parts). 1985.

1952–1954, vol. 15: *Korea* (two parts). 1984.

1952–1954, vol. 16: *The Geneva Conference.* 1981.

1955–1957, vols. 2 & 3: *China.* 1986.

U.S. Department of State. *United States Policy in the Korean Conflict.* Washington, D.C.: Government Printing Office, 1951.

U.S. Department of State. *United States Policy in the Korean Crisis,* Washington, D.C.: Government Printing Office, 1950.

U.S. President. *Public Papers of the Presidents of the United States: Harry S. Truman. Dwight D. Eisenhower.* Washington, D.C.: Government Printing Office, 1965–66, 1960–61.

Oral Histories

Almond, Edward, M. U.S. Army Military History Institute, Carlisle Barracks, Pennsylvania.

Ayers, Eben A. Harry S. Truman Library, Independence, Missouri.

Battle, Lucius. Harry S. Truman Library, Independence, Missouri.

Bibliography

Bell, David E. Harry S. Truman Library, Independence, Missouri.
Bendetsen, Karl. Harry S. Truman Library, Independence, Missouri.
Bohlen, Charles. Dwight D. Eisenhower Library, Abilene, Kansas.
Bolté, Charles. U.S. Army Military History Institute, Carlisle Barracks, Pennsylvania.
Bowie, Robert R. Dwight D. Eisenhower Library, Abilene, Kansas.
Clark, Mark. Eisenhower Administration Oral History Project, Butler Library, Columbia University, New York, New York.
Clark, Mark. Oral History. U.S. Army Military History Institute, Carlisle Barracks, Pennsylvania.
Clubb, O. Edmund. Harry S. Truman Library, Independence, Missouri.
Elsey, George M. Harry S. Truman Library, Independence, Missouri.
Finletter, Thomas K. Harry S. Truman Library, Independence, Missouri.
Flanders, Ralph. Dwight D. Eisenhower Library, Abilene, Kansas.
Franks, Lord Oliver. Harry S. Truman Library, Independence, Missouri.
Gross, Ernest. Oral History Project, Butler Library, Columbia University, New York, New York.
Henderson, Loy. Harry S. Truman Library, Independence, Missouri.
Hickerson, John D. Harry S. Truman Library, Independence, Missouri.
Jessup, Philip. Oral History Project, Butler Library, Columbia University, New York, New York.
Johnson, U. Alexis. Harry S. Truman Library, Independence, Missouri.
Judd, Walter H. Oral History Project, Butler Library, Columbia University, New York, New York.
Knowland, William F. Oral History Project, Butler Library, Columbia University, New York, New York.
Koo, V. K. Wellington. Chinese Oral History Project, Butler Library, Columbia University, New York, New York.
Matthews, H. Freeman. Harry S. Truman Library, Independence, Missouri.
Muccio, John J. Harry S. Truman Library, Independence, Missouri.
Murphy, Charles S. Harry S. Truman Library, Independence, Missouri.
Murphy, Robert D. Dwight D. Eisenhower Library, Abilene, Kansas.
Pace, Frank. Harry S. Truman Library, Independence, Missouri.
Pace, Frank. U.S. Army Military History Institute, Carlisle Barracks, Pennsylvania.
Princeton Seminars, 1953–1954, Dean Acheson Papers. Harry S. Truman Library, Independence, Missouri.
Ridgway, Matthew B. Oral History Project, Butler Library, Columbia University, New York, New York.
Ridgway, Matthew B. U.S. Army Military History Institute, Carlisle Barracks, Pennsylvania.
Robertson, Walter S. Eisenhower Administration Oral History Project, Butler Library, Columbia University, New York, New York.
Sprouse, Philip. Harry S. Truman Library, Independence, Missouri.
Taylor, Maxwell. U.S. Army Military History Institute, Carlisle Barracks, Pennsylvania.

Newspaper Collections and Radio Monitoring Reports

BBC Monitoring Reports, Summary of World Broadcasts, Part 5: Far East. Reading, Berkshire.

British Library Reference Division—Newspaper Library, Colingdale, London, England.
Butler Library, Columbia University, New York, New York.
Current Background. U.S. Consulate General, Hong Kong.
Survey of the China Mainland Press. U.S. Consulate General, Hong Kong.

Rand Reports

Goldhamer, Herbert. "Communist Reaction in Korea to American Possession of the A-Bomb and Its Significance for U.S. Political and Psychological Warfare." August 1952.
———. "The Korean Armistice Conference." December 1951.

SECONDARY WORKS

Books

Acheson, Dean. *Present at the Creation: My Years in the State Department*. New York: Norton, 1969.
Adams, Sherman. *Firsthand Report: The Inside Story of the Eisenhower Administration*. London: Hutchinson, 1962.
Alexander, Bevin. *Korea: The First War We Lost*. New York: Hippocrene Books, 1986.
Alexander, Charles C. *Holding the Line: The Eisenhower Era, 1952–1961*. Bloomington: Indiana University Press, 1975.
Allison, Graham T. *Essence of Decision: Explaining the Cuban Missile Crisis*. Boston: Little Brown, 1971.
Allison, John M. *Ambassador from the Prairie or Allison Wonderland*. Boston: Houghton Mifflin, 1973.
Alsop, Joseph, Stewart Alsop. *The Reporter's Trade*. London: Bodley Head, 1960.
Ambrose, Stephen E. *Eisenhower: Soldier, General of the Army, President-Elect, 1890–1952*. New York: Simon & Schuster, 1983.
———. *Eisenhower the President*. London: Allen & Unwin, 1984.
Appleman, Roy E. *South to the Naktong, North to the Yalu*. Washington, D.C.: Government Printing Office, 1961.
Aronson, James. *The Press and the Cold War*. Indianapolis, Ind.: Bobbs-Merrill, 1970.
Attlee, Clement. *Twilight of Empire: Memoirs of Prime Minister Clement Attlee*. New York: A. S. Barnes, 1962.
Bailey, Sydney. *How Wars End: The United Nations and the Termination of Armed Conflict*. Oxford: Clarendon Press, 1982.
Baldwin, Frank, ed. *Without Parallel: The American-Korean Relationship since 1945*. New York: Pantheon, 1975.
Barnet, Richard J. *Roots of War: The Men and Institutions behind U.S. Foreign Policy*. Harmondsworth: Penguin, 1971.
Bernstein, Barton J., ed. *Politics and Policies of the Truman Administration*. Chicago: Quadrangle Books, 1970.
Betts, Richard K. *Nuclear Blackmail and Nuclear Balance*. Washington, D.C.: Brookings Institution, 1987.
———. *Soldiers, Statesmen and Cold War Crises*. Cambridge: Harvard University Press, 1977.

[256]

Biderman, Albert D. *March to Calumny: The Story of American POW's in the Korean War.* London: Macmillan, 1963.

Blair, Clay. *The Forgotten War: America in Korea, 1950–1953.* New York: Times Books, 1987.

Blaker, Michael. *Japanese International Negotiating Style.* New York: Columbia University Press, 1977.

Blum, Robert M. *Drawing the Line: The Origin of the American Containment Policy in East Asia.* New York: Norton, 1982.

Boardman, Robert. *Britain and the People's Republic of China, 1949–1974.* London: Macmillan, 1976.

Bohlen, Charles E. *Witness to History, 1929–1969.* New York: Norton, 1973.

Borden, William S. *The Pacific Alliance: United States Foreign Economic Policy and Japanese Trade Recovery, 1947–1954.* Madison: University of Wisconsin Press, 1984.

Borg, Dorothy, and Waldo Heinrichs, eds. *Uncertain Years: Chinese-American Relations, 1947–1950.* New York: Columbia University Press, 1980.

Borisov, O. B., and B. T. Koloskov. *Sino-Soviet Relations, 1945–1973.* Bloomington: University of Indiana Press, 1975.

Bowles, Chester. *Ambassador's Report.* London: Victor Gollancz, 1954.

Bradley, Omar N., and Clay Blair. *A General's Life: An Autobiography.* New York: Simon & Schuster, 1983.

Brands, Henry W., Jr. *Cold Warriors: Eisenhower's Generation and American Foreign Policy.* New York: Columbia University Press, 1988.

Brett, Edward A. *The World Economy since the War.* London: Macmillan, 1985.

Brodie, Bernard. *War and Politics.* London: Macmillan, 1973.

Buhite, Russell D. *Soviet-American Relations in Asia, 1945–1954.* Norman: University of Oklahoma Press, 1981.

Burchett, Wilfred. *At the Barricades.* London: Quartet Books, 1980.

Burchett, Wilfred, and Alan Winnington. *Koje Unscreened.* Peking: Foreign Languages Press, 1953.

Cable, James. *The Geneva Conference of 1954 on IndoChina.* London: Macmillan, 1986.

Cagle, Malcolm W., and Frank A. Manson. *The Sea War in Korea.* Annapolis, Md.: U.S. Naval Institute, 1957.

Cameron, James. *Point of Departure.* Stocksfield, Northumberland: Oriel Press, 1967.

Caridi, Ronald J. *The Korean War and American Politics: The Republican Party as a Case Study.* Philadelphia: University of Pennsylvania Press, 1968.

Carlton, David. *Anthony Eden: A Biography.* London: Allen & Unwin, 1986.

Caute, David. *The Great Fear: The Anti-Communist Purge under Truman and Eisenhower.* New York: Simon & Schuster, 1978.

Challener, Richard D., ed. *The Legislative Origins of American Foreign Policy.* U.S. Senate Foreign Relations Committee (Historical Series). Reviews of the World Situation, 1949–1950. New York: Garland Publishing, 1979.

Cho, Soon Sung. *Korea in World Politics, 1940–1950.* Los Angeles: University of California Press, 1967.

Choy, Bong-youn. *Korea—A History.* Rutland, Vt. and Tokyo: Charles E. Tuttle, 1971.

Clark, Mark W. *From the Danube to the Yalu.* New York: Harper & Row, 1954.

Clubb, O. Edmund. *Twentieth Century China.* New York: Columbia University Press, 1964.

Coddington, Alan. *Theories of the Bargaining Process.* London: Allen & Unwin, 1968.

Cohen, Warren I. *Dean Rusk.* The American Secretaries of State and Their Diplomacy, no. 19. Totowa, N.J.: Cooper Square Publishers, 1980.

————, ed. *New Frontiers in American-East Asian Relations: Essays Presented to Dorothy Borg*. New York: Columbia University Press, 1983.

Cohen, Warren I., and Akira Iriye, eds. *The Great Powers in East Asia*. New York: Columbia University Press, 1990.

Collins, J. Lawton. *War in Peacetime: The History and Lessons of Korea*. Boston: Houghton Mifflin, 1969.

Colville, John. *The Fringes of Power: 10 Downing Street Diaries, 1939–1955*. New York: Norton, 1986.

Cook, Blanche Wiesen. *The Declassified Eisenhower: A Divided Legacy*. Garden City, N.Y.: Doubleday, 1981.

Cotton, James, and Ian Neary, eds. *The Korean War in History*. Manchester: Manchester University Press, 1989.

Crosbie, Philip. *Three Winters Cold*. Dublin: Browne and Nolan, 1955.

Cumings, Bruce. *The Origins of the Korean War: Liberation and the Emergence of Separate Regimes, 1945–1947*. Princeton, N.J.: Princeton University Press, 1981.

————, ed. *Child of Conflict: The Korean-American Relationship, 1943–1953*. Seattle: University of Washington Press, 1983.

Cutforth, Rene. *Korean Reporter*. London: Allen Wingate, 1952.

Dallek, Robert. *The American Style of Foreign Policy*. New York: Alfred A. Knopf, 1983.

Davies, John Paton. *Dragon by the Tail*. New York: Norton, 1972.

Davies, S. J. *In Spite of Dungeons*. London: Hodder and Stoughton, 1954.

Dayal, Shiv. *India's Role in the Korean Question*. Delhi: Chand, 1959.

Dean, William F. (as told to William L. Worden). *General Dean's Story*. New York: Viking, 1954.

Delessert, Christiane S. *Release and Repatriation of Prisoners of War at the End of Active Hostilities*. Zurich: Schulthess Polygraphischer Verlag, 1977.

Devine, Donald. *The Political Culture of the United States*. Boston: Little Brown, 1972.

Divine, Robert A. *Eisenhower and the Cold War*. New York: Oxford University Press, 1981.

————. *Foreign Policy and U.S. Presidential Elections, 1952–60*. New York: New Viewpoints, 1974.

Dobbs, Charles M. *The Unwanted Symbol: American Foreign Policy, the Cold War and Korea, 1945–1950*. Kent, Ohio: Kent State University Press, 1981.

Domes, Jurgen. *Peng Te-huai: The Man and the Image*. Stanford, Calif.: Stanford University Press, 1985.

Donovan, Robert J. *Eisenhower: The Inside Story*. New York: Harper, 1956.

Dower, John W. *War without Mercy: Race and Power in the Pacific War*. New York: Pantheon, 1986.

Dulles, Foster Rhea. *American Policy toward Communist China: The Historical Record, 1949–1969*. New York: Thomas Y. Crowell, 1972.

Eden, Anthony. *Full Circle*. London: Cassell, 1960.

Eisenhower, Dwight D. *The White House Years: Mandate for Change, 1953–56*, vol. 1. Garden City, N.Y.: Doubleday, 1963.

Ekwall, Robert B. *Faithful Echo*. New York: Twayne Publishers, 1960.

Elliott, Mark R. *Pawns of Yalta: Soviet Refugees and America's Role in their Repatriation*. Urbana: University of Illinois Press, 1982.

Etzold, Thomas H., and John L. Gaddis. *Containment: Documents on American Policy and Strategy, 1945–1950*. New York: Columbia University Press, 1978.

Farrar-Hockley, Captain Anthony. *The Edge of the Sword*. London: Frederick Muller, 1954.

Ferrell, Robert H. *George C. Marshall.* New York: Cooper Square Publishers, 1966.
———. *Harry S. Truman and the Modern American Presidency.* Boston: Little Brown, 1983.
———, ed. *The Diary of James C. Hagerty.* Bloomington: Indiana University Press, 1983.
———, ed. *The Eisenhower Diaries.* New York: Norton, 1981.
———, ed. *Off the Record: The Private Papers of Harry S. Truman.* New York: Harper & Row, 1980.
Field, James, A. *History of United States Naval Operations: Korea.* Washington, D.C.: Government Printing Office, 1962.
Finletter, Thomas K. *Power and Policy: US Foreign Policy and Military Power in the Hydrogen Age.* New York: Harcourt Brace, 1954.
Fleming, David F. *The Cold War and its Origins 1917–1960.* 2 vols. Garden City, N.Y.: Doubleday, 1961.
Fogdick, Dorothy. *Common Sense and World Affairs.* New York: Harcourt Brace, 1955.
Foot, Rosemary. *The Wrong War: American Policy and the Dimensions of the Korean Conflict, 1950–1953.* Ithaca, N.Y.: Cornell University Press, 1985.
Forsythe, David P. *Humanitarian Politics: The International Committee of the Red Cross.* Baltimore: Johns Hopkins University Press, 1977.
Freedman, Lawrence. *The Evolution of Nuclear Strategy.* London: Macmillan, 1983.
Freeland, Richard H. *The Truman Doctrine and the Origins of McCarthyism; Foreign Policy, Domestic Politics, and Internal Security, 1946–1948.* New York: Alfred A. Knopf, 1972.
Futrell, Robert F. *The United States Air Force in Korea, 1950–53.* New York: Duell, Sloan and Pearce, 1961.
Gaddis, John L. *The Long Peace: Inquiries into the History of the Cold War.* New York: Oxford University Press, 1987.
———. *Strategies of Containment: A Critical Appraisal of Post-War American National Security Policy.* New York: Oxford University Press, 1982.
Gallicchio, Marc. *The Cold War Begins in Asia.* New York: Columbia University Press, 1988.
Gallup Poll. *Vol II: Public Opinion 1949–1953.* New York: Random House, 1972.
Gardner, Lloyd C. *Approaching Vietnam.* New York: Norton, 1988.
———, ed. *The Korean War.* Chicago: Quadrangle Books, 1972.
Garthoff, Raymond L. ed. *Sino-Soviet Military Relations.* New York: Praeger, 1966.
George, Alexander L. *The Chinese Communist Army in Action: The Korean War and Its Aftermath.* New York: Columbia University Press, 1967.
George, Alexander L., David K. Hall, and William E. Simons. *The Limits of Coercive Diplomacy.* Boston: Little Brown, 1971.
George, Alexander L., and Richard Smoke. *Deterrence in American Foreign Policy: Theory and Practice.* New York: Columbia University Press, 1974.
Gittings, John. *The Role of the Chinese Army.* London: Oxford University Press, 1967.
Goodman, Allen E. *The Lost Peace: America's Search for a Negotiated Settlement of the Vietnam War.* Stanford, Calif.: Hoover Institution Press, 1978.
———, ed. *Negotiating While Fighting: The Diary of Admiral C. Turner Joy at the Korean Armistice Conference.* Stanford, Calif.: Hoover Institution Press, 1978.
Goodrich, Leland M. *Korea: A Study of United States Policy in the United Nations.* New York: Council on Foreign Relations, 1956.
Gopal, Sarvepalli. *Jawaharlal Nehru: A Biography,* vol. 2: *1947–56.* London: Jonathan Cape, 1979.

Gordenker, Leon. *The United Nations and the Peaceful Unification of Korea: The Politics of Field Operations, 1947–1950.* The Hague: Martinus Nijhoff, 1959.

Gosnell, Harry F. *Truman's Crises: A Political Biography of Harry S. Truman.* Westport, Conn.: Greenwood Press, 1980.

Goulden, Joseph C. *Korea: The Untold Story of the War.* New York: Times Books, 1982.

Graebner, Norman A. *The New Isolationism.* New York: Ronald Press, 1956.

———, ed. *The National Security: Its Theory and Practice, 1945–1960.* New York: Oxford University Press, 1986.

Gravel, Senator M. *The Pentagon Papers: The Defense Department History of the United States Decision Making on Vietnam.* Boston: Beacon Press, 1971.

Greenstein, Fred I. *The Hidden-Hand Presidency: Eisenhower as Leader.* New York: Basic Books, 1982.

Guttmann, Allen, ed. *Korea and the Theory of Limited War.* Boston: Heath, 1967.

Halliday, Jon, and Bruce Cumings. *Korea: The Unknown War.* London: Viking, 1988.

Halperin, Morton H. *Bureaucratic Politics and Foreign Policy.* Washington, D.C.: Brookings Institution, 1974.

Hamby, Alonzo L. *Beyond the New Deal: Harry S. Truman and American Liberalism.* New York: Columbia University Press, 1973.

Hansen, Kenneth A. *Heroes behind Barbed Wire.* Princeton, N.J.: Van Nostrand, 1957.

Hastings, Max. *The Korean War.* London: Michael Joseph, 1987.

Haynes, Richard F. *The Awesome Power: Harry S. Truman as Commander in Chief.* Baton Rouge: Louisiana State University Press, 1973.

Heller, Francis H., ed. *The Korean War: A 25 Year Perspective.* Lawrence: Regents Press of Kansas, 1977.

Henderson, Gregory. *Korea: The Politics of the Vortex.* Cambridge: Harvard University Press, 1968.

Hermes, Walter C. *Truce Tent and Fighting Front,* Washington, D.C.: Government Printing Office, 1966.

Higgins, Trumbull. *Korea and the Fall of MacArthur: A Précis in Limited War.* New York: Oxford University Press, 1960.

Hoopes, Townsend. *The Devil and John Foster Dulles.* Boston: Little Brown, 1973.

Hsieh, Alice L. *Communist China's Strategy in the Nuclear Era.* Englewood Cliffs, N.J.: Prentice Hall, 1962.

Hughes, Emmet J. *The Ordeal of Power: A Political Memoir of the Eisenhower Years.* New York: Atheneum, 1963.

Hunt, Michael. *Ideology and US Foreign Policy.* New Haven: Yale University Press, 1987.

Hwang, Byong-moo, and Melvin Gurtov. *China under Threat: The Politics of Strategy and Diplomacy.* Baltimore: Johns Hopkins University Press, 1980.

Iklé, Fred. *How Nations Negotiate.* New York: Harper & Row, 1964.

Ireland, Timothy P. *Creating the Entangling Alliance: The Origins of the North Atlantic Treaty Organization.* London: Aldwych Press, 1981.

Jackson, Robert. *Air War over Korea.* London: Ian Allan, 1973.

Jebb, Gladwyn. *The Memoirs of Lord Gladwyn.* New York: Weybright and Talley, 1972.

Jencks, Harlan. *From Muskets to Missiles: Politics and Professionalism in the Chinese Army, 1945–1981.* Boulder, Colo.: Westview Press, 1982.

Jervis, Robert. *Perception and Misperception in International Politics.* Princeton, N.J.: Princeton University Press, 1976.

Johnson, U. Alexis (with J. O. McAllister). *The Right Hand of Power.* Englewood Cliffs, N.J.: Prentice Hall, 1984.

Jones, Francis. *No Rice for Rebels: A Story of the Korean War.* London: Bodley, 1956.

Joy, Admiral C. Turner. *How Communists Negotiate.* New York: Macmillan, 1955.

Jurike, Stephen, Jr., ed. *From Pearl Harbor to Vietnam: The Memoirs of Admiral Arthur W. Radford.* Stanford, Calif.: Hoover Institution Press, 1975.

Kalicki, Jan. *The Pattern of Sino-American Crises.* London: Cambridge University Press, 1975.

Kaplan, Stephen S., et al. *Diplomacy of Power: Soviet Forces as a Political Instrument.* Washington, D.C.: Brookings Institution, 1981.

Karig, Walter, Malcolm W. Cagle, and Frank A. Manson. *Battle Report: The War in Korea.* New York: Rhinehart, 1952.

Kaufman, Burton I. *The Korean War: Challenges in Crisis, Credibility, and Command.* Philadelphia: Temple University Press, 1986.

Kelman, Herbert C., ed. *International Behavior: A Social-Psychological Analysis.* New York: Holt, Rinehart and Winston, 1965.

Kennan, George F. *Memoirs, 1925–1950,* vol. 1. Boston: Little Brown, 1967.

——. *Memoirs, 1950–1963,* vol. 2. Boston: Little Brown, 1972.

Keohane, Robert. *After Hegemony: Cooperation and Discord in the World Political Economy.* Princeton, N.J.: Princeton University Press, 1984.

Khrushchev, Nikita. *Khrushchev Remembers.* Boston: Little Brown, 1970.

Kinkaid, Eugene. *Why They Collaborated.* London: Longman, 1960.

Knox, Donald. *The Korean War: Pusan to Chosin.* Boston: Harcourt, Brace, Jovanovich, 1986.

Kolko, Joyce, and Gabriel Kolko. *The Limits of Power: The World and United States Foreign Policy, 1945–1954.* New York: Harper & Row, 1972.

Kraslow, David, and Stuart H. Loory. *The Secret Search for Peace in Vietnam.* New York: Vintage Books, 1968.

LaFeber, Walter. *America, Russia and the Cold War, 1945–1980.* New York: Wiley, 1980.

Lall, Arthur. *How Communist China Negotiates.* New York: Columbia University Press, 1968.

Larson, Deborah Welch. *Origins of Containment: A Psychological Explanation.* Princeton, N.J.: Princeton University Press, 1985.

Lauren, Paul G., ed. *Diplomacy: New Approaches in History, Theory and Policy.* New York: Free Press, 1979.

Lebow, Richard N. *Between Peace and War: The Nature of International Crisis.* Baltimore: Johns Hopkins University Press, 1981.

Leckie, Robert. *Conflict: The History of the Korean War, 1950–1953.* New York: Putman, 1962.

Lewis, John Wilson, and Xue Litai. *China Builds the Bomb.* Stanford: Stanford University Press, 1988.

Lewy, Guenter. *America in Vietnam.* New York: Oxford University Press, 1978.

Lisgor, Nancy, and Frank Lipsius. *A Law unto Itself: The Untold Story of the Law Firm Sullivan and Cromwell.* New York: William Morrow, 1988.

MacArthur, Douglas A. *Reminiscences.* New York: McGraw Hill, 1964.

McCormack, Gavan. *Cold War, Hot War: An Australian Perspective on the Korean War.* Sydney: Hale & Iremonger, 1983.

MacDonald, Callum A. *Korea: The War before Vietnam.* London: Macmillan, 1986.

McLellan, David S. *Dean Acheson: The State Department Years.* New York: Dodd, Mead, 1976.

Mahurin, Walker M. *Honest John: The Autobiography of Walker M. Mahurin.* New York: Putman, 1962.

Manchester, William. *American Caesar: Douglas MacArthur, 1880–1964*. New York: Dell, 1978.

Mao Tse-tung (Mao Zedong). *Selected Works*, vols. 4 and 5. Peking: Foreign Languages Press, 1969, 1977.

Matray, James I. *The Reluctant Crusade: American Foreign Policy in Korea, 1941–1950*. Honolulu: University of Hawaii Press, 1985.

May, Ernest R. *"Lessons" of the Past: The Use and Misuse of History in American Foreign Policy*. New York: Oxford University Press, 1973.

———. *The Truman Administration and China, 1945–1949*. Philadelphia: Lippincott, 1975.

May, Ernest R., and James C. Thomson, Jr. *American–East Asian Relations: A Survey*. Cambridge: Harvard University Press, 1972.

Mayers, David Allen. *Cracking the Monolith: US Policy Against the Sino-Soviet Alliance, 1949–1955*. Baton Rouge: Louisiana State University Press, 1986.

Meyers, Samuel M., and Albert B. Biderman, eds. *Mass Behavior in Battle and Captivity: The Communist Soldier in the Korean War*. Chicago: University of Chicago Press, 1968.

Momyer, General William W. *Air Power in Three Wars*. New York: Arno Press, 1980.

Mueller, John E. *War, Presidents and Public Opinion*. New York: John Wiley, 1973.

Munro, John A., and Alex I. Inglis, eds. *Mike: The Memoirs of the Right Honourable Lester B. Pearson*, vol. 2: *1948–1957*. Toronto: University of Toronto Press, 1973.

Murphy, Robert. *Diplomat Among Warriors*. Garden City, N.Y.: Doubleday, 1964.

Nagai, Yonosuke, and Akira Iriye, eds. *The Origins of the Cold War in Asia*. New York: Columbia University Press, 1977.

Nicolson, Harold. *Diplomacy*. London: Thornton Butterworth, 1939.

Nie Jung-chen (Nie Rongzhen). *Huiyi Lu* (Memoirs). Peking: PLA Publishers, 1984.

Noble, Harold Joyce. *Embassy at War*. Seattle: University of Washington Press, 1975.

O'Neill, Robert. *Australia in the Korean War, 1950–1953*, Vol. 1: *Strategy and Diplomacy*. Canberra: Australian War Memorial and Australian Govt. Publishing Services, 1981.

Osgood, Robert. *Limited War*. Chicago: University of Chicago Press, 1956.

Oshinsky, David. *A Conspiracy So Immense: The World of Joe McCarthy*. New York: Free Press, 1983.

Paige, Glenn D. *The Korean Decision*. New York: Free Press, 1968.

Panikkar, Kavalam, M. *In Two Chinas: Memoirs of a Diplomat*. London: Allen & Unwin, 1955.

Pasley, Virginia. *22 Stayed*. London: Allen, 1955.

Pasqualini, Jean. *Prisoner of Mao*. New York: Coward, McCann & Geoghegan, 1973.

Patterson, James T. *Mr Republican: A Biography of Robert A. Taft*. Boston: Houghton Mifflin, 1972.

Peng Te-huai (Peng Dehuai). *Memoirs of a Chinese Marshal: The Autobiographical Notes of Peng Dehuai*. Peking: Foreign Languages Press, 1984.

Phillips, Cabell. *The Truman Presidency*. New York: Macmillan, 1966.

Poots, Rutherford M. *Decision in Korea*. New York: McBridge, 1954.

Porter, Brian. *Britain and the Rise of Communist China: A Study of British Attitudes, 1945–1954*. London: Oxford University Press, 1967.

Porter, Gareth. *A Peace Denied: The United States, Vietnam, and the Paris Agreement*. Bloomington, Ind.: Indiana University Press, 1975.

Pruessen, Ronald W. *John Foster Dulles: The Road to Power*. New York: Free Press, 1982.

Pye, Lucian. *Chinese Commercial Negotiating Style*. Cambridge, Mass.: Oelgeschlager, Gunn & Hain, 1982.

Randle, Robert F. *The Origins of Peace: A Study of Peacemaking and the Structure of Peace Settlements*. New York: Free Press, 1973.

Rangarajan, L. N. *The Limitation of Conflict: A Theory of Bargaining and Negotiation*. London: Croom Helm, 1985.

Rankin, Karl Lott. *China Assignment*. Seattle: University of Washington Press, 1964.

Reardon-Anderson, James. *Yenan and the Great Powers*. New York: Columbia University Press, 1980.

Rees, David. *Korea: The Limited War*. New York: St. Martin's Press, 1964.

Reeves, Thomas C. *The Life and Times of Joe McCarthy: A Biography*. New York: Stein & Day, 1982.

Reichard, Gary W. *Politics as Usual: The Age of Truman and Eisenhower*. Arlington Heights, Ill.: Harlan Davidson, 1988.

Reid, Escott. *Envoy to Nehru*. Oxford: Oxford University Press, 1981.

Ridgway, Matthew B. *The Korean War*. Garden City, N.Y.: Doubleday, 1967.

Rosas, Allan. *The Legal Status of Prisoners of War: A Study in International Humanitarian Law Applicable in Armed Conflicts*. Helsinki: Suomalainen Tiedeakatemic, 1976.

Rovere, Richard H., and Arthur M. Schlesinger, Jr. *The MacArthur Controversy and American Foreign Policy*. New York: Noonday Press, 1965.

Scalapino, Robert A., and Chong-sik Lee. *Communism in Korea*, part 1. Berkeley: University of California Press, 1972.

Schaller, Michael. *The American Occupation of Japan*. New York: Oxford University Press, 1985.

Schelling, Thomas C. *The Strategy of Conflict*. London: Oxford University Press, 1960.

Schilling, Warner R., Paul Hammond, and Glenn H. Snyder. *Strategy, Politics and Defense Budgets*. New York: Columbia University Press, 1962.

Schnabel, James F. *Policy and Direction: The First Year*. Washington, D.C.: Government Printing Office, 1972.

Schoenbaum, Thomas J. *Waging Peace and War: Dean Rusk in The Truman, Kennedy and Johnson Years*. New York: Simon & Schuster, 1988.

Segal, Gerald. *Defending China*. London: Macmillan, 1986.

Shuckburgh, Evelyn. *Descent to Suez: Diaries, 1951–56*. London: Weidenfeld and Nicolson, 1986.

Shulman, Marshall D. *Stalin's Foreign Policy Reappraised*. Cambridge: Harvard University Press, 1963.

Sigal, Leon. *Fighting to a Finish: The Politics of War Termination in the United States and Japan, 1945*. Ithaca, N.Y.: Cornell University Press, 1988.

Simmons, Robert. *The Strained Alliance: Peking, Pyongyang, Moscow and the Politics of the Korean Civil War*. New York: Free Press, 1975.

Smith, Gaddis. *Dean Acheson*. New York: Cooper Square, 1972.

Snyder, Glenn H., and Paul Diesing. *Conflict among Nations: Bargaining, Decision-Making, and System Structure in International Crises*. Princeton, N.J.: Princeton University Press, 1977.

Spanier, John W. *The Truman-MacArthur Controversy and the Korean War*. Cambridge: Harvard University Press, 1959.

Stairs, Denis. *The Diplomacy of Constraint: Canada, the Korean War and the United States*. Toronto: University of Toronto Press, 1974.

Stebbins, Richard P. *The United States in World Affairs*. New York: Council on Foreign Relations, 1950–54.

Steel, Ronald. *Walter Lippmann and the American Century*. Boston: Little Brown, 1980.

Stewart, James T. *Air Power—The Decisive Force in Korea*. Princeton, N.J.: Van Nostrand, 1957.

Stoessinger, John G. *Nations into Darkness: China, Russia and America.* New York: Random House, 1978.

Stone, Isidor F. *The Hidden History of the Korean War.* New York: Monthly Review Press, 1952.

Stories of the Chinese People's Volunteers. Peking: Foreign Languages Press, 1960.

Stueck, William Whitney, Jr. *The Road to Confrontation: American Policy toward China and Korea, 1947–1950.* Chapel Hill: University of North Carolina Press, 1981.

Taubman, William. *Stalin's American Policy.* New York: Norton, 1982.

Taylor, Maxwell D. *Swords and Plowshares.* New York: Norton, 1972.

Thies, Wallace. *When Governments Collide: Coercion and Diplomacy in the Vietnam Conflict, 1964–68.* Berkeley: University of California Press, 1980.

Thorne, Christopher. *American Political Culture and the Asian Frontier, 1943–1973.* London: The British Academy Sarah Tryphena Phillips Lecture, 1988.

———. *The Issue of War: States, Societies, and the Far Eastern Conflict of 1941–1945.* London: Hamish Hamilton, 1985.

Tolstoy, Nikolai. *Victims of Yalta.* London: Hodder and Stoughton, 1977.

Trevelyan, Humphrey. *Living with the Communists.* Boston: Gambit, 1971.

Truman, Harry S. *Memoirs.* vol. 2: *Years of Trial and Hope, 1946–1952.* Garden City, N.Y.: Doubleday, 1956.

Tucker, Nancy Bernkopf. *Patterns in the Dust: Chinese-American Relations and the Recognition Controversy, 1949–1950.* New York: Columbia University Press, 1983.

Tunstall, Jeremy. *I Fought in Korea.* London: Lawrence & Wishart, 1953.

Ulam, Adam B. *Expansion and Coexistence: Soviet Foreign Policy, 1917–1973.* New York: Praeger, 1974.

———. *The Rivals: America and Russia Since World War II.* New York: Viking, 1971.

Ungar, Sanford J., ed. *Estrangement: America and the World.* New York: Oxford University Press, 1985.

Vandenburg, Arthur H. Jr., ed. *The Private Papers of Senator Vandenburg.* Boston: Houghton Mifflin, 1952.

Vatcher, William H., Jr. *Panmunjom: The Story of the Korean Military Armistice Negotiations.* New York: Praeger, 1958.

Warr, Peter. *Psychology and Collective Bargaining.* London: Hutchinson, 1973.

White, William Lindsay. *The Captives of Korea: An Unofficial White Paper on the Treatment of War Prisoners.* New York: Scribners, 1957.

Whiting, Allen S. *China Crosses the Yalu: The Decision to Enter the Korean War.* Stanford, Calif.: Stanford University Press, 1960.

Whitney, Courtney. *MacArthur: His Rendezvous with History.* New York: Knopf, 1956.

Whitson, William. *The Chinese High Command.* New York: Praeger, 1973.

Williams, Philip M., ed. *The Diary of Hugh Gaitskell, 1945–1956.* London: Jonathan Cape, 1983.

Williams, William A. *Empire as a Way of Life.* New York: Oxford University Press, 1980.

Willoughby, Charles A., and John Chamberlain. *MacArthur, 1941–1951.* New York: McGraw-Hill, 1954.

Wu Hsiu-chuan (Wu Xiuquan). *Eight Years in the Ministry of Foreign Affairs.* Peking: New World Press, 1985.

Young, John W., ed. *The Foreign Policy of Churchill's Peacetime Administration, 1951–1955.* Leicester: Leicester University Press, 1988.

Young, Kenneth. *Diplomacy and Power in Washington-Peking Dealings, 1953–1967.* Chicago: The University of Chicago Center for Policy Study, 1967.

Bibliography

——. *Negotiating with the Chinese Communists: The United States Experience, 1953–1967.* New York: McGraw-Hill, 1968.
Young, Oran R., ed. *Bargaining: Formal Theories of Negotiation.* Urbana: University of Illinois Press, 1975.
Zartman, I. William. *The 50% Solution.* Garden City, N.Y.: Anchor Press, 1976.
——, ed. *The Negotiation Process: Theories and Applications.* Beverly Hills, Calif.: Sage, 1978.
Zartman, I. William, and Maureen R. Berman. *The Practical Negotiator.* New Haven: Yale University Press, 1982.

Articles

Bacchus, Wilfred. "The Relationship Between Combat and Peace Negotiations: Fighting While Talking in Korea, 1951–1953." *Orbis* 17, no. 2 (Summer 1973).
Bernstein, Barton J. "New Light on the Korean War." *International History Review,* 3 (April 1981).
——. "The Policy of Risk: Crossing the 38th Parallel and Marching to the Yalu." *Foreign Service Journal,* March 1977.
——. "The Struggle over the Korean Armistice: Prisoners of Repatriation?" In Bruce Cumings, ed., *Child of Conflict: The Korean-American Relationship, 1943–1953.* Seattle: University of Washington Press, 1983.
——. "Syngman Rhee: The Pawn as Rook: The Struggle to End the Korean War." *Bulletin of Concerned Asian Scholars* 10, no. 1 (1978).
——. "Truman's Secret Thoughts on Ending the Korean War." *Foreign Service Journal,* November 1980.
——. "The Week We Went to War: American Intervention and the Korean Civil War." *Foreign Service Journal,* January 1977.
Blechman, Barry M., and Robert Powell. "What in the Name of God Is Strategic Superiority?" *Political Science Quarterly* 97 (Winter 1982–83).
Brands, Henry W., Jr. "The Dwight D. Eisenhower Administration, Syngman Rhee and the 'Other' Geneva Conference of 1954." *Pacific Historical Review* 61 (February 1987).
Buhite, Russell D. "Major Interests: American Policy Toward China, Taiwan and Korea, 1945–1950." *Pacific Historical Review* 47, no. 3 (1978).
Bullen, Roger. "Great Britain, the United States and the Indian Armistice Resolution on the Korean War: November 1952." In *Aspects of Anglo-Korean Relations, International Studies* (International Centre for Economics and Related Disciplines, London School of Economics and Political Science), 1984/1.
Calingaert, Daniel. "Nuclear Weapons and the Korean War." *Journal of Strategic Studies* 11, no. 3 (June 1988).
Carpenter, William M. "The Korean War: A Strategic Perspective." *Comparative Strategy* 2, no. 4 (1980).
Cohen, Warren I. "Conversations with Chinese Friends: Zhou Enlai's Associates Reflect on Chinese-American Relations in the 1940s and the Korean War." *Diplomatic History* 11 (Summer 1987).
Cottrell, Alvin J., and James E. Dougherty. "The Lessons of Korea: War and the Power of Man." *Orbis* 2 (Spring 1958).
Cox, Robert W. "Social Forces, States and World Orders: Beyond International Relations Theory." In *Millennium: Journal of International Studies* 10 (Summer 1981).

Dingman, Roger. "Atomic Diplomacy during the Korean War." *International Security*, 13, no. 3, (Winter 1988–89).

———. "Truman, Attlee and the Korean War Crisis." In *The East Asian Crisis, 1945–1951, International Studies* (International Centre for Economics and Related Disciplines, London School of Economics), 1982/1.

Dockrill, Michael L. "The Foreign Office, Anglo-American Relations and the Korean War, June 1950–June 1951." *International Affairs* (London), 62 (1986).

Endicott, Stephen L. "Germ Warfare and the 'Plausible Denial': The Korean War 1952–1953." *Modern China* 5, no. 1 (January 1979).

Farrar, Peter. "Britain's Proposal for a Buffer Zone South of the Yalu in November 1950: Was It a Neglected Opportunity to End the Fighting in Korea?" *Journal of Contemporary History* 18 (1983).

Foot, Rosemary. "Anglo-American Relations in the Korean Crisis: The British Effort to Avert an Expanded War, December 1950–January 1951." *Diplomatic History* 10, no. 1 (1986).

———. "Nuclear Coercion and the Ending of the Korean Conflict." *International Security* 13, no. 3, (Winter 1988–89).

———. "The Search for a Modus-Vivendi: Anglo-American Relations and China Policy in the Eisenhower Era." In Warren I. Cohen and Akira Iriye, eds. *The Great Powers and East Asia*. New York: Columbia University Press, 1990.

Friedman, Edward. "Nuclear Blackmail and the End of the Korean War." *Modern China* 1, no. 1 (January 1975).

———. "Problems in Dealing with an Irrational Power: America Declares War on China." In *America's Asia: Dissenting Essays on Asian-American Relations,* ed. Mark Selden and Edward Friedman. New York: Random House, 1971.

Gaddis, John L. "Reconsiderations—Was the Truman Doctrine a Real Turning Point?" *Foreign Affairs* 52 (January 1974).

Gill, Stephen. "American Hegemony: Its Limits and Prospects in the Reagan Era." In *Millennium: Journal of International Studies* 15, (Winter 1986).

Gittings, John. "Talks, Bombs and Germs—Another Look at the Korean War." *Journal of Contemporary Asia* 5, no. 2 (1975).

Gray, Colin S. "National Style in Strategy: The American Example." *International Security* 6 (Fall 1981).

Gutteridge, J. A. C. "The Repatriation of Prisoners of War." *International and Comparative Law Quarterly* 2 (1953).

Halliday, Jon. "Anti-Communism and the Korean War, 1950–1953." In Ralph Miliband et al., eds., *The Socialist Register*. London: Merlin Press, 1984.

———. "The Korean War: Some Notes on Evidence and Solidarity." *Bulletin of Concerned Asian Scholars* 11, no. 3 (1979).

———. "What Happened in Korea? Rethinking Korean History, 1945–1953." *Bulletin of Concerned Asian Scholars* 5, no. 3 (1973).

Harris, William R. "Chinese Nuclear Doctrine: The Decade Prior to Weapons Development (1945–1955)" *China Quarterly* 21 (January–March 1965).

Holsti, Ole. "The 'Operational Code' Approach to the Study of Political Leaders: John Foster Dulles' Philosophical and Instrumental Beliefs." *Canadian Journal of Political Science* 3 (March 1970).

Horner, Charles. "The Production of Nuclear Weapons." In William W. Whitson, ed., *The Military and Political Power in China in the 1970s*. New York: Praeger, 1972.

Hsieh, Alice L. "China's Secret Military Papers: Military Doctrine and Strategy." *China Quarterly* 18 (April–June 1964).

Immerman, Richard H. "Eisenhower and Dulles: Who Made the Decisions." *Political Psychology* 1 (Autumn 1979).

Jervis, Robert. "The Impact of the Korean War on the Cold War." *Journal of Conflict Resolution* 24, no. 4 (December 1980).

Keefer, Edward C. "President Dwight D. Eisenhower and the End of the Korean War." *Diplomatic History* 10 (Summer 1986).

Koh, Biyung Chul. "The Korean War as a Learning Experience for North Korea." *Korea and World Affairs* 3, no. 3 (Fall 1979).

LaFeber, Walter. "Crossing the 38th: The Cold War in Microcosm." In Lynn Miller and Ronald W. Pruessen, eds., *Reflections on the Cold War*. Philadelphia: Temple University Press, 1974.

Leffler, Melvyn P. "The American Conception of National Security and the Beginnings of the Cold War, 1945–1948." *American Historical Review* 89 (April 1984).

Lofgren, Charles A. "Mr. Truman's War: A Debate and Its Aftermath." *Review of Politics* 31 (April 1969).

McLellan, David S. "Dean Acheson and the Korean War." *Political Science Quarterly* 83, no. 1 (March 1968).

Matray, James. "America's Reluctant Crusade: Truman's Commitment of Combat Troops in the Korean War." *Historian* 42, no. 3 (May 1980).

———. "Truman's Plan for Victory: National Self-Determination and the 38th Parallel Decision in Korea." *Journal of American History* 66 (September 1979).

Mushakoji, Kinhide. "The Strategies of Negotiation: An American-Japanese Comparison." In J. A. LaPonce and Paul Smoker, eds., *Experimentation and Simulation in Political Science*. Toronto: University of Toronto Press, 1972.

Ogley, Roderick. "The United Nations and East-West Relations." *Institute for the Study of International Organization*, Brighton, University of Sussex, ISIO Monographs, first series, no. 6 (1972).

Park, Hong-kyu. "Korean War Revisited—Survey of Historical Writing." *World Affairs* 137, no. 4 (Spring 1975).

Pelz, Stephen E. "When the Kitchen Gets Hot, Pass the Buck: Truman and Korea in 1950." *Reviews in American History,* 6 (December 1978).

Reichard, Gary W. "Divisions and Dissent: Democrats and Foreign Policy, 1952–1956." *Political Science Quarterly* 93 (Spring 1978).

Rosenberg, David A. "The Origins of Overkill: Nuclear Weapons and American Strategy, 1945–1960." *International Security* 7, no. 4 (Spring 1983).

———. "US Nuclear Stockpile 1945 to 1950." *Bulletin of the Atomic Scientists* 38, no. 5 (May 1982).

Schein, Edgar H. "The Chinese Indoctrination Program for Prisoners of War: A Study of Attempted 'Brainwashing'." *Psychiatry,* 1956.

Smith, Gaddis. "Reconsiderations: The Shadow of John Foster Dulles." *Foreign Affairs* 52 (January 1974).

Steinberg, Blema A. "The Korean War and Indian Neutralism." *Orbis,* part 8 (Winter 1965).

Stueck, William W., Jr. "The Korean War as International History." *Diplomatic History* 10 (Fall 1986).

———. "The Limits of Influence: British Policy and American Expansion of the War in Korea." *Pacific Historical Review* 55 (February 1986).

———. "The Soviet Union and the Origins of the Korean War." *World Politics* 28 (1975–1976).

Swartout, Robert, Jr. "American Historians and the Outbreak of the Korean War: An Historiographical Essay." *Asia Quarterly* 1 (1979).

Warner, Geoffrey. "The Korean War." *International Affairs,* 56 (January 1980).

Wells, Samuel F., Jr., "The Origins of Massive Retaliation." *Political Science Quarterly* 96 (Spring 1981).

———. "Sounding the Tocsin: NSC 68 and the Soviet Threat." *International Security* 4, no. 2 (Fall 1979).

Whiting, Allen S. "The Use of Force in Foreign Policy by the People's Republic of China." *Annals of the American Academy of Political and Social Science* 402 (July 1972).

Wiltz, John E. "The MacArthur Hearings of 1951: The Secret Testimony." *Military Affairs* 39 (December 1975).

Wubben, Harold H. "American Prisoners of War in Korea: A Second Look at the 'Something New in History' Theme." *American Quarterly* 22 (Spring 1970).

Dissertations

Elowitz, Larry. "Korea and Vietnam: Limited War and the American Political System." University of Florida, 1972.

Flint, Roy K. "The Tragic Flaw: MacArthur, the Joint Chiefs and the Korean War." Duke University, 1975.

Kotch, John. "The Origins of the American Security Commitment to Korea." Columbia University, 1975.

Mantell, Matthew. "Opposition to the Korean War: A Study in American Dissent." New York University, 1973.

Mauck, Kenneth R. "The Formation of American Foreign Policy in Korea, 1945–1953." University of Oklahoma, 1978.

Ryan, Mark A. "Chinese Attitudes toward Nuclear Weapons: China and the United States during the Korean War." Georgetown University, 1986.

Weiss, Lawrence S. "Storm around the Cradle: The Korean War and the Early Years of the People's Republic of China, 1949–1953." Columbia University, 1981.

Wilhelm, Alfred Donovan, Jr. "Sino-American Negotiations: The Chinese Approach." University of Kansas, 1986.

Index

Acheson, Dean: attitude toward negotiations, 10, 14–15, 22–24, 30–31, 54, 68–69, 130, 210–211; crossing 38th Parallel, 25; demilitarized zone south of Yalu, 27; at MacArthur Hearings, 45; on nonforcible repatriation, 88 92, 147–50; relations with Marshall, 64; relations with Truman, 15, 91, 149, 157; at United Nations, 6, 155–158

Agenda, framing of, 44–46

Alexander, Lord, 134

Allison, John M., 144, 218

Attlee, Clement, 7, 28–30, 172

Australia, 5–6, 65, 81, 201; on nonforcible repatriation, 93, 100, 110, 133–134, 153, 168, 172, 209

Barrett, Edward G., 90

Belande, Victor, 27

Bevin, Ernest, 22–23, 27

Boatner, Haydon E., 129, 131, 237n.

Bohlen, Charles E., 22–23, 36, 41, 56, 69–70, 79, 160, 165, 177, 182, 214; on nonforcible repatriation, 90, 99

Bohlen-Bradley visit to Korea, 51–52, 57–58, 66, 105

Bolté, Charles L., 27, 57

Bradley, Omar F., 30, 57–58, 81, 137, 150, 163, 214; on nonforcible repatriation, 90, 99

Britain, 5–6; negotiating initiatives, 20–22, 27, 66; on nonforcible repatriation, 92, 100, 110, 134–135, 153, 155–157, 168, 171–172, 175, 209; perceptions of U.S. policies, 50, 65–67, 80; at political conference on Korea, 201,

203–204; Rhee's release of non-repatriate POWs, 184. *See also* Greater Sanction; *entries for individuals in U.K. government*

Brooks, Joseph, 113

Burke, Arleigh, 59–60, 104

Cabell, Charles P., 146

Cadwell, Victor, 120

Canada, 5; on nonforcible repatriation, 92–93, 134, 153, 168, 171–172, 175, 209; at political conference on Korea, 201

Ceasefire line, establishment of (item 2), 45–48, 52–53, 56–60, 71, 207

Central Intelligence Agency, 90

Chase, A. Sabin, 113, 117, 220

Chiang Kai-shek, 23, 76, 192–193, 219

Chiao Kuan-hua, 12, 17

Chinese attitude toward nuclear weapons, 178–80, 222

Chinese negotiating style, 16–17, 44, 54, 70–71, 226n.

Chinese-North Korean relations, 18, 50, 70–71

Chinese objectives, 19, 28–30, 40, 71–73, 98, 181, 217–218. *See also* Chou En-lai; *entries for individual agenda items*

Chou En-lai, 29, 72, 205, 219; discussions with Indian officials, 26, 132–133, 137, 154, 170, 186, 195, 214, 217; March 30 statement, 168; in Moscow, 147, 167, 183

Churchill, Winston, 92, 101, 160, 172

Civil information and education program, 113–117, 134–135, 216

Library of Congress Cataloging-in-Publication Data

Foot, Rosemary, 1948–
  A substitute for victory: the politics of peacemaking at the Korean armistice talks /
Rosemary Foot.
      p.   cm. — (Cornell studies in security affairs)
  Includes bibliographical references.
  ISBN 0–8014–2413–5 (alk. paper)
  1. Korean War, 1950–1953—Armistices. I. Title. II. Series.
DS921.7.F66   1990
951.904'2—dc20   89–45973